COMPASSION

A New Philosophy of the Other

VIBS

Volume 134

Robert Ginsberg
Founding Editor

Peter A. Redpath
Executive Editor

COMPASSION

A New Philosophy of the Other

Werner J. Krieglstein

Amsterdam – New York, NY 2002

The paper on which this book is printed meets the requirements of "ISO 9706:1994, Information and documentation - Paper for documents - Requirements for permanence".

ISBN: 90-420-0903-9
Printed in The Netherlands

To Maryann,
Robin, Mark, Daniel, Thomas, and Michael

CONTENTS

EDITORIAL FOREWORD

In my recent book *Tomorrow's Children*, I said that practicing caring and care giving helps meet our human needs for meaning, for spiritual awareness, for larger purpose. The deeply imbedded human yearning for connection that is the evolutionary mainspring for love is also the evolutionary mainspring for spirituality – for the sense of awe and wonder that comes from the intuitive understanding that we are not isolated blips on the evolutionary screen, that we are in a mysterious, and truly miraculous, way actively interconnected with all that is, was, and can be.

Krieglstein makes this basic concept of connectedness and compassionate caring the central theme of his new philosophy, which he calls Transcendental Perspectivism. Drawing from major tenets of modern feminism, Krieglstein puts compassion into the center of any future philosophizing. He argues that the last three hundred years of Western philosophy have shown the dead end of a philosophical system that in the name of truth set out to dominate other cultures, and in the end even justified the relentless exploitation and destruction of all of nature.

In my cultural transformation theory, first introduced in my book *The Chalice and The Blade,* I argued that the domination principle must be overcome if humanity is to survive. I showed ways how the partnership model can be used to eventually replace domination and rejuvenate humanity. For this reason I have been instrumental in establishing an educational program to teach partnership education. *Tomorrow's Children* offers a variety of models to include partnership education in the curriculum of each school.

Krieglstein offers a wealth of examples from many different academic fields to show how connecting and caring have already become the central focus of many fields of human inquiry, even while academic philosophy has been slow to catch up with a proper analysis of these encouraging human endeavors. In my writings I have emphasized the understanding that we are partners on this planet with nature, inextricably connected with our Mother Earth. Drawing on findings from Chaos theory, Quantum Physics, and my cultural transformation theory, Krieglstein argues that this partnership may even include the possibility of communication with what has traditionally been called inorganic or inanimate materia. He cites progressive scientists who today believe that life is not a blind accident in an otherwise not-aware and non-caring universe, but that we can envision the possibility of a seamless connectedness of the whole universe, from the smallest atom to the largest stars and galaxies. Some scientists support this panpsychic view. They believe that have found evidence of awareness or, as Krieglstein says, an inner perspective, even in the smallest particles such as quarks, and electrons, perhaps even in the space that surrounds us. Such quantum animism would open up the possibility of communication, a spiritual form of partnership, with the whole universe.

Building on this spiritual partnership, Krieglstein proposes nothing less than to develop a new cosmic spirituality. Inspired by universal connectedness, a future person of faith is able to move between different creeds and religions and take the best from each. In his partnership ethics, Krieglstein suggests that to facilitate human interaction we must temporarily eclipse our own selfish interests and put ourselves into the service of others. This sends a powerful signal of the willingness to cooperate to all participants in this new community.

Much of Krieglstein's work focuses on the reasons why we have lost community and why it is absolutely necessary for our evolutionary survival to regain a sense for community and to practice communal care. He demonstrates how at different levels of evolution, beginning with simple electrons, through algae and one-cell organisms, and at many more complex stages of the animal kingdom, individuals have cooperated and in million ways tried to come together in communal activities. He suggests that at rare occasions during such communal rituals, a critical mass of individuals may have decided to stay together instead of dispersing. These incidences of collective orchestrations, as Krieglstein calls it, may constitute those rare moments of evolutionary self-organization, when a new individual is born that is now able to operate on a higher and yet unexplored dimension.

Krieglstein puts self-organizing processes in the center of his new worldview. This may be Krieglstein's greatest achievement, to have put a new spin on Darwin's otherwise blindly operating system known as the survival of the fittest. David Loye in *Darwin's Lost Theory of Love* pointed at the widely recognized principle of self-organization as a third evolutionary candidate in addition to natural selection and random variation "for being a prime shaper of our lives." Krieglstein makes a convincing case that self-organization is not only found in natural processes involving life but is at work at all levels of the universe, from the smallest particles to the largest galaxies.

Using the demise of the Easter Island as an example, Krieglstein paints a dark picture of the fatal course of humanity if the current dominator paradigm is not abandoned. He has a clear vision of a bright future of all life on earth if the new principles of partnership are learned, practiced, and implemented in education, social life, and the business world. To this end, he reviews the great achievements of twentieth-century's most progressive movements.

Krieglstein's book is above all a call to action. Transcendental Perspectivism as a philosophy with a primary focus on connecting poses an ethical demand to correct the ills of humanity on earth.

Riane Eisler
Carmel, California

GUEST FOREWORD

In the midst of immense scientific advances the question of life, of a life-giving force, and the simple question of how to live a happy and fulfilled life persist and await answers today as ardently and restlessly as ever. Through the centuries philosophers have pondered on the depths of truth and existence, producing theories that have been named with numerous isms. Reasoning has been the main tool in this pondering, while the expanse of feelings has been left to linger in the shadows. Will our time succeed in bringing a new balance and harmony to these two different spheres of the human mind, in particular with regard to our relation with nature, with each other, and with our own inner selves, with an outcome of rendering more happiness to everyday life in families and communities? Here, outstandingly, Krieglstein comes forward with new, comprehensive and boldly creative ideas.

Transcendental Perspectivism, as Krieglstein calls his worldview, is a holistic approach to seeing the living connectedness of human beings and the universe. Compassion to Krieglstein means a new way of respecting and enjoying life. The concept embraces all religious, philosophic, ethic, aesthetic, and creative aspects of life. He bases his thinking firmly on the latest Western discoveries in natural and human sciences, from areas such as quantum physics, chaos theory, and the psychology of emotional intelligence. Krieglstein, with an extraordinary knowledgeable skill, also combines into the whole of his philosophy concepts of Eastern thought and the ancient wisdom of many cultures. His views are truly transcultural and interdisciplinary. For him the time of domination and dominating theories as well as of cultural discrimination is over. A new era of partnership and mutual cooperation must emerge if the survival of humankind is to be guaranteed. This survival requires a third enlightenment, which is related to the quality of life. The question is about emotional survival, and, according to Krieglstein, this issue should become a constitutive part of all sectors of our lives, a pivotal element of family and community. Emotional survival is not possible without a renewed understanding of compassion, and the ability to merge spiritually with another. Compassion should be extended to all humankind and to all nature.

The book is not only academically well reflected and documented, it also gives a great number of examples from everyday situations to demonstrate the path to a happier, more fulfilling life in a community. What is needed first and foremost is a new, compassionate and open-hearted awareness to the spiritual dimension of life, to see and feel intuitively the miraculous life force in our entire environment, natural and human. Krieglstein wonderfully convinces us throughout his book that life energy exists in the cosmos, in the nature and in us, which is full of beauty and joy and which we have to find access to.

Through this access we can advance to a higher spiritual consciousness of the Universe and at the same time create a sounder and more richly satisfying community, enhancing a dream of a cosmic community through collective orchestration. Questions still exist on what the ideal future cosmic community will be like, but Krieglstein's vision enlightens the way.

It was a great enjoyment for me to read Krieglstein's inspiring book. So many beautiful and delightful wonders exist, concealed in miracles around us and within our souls. We can be grateful to all those who open our minds to see them and who create new vistas of the invisible sides of the Spiritual in our existence. Krieglstein is one of them.

Sonja Servomaa
Researcher in Asian Philosophy of Art and Aesthetics,
University of Helsinki, Finland

" . . . in today's multicultural world, the truly reliable path to coexistence, to peaceful coexistence and creative cooperation, must start from what is at the root of all cultures and what lies infinitely deeper in human hearts and minds than political opinion, convictions, antipathies, or sympathies: it must be rooted in self-transcendence. Transcendence as a hand reached out to those close to us, to foreigners, to the human community, to all living creatures, to nature, to the universe; transcendence as a deeply and joyously experienced need to be in harmony even with what we ourselves are not, what we do not understand, what seems distant from us in time and space, but with which we are nevertheless mysteriously linked because, together with us, all this constitutes a single world. Transcendence as the only real alternative to extinction."

Vaclav Havel

INTRODUCTION
Virtual Gorillas

Visualize this: you are in the midst of a rain forest. You are part of a group of apes foraging in the under wood. You are a member of a group of primates, gorillas, about sixteen of them. A silverback might charge at you any time if you misbehave. He is the leader of the pack. The silverback keeps a close eye on you. Do you behave properly? Or are you out of line? Are you acting in a way the group does not approve? Or are you even challenging the mighty silverback's authority? A warning cough means "back off." You are startled. You scramble to find the reverse button on your controls. You manage to escape.

Next you are in a library, with a book on animal behavior, studying an article on peace making among primates. A little later, you put on your helmet again and enter their world, the habitat of our closest relatives. You are ready to test the techniques you just learned, ready for peace. The helmet is your tool that can transport you into the midst of a primate group. It can give you first-hand experience of what so far you have only been able to learn from books, in theory. You can become one of them.

This kind of interaction between theory and practical experience has been made possible by an invention called virtual reality, an auspicious union between sophisticated computer technology and modern game design. "Virtual Gorillas"[1] is the newest attraction at the Atlanta Zoo. The creatures in this novel exhibit – a few dozen Gorillas – are not even alive. They "exist only in a virtual electronic world, a world visitors can enter by donning a helmet that presents a three dimensional view of the gorilla habitat."[2] With a control stick, a user "walks" among the apes, becoming an adolescent gorilla.

Learning to see and experience the world through the eyes of others is Perspectivism in action. Our use of modern technology makes an ancient dream of humanity (expressed in the visions of shamans and witch doctors) possible. When early human beings observed birds in the sky, they dreamed about flying. Like fish, they learned how to swim; like spiders, they learned how to weave; and like snakes, they learned how to strike with poisonous venom. Imitating birds, they learned how to sing, and how to attract and please a lover.

Early human beings moved out of Africa, the ancient cradle where humanity first evolved, into new and often hostile territory. Some of those ancestors traveled along the landmasses into Asia; others came to the vast expanses of Northern Europe and Siberia. In the boundless steppes of the

North, they had to prove, in new ways, their tremendous ability to adapt. Back in Africa, the land had given them a near limitless supply of food in the form of plants, fruits, berries, and nuts, but the Northern steppes were harsh and unfriendly.

Here they found that their animal brothers and sisters had made that move long before them. They encountered animals that had adapted many thousands of years earlier and now thrived in their new climate. When they came to the forests and swamps of Old Europe, they discovered that the bear was already there. When they came to Siberia, they encountered the wolf and the elk. To survive they learned how to imitate those animals. They observed the bear, the wolf, and the elk, and learned from them. Like the bear, they took refuge in mountain caves and in hollow trees. From the dead bear, they took the fur to keep warm. From the wolf, they learned how to stalk weaker animals and use them for food. Like the reindeer and the elk, they learned to migrate as seasons changed.

The human beings needed new sources of food in each new climate. In those northern worlds, meat became the main staple of nutrition, especially during the long and harsh winters. They watched the animals and what they ate. If it was good for them, human beings could trust it as well. Our ancestors journeyed over this wondrous earth, from which they believed everything was born and to which all will return, and they revered her as a goddess.

Delivered to us from ancient times, myths and stories report these encounters with animals. They became part of the narrative we call mythology or religion. Often these early human beings attributed divine and magical powers to their animal friends. They must have been in awe when they watched how the animals mastered the environment with infinite skills.

As human beings learned all those skills from animals, a strange rift began to develop. Perhaps it was our mind that first separated us from the animal world. Some say it was a divine mission: a special message human beings had received from a distant god. Or was it guilt over killing animals and using them as food that created the distance? We will never know exactly what caused the initial rift between human beings and the natural world.

Ever since this chasm occurred, human beings have had a deep yearning for the sources, a desire to regain a connection to nature and the animal world. Songs and stories spoke of this longing to see the world through animal eyes, to feel their emotions, to connect to the earth again like only animals can do. Psychologists have called this the desire for oneness in the womb. Philosophically, it became known as the yearning for the other.

People put on masks and pretended to be like animals. They took mind-altering substances to experience magic and slip into the animal world. In dreams, trances, and hallucinations, human beings imagined they were animals. Many desired to return after death as a specific animal. Those who were able to assume an animal role often enjoyed great influence and power.

They were the shamans and prophets, the ancestors of the modern priests: poets, healers, and educators.

The European Enlightenment moved away from the magic that surrounded those early human beings who lived in a virgin world. Disconnected from the earth, modern human beings, children of that Enlightenment, still yearn to find their way back to the sources, to transcend the narrow boundaries of the self and become one with the other, one with the earth, one with the universe. Is it possible that technology can help us along this path?

This book is an exploration of our world as the other. Perspectivism is a new philosophy in search of this other. Transcendental Perspectivism expresses the belief in the reality of the other, a reality that transcends our limited self. Transcendental Perspectivism is the attempt to find a way out of the extreme individualistic isolation of modern times.

In my journey toward the other, I asked these central questions: why are we so disconnected from the earth? Why do we see ourselves so separate from nature? How might we find our way back into community, with our fellow human beings, with the animals that populate this world, and even with the universe?

When I started out on this path of exploration, I was hardly aware in how many different ways we modern human beings have already begun to reverse the direction of the Western mind into isolation. While some people may find a romantic element in my philosophy, I must point out that my optimism about the world, the universe, and about our human journey in it is not sentimental at all. Basic optimism, I believe, is justified, and necessary for survival. I also believe that a union with nature is possible and desirable. I do not believe that this union is, by necessity, closed to our understanding, and therefore irrational. When transcending the boundaries of the analytically reflecting mind, the tools of understanding and science do not necessarily lose their validity. Therefore, this new Enlightenment cannot be a falling back into dark irrationality but must ultimately be a tool for thoughtful awareness and empowerment.

PART I

TRANSCENDENTAL PERSPECTIVISM:
A NEW ENLIGHTENMENT

One

THE VOODOO CONNECTION

> Modern civilization has bred a race with brains
> like those of rabbits. And we who are the heirs
> of the witch doctor and the voodoo, we artists
> who have been so long the despised are about to
> take over control.
>
> Ezra Pound

I am looking at the world with an artist's eye. My experience of the other is aesthetic. As an artist I can find the world whole. The more I am connected the better my art. Naïve artists, from Homer to Shakespeare and Goethe, experienced the world from the first-person perspective. Uneasily, the artists after the Renaissance followed the move of science and adopted a third person perspective, an objective view of the world as it was expressed in the great novels of the nineteenth century. It became the rule for art during modernism. Postmodernism, in many ways, rediscovered the first-person perspective, in literature, criticism, and even science. But for many, a vital ingredient of naivety has been lost, perhaps forever. The self-centeredness of the first person perspective has turned into narcissism. Extreme individualism has made us even more aware of the loss of wholeness, the loss of community, the loss of family, the loss of the other. Without a simultaneous discovery of the perspective of the second person, the perspective of the living other, the first person perspective remains self serving and vain. Rediscovering this perspective is the goal of Transcendental Perspectivism, and as we will see in the following pages, the groundwork has been laid and the direction is given.

When Karen McCarthy-Brown, an anthropologist from New York, decided to study Voodoo, she befriended Mama Lola – a Voodoo priestess in Brooklyn. While observing Mama Lola and her practices, McCarthy-Brown undertook several journeys to Haiti. There she met with other Voodoo practitioners. She recorded their stories, took notes, and used all the customary tools of a professional anthropologist.

By the time McCarthy-Brown sat down to write her book she had to confess that she had become a Voodoo practitioner herself. In the introduction, McCarthy-Brown contends that the only way she could give an "objective" account of Voodoo was by personally identifying herself with the major tenets of Voodoo doctrine. As her friendship with Mama Lola grew, the author says, a shift took place "in the way I understood my professional work . . . . I soon found that I could not claim a place in her Voodoo family and remain a detached observer."[1]

This anthropologist, trained in the pursuit of academic objectivity, soon realized that "the heart of the system, its ability to heal, would remain closed" to her, if she persisted in studying Voodoo objectively – in the traditional sense. Karen McCarthy-Brown had to become a believer herself.

Enter the Age of Perspectivism.

A Native American saying goes: You have to walk a mile in my moccasins before you can understand me. Similar ideas were already expressed in the Kabbalistic literature of ancient Judaism.

This practice of getting deeply and emotionally involved in other people and in the subject we set out to understand is the essence of a philosophy I call Perspectivism. Recent developments, not only in academia, but also in all forms of cultural and cross-cultural life, seem to indicate the widespread use of this new philosophy.

Reviewing a recent publication titled *Searching the Scriptures: A Feminist Commentary,* Miriam Theresa Winter, a professor of liturgy/worship, spirituality, and feminist studies at Hartford Seminary, concedes that she examines biblical texts from a "liberation perspective" which purposely is grounded in a "hermeneutics of suspicion."[2] The premise of the book is that the biblical writings do not represent an objective, even divinely-controlled report of the biblical events, but are the result of a particular advocacy, namely the advocacy of those who try to "foster women's and marginalized men's subordination and exploitation."[3] By reading both canonical and non-canonical texts next to each other and "against the grain of tradition" the book, according to Winter, puts "women at 'the center of the frame' within a variety of interpretive frameworks so that women's reality, implicit in the text, might more clearly emerge." Winter says:

> Particularly effective is the use of a rhetorical analysis, which takes as its starting point the fact that the scriptural text under consideration was written in response to an argument or debate in order to persuade an audience to adopt the writer's point of view. Once we see that the writer's perspective is only one among many competing voices in a real life situation, commentators take us a step further by reconstructing the arguments "on the other side of the text," often allowing invisible women to speak.[4]

By reading the scriptures in such a comparative and critical way, Winter employs a Perspectivist methodology. Winter's method allows her to restore the lost voices of women to their proper historical place. These voices were lost because of a falsely objectified reading of the same scriptures by religious dogmatists who allow their opinions to masquerade as "the truth."

A popular television series with the title *How the West Was Lost* was announced in the following way: "In school we were taught history only from one point of view: from the point of view of the Western Europeans who came to this continent as conquerors. Now Discovery Channel tells the story from the point of view of those who were already here." In rewriting a major part of American history by giving a voice to the other side, Perspectivism is at work.

A major network reports the daily news as compiled by broadcasting stations around the world, "as seen from their perspective."[5]

In a similar way Perspectivist methodology swept through the halls of postmodern literature. In an article on "Bringing the Personal into Scholarship" another anthropologist, Ruth Behar from the University of Michigan, asks the provocative question: "Dare We Say 'I'?"[6] Her article deals with the controversial, but increasingly more popular, method of bringing the personal, autobiographical voice into research papers and scholarly works. She does this not only as a "feminist or minority-group pastime" but because "modern writing wishes to speak in a plain language that will be understood by a large audience."[7] Her main points, she claims, are theoretically based and philosophically reasoned. Behar claims that what draws her and other scholars to write personally is "a desire to abandon the alienating 'metalanguage' that closes instead of opening the doors of academe to all those who wish to enter."[8] Behar says:

> Personal writing represents a sustained effort to democratize the academy. Indeed, it emerges from the struggles of those traditionally excluded from the academy, such as women and members of minority groups, to find a voice that acknowledges both their sense of difference and their belated arrival on the scholarly scene. "Yes, we are here," so many of the personal texts seem to assert, "but we are not who you think we are!"[9]

The implied goal of such personalized writing is to add another perspective to the ongoing dialogue of multiple perspectives that has replaced the earlier search for objectivity. This is a perspective that includes both the I and the You.

"Call it sentimentality," Behar proclaims, "I think a growing number of scholars have become impatient with cold-blooded analysis, which places the observer, and therefore the reader, at a safe, clinical, Mr. Spockian distance from the observed."[10]

She cautiously concludes: "Obviously, personal writing isn't a cure for all the inadequacies of scholasticism. And, as with any new paradigm, the criteria for evaluating personal writing is still hazy and uncertain."[11]

Personalized research and writing that insists on a variety of perspectives is by no means limited to one academic discipline, or for that matter, to the academic world alone. Perspectivist thinking now spans the gamut of modern life in general. It more recently has even taken hold in the sciences. Perspectivism is found in ethical theory, psychology, sociology, and biology. Social workers and psychologists practice Perspectivism as a matter of professionalism; even mathematicians speak about the mathematical perspective. Perspectivist thinking is also taking hold in the cathedral of objectivity, the so-called hard sciences.

In physics, especially in theoretical and particle physics, the object of verifiable research, the material world, has slipped away as scientists penetrate deeper and deeper into the mysteries of *materia*. What was still unthinkable for Albert Einstein has become almost commonplace among modern physicists. When it comes to telling the story of how the universe came into being, a new consensus emerges. The smallest units of our material world seem to emanate out of nothingness and in the grand scheme of things nothingness and something appear convertible. To some scientists, the properties of the smallest particles that make up our world do not at all need to be fixed by eternal laws, as traditional scientists assumed. They seem to depend instead on a mysterious gauge field underlying our reality from which each particle draws its peculiar character.

Many scientists agree that in the face of these mysteries not one but a multitude of stories might be correct. This phenomenon at the base of our understanding of the natural world has rightly been called post-modern physics. In *Superstrings and the Search for the Theory of Everything*,[12] David Peat says that theories in physics have lost direct contact with reality. Theories are no longer tested in experimental laboratories, but by their aesthetics, mathematical consistency and by their connection with other theories. As we will discuss later, a monumental shift has taken place in the hall of the so-called objective sciences. Many scientists today believe that the center of traditional objectivity, the material world is barred to our objective understanding.

Such a shift at the basis of science exerts its impact on all areas of modern life. Under the old paradigm of objective science, Perspectivist thinking, when it occurred in the arts and the humanities for instance, was treated as a pre-scientific shortcoming. Perspectivism marked those academic fields, which had not yet reached the kind of objectivity that was thought to be characteristic of the physical sciences. Psychology, sociology, and the humanities, in which some level of Perspectivist thinking has always been the rule, traditionally tried to hide their so-called "unscientific" underpinnings. The last shift in scientific thinking, however, strongly suggests that Perspectivist thinking may be the rule of the universe instead of being its exception.

Biology, for example, in the past, was eager to emulate the physical sciences in the attempt to become objective. Influenced by positivistic science, biology drew a picture of animals and their behavior in totally automatic, functional terms. Under the old paradigm of objective science, to speak of animals' feelings, their pain, loneliness, and joys, in human terms was generally considered irresponsible science. More recently, scientists have been rethinking the value and place of so-called anthropomorphism.[13] Kim McDonald, in an article in the *Chronicle of Higher Education*, claims that anthropomorphism, which has long been considered taboo, "is now being recognized as an important scientific tool in animal-behavior studies."[14] Says McDonald: "A growing number of ethologists think it is wrong simply to dismiss anthropomorphic thinking outright. They have begun arguing in journals and other scholarly publications that anthropomorphism, when used selectively, can be a valuable scientific tool."[15]

In order to enhance our relationship with animals, Perspectivism suggests trying to see the world through their eyes. Perspectivism encourages the researcher to identify with the world of the animal, including its emotions, hopes, pleasures, and pains. In evaluating an animal's action, the researcher should ask: "What makes sense from the perspective of the animal?"

When trying to figure out reasons for a hognose snake's strange behavior, Gordon M. Burghardt, a psychology professor at the University of Tennessee, admits that his scientific research would have gone nowhere had he not been able to "imagine" himself in the situation of the snake. From that perspective, he then asked the question: "What makes sense?" Objectivism, in contrast, usually asked: "What makes sense from our human perspective?" The new Perspectivist scholarship first identifies with the object of the study (be it another person, animal, or plant) and then asks what makes sense from that point of view – from that perspective.

By granting a subjective perspective to the "objects" in nature, we accept in the other a living and changing point of view instead of that of a dead construct. By encouraging such communication, Perspectivist thinking reshapes our relationship with nature. Under the old paradigm of objective truth, nature was degraded into a mere thing. Animals were identified as soulless creatures, which do not feel pain because they have no concept of pain. They were considered mere automatons created for our use. Perspectivism establishes a new respect for animals and plants, because it invites us to seek compassionate identification with the plight of the natural world. Perspectivism introduces a new type of holistic anthropomorphism. Perspectivism allows us to see human beings, with their minds and their emotional attachments, as part of the natural world instead of separate from it. Since we are part of it, we may not find it strange that nature repeats some of the emotions we feel and the actions we perform.

For too long we believed that language is particular to human beings. We now have found that many animal species have quite developed ways of communicating with each other. We have found that animals can trick each other, play games with each other and even that animals teach each other moral standards. Western philosophers have long assumed that morality was exclusively human, a result of our ability to reason. Ethical laws, from a religious, mythological perspective, were supposed to be a special gift from God, an endowment from a transcendent heaven to save humanity from evil. Today scientists talk about the evolution of ethics, from simple ethical behavior to a more complex one among primates.

In the last part of my book, I will show how Perspectivism redefines our understanding of the material world. Perspectivist philosophy searches for a plausible theory that lets us not only understand, but also eventually identify with so-called inanimate objects. This was common among primal people, who believed that spirits inhabited the whole world. Such animistic beliefs were eradicated by orthodox religions, enlightened reason, and scientific discoveries. Can we learn a new way of communicating again with those things we ordinarily consider inanimate, soulless, inorganic, or dead? Are we able, as modern human beings, to reconnect with nature, the earth, and even with the universe?

While primal people practiced a respectful dialogue with the forces of nature inherent in volcanoes, mountains, rocks, and the sea, we severed this connection with our scientific paradigm. By promoting ideas of pan-spiritualism and quantum animism, Perspectivism teaches us to reconnect ourselves with the natural world. Perspectivism suggests re-spiritualizing our relationship with the world of "mere things." Quantum Animism promotes the idea that physical objects at the quantum level exist not as little blocks of dead material, but as conscious events. Communicating with all parts of the universe is shamanistic practice and in a deep sense, Transcendental Perspectivism is the philosophy of the shamans.

Two

THE SACRED WHEEL

> Earth cannot be changed for the better unless we
> achieve a transformation in the consciousness of
> individuals and in public life.
> Parliament of World Religions

Transcendental Perspectivism promotes spiritual awareness. Connecting with
the universe is at the heart of any spirituality. Spirituality without a second
person perspective, a perspective of the other, would be lifeless. Unfortunately, we often find this kind of lifeless practice among traditional religiosity. But far from discrediting religions, Transcendental Perspectivism embraces the best of all religions. A remarkable event, that demonstrates such a
unity in diversity among the world religions, took place during the last part of
the twentieth century in Chicago.

In 1993, Chicago hosted the Second Parliament of World Religions.
Commemorating the First Parliament of World Religions, which was held
there in 1893, the Second Parliament attracted representatives from over
sixty different religious creeds and sects. They came together to discuss, interact, celebrate, and criticize.

Because of the sheer number of lectures, performances, meetings, and
other offerings, taking part in the parliament could easily have left participants with an overwhelming sense of disorientation. For this reason, we
could conclude that the conference copied the liberal marketplace; it was a
smorgasbord of images and ideas. The rainbow-like presence of most traditional world religions and the participation of many fringe groups (such as
futurologists, neo-pagans, UFO-theorists, theosophical anthropologists, and
secular humanists) however, resulted in a celebration of multiculturalism and
a mega-spirituality worthy of such a global event.

At the final gathering in Grant Park, a document on world ethics was
read that had been put together by a representative number of the religious
leaders present at the parliament. Recalling the Human Rights Declaration of
the United Nations in 1948, the Global Ethics document affirmed the "fundamental unity of the human family on Earth." The Global Ethics declaration
stated that religious leaders wished "to confirm and deepen" from "the perspective of an ethic: the full realization of the intrinsic dignity of the human
person, the inalienable freedom and equality in principle of all human beings,
and the necessary solidarity and interdependence of all humans with each
other."[1]

The authors of the document expressed their full awareness of the
bloodstained history of church relationships that is filled with hostility, intol-

erance, and outright warfare. The leaders affirmed that they "do not wish to gloss over or ignore the serious differences among the individual religions. However, they should not hinder us from proclaiming publicly those things which we already hold in common and which we jointly affirm, each on the basis of our own religious or ethical grounds."[2]

The forward-looking and ecumenical quality expressed in this document of Global Ethics became even more evident in a publication about the parliament that gave public voice to each participating group. This book, *A Sourcebook for the Community of Religions*,[3] demonstrated a point of unity between the participating sections that made this event truly remarkable. The authors asked each contributor to briefly identify the elements within their faith that would address the most burning issues facing humanity at the end of the twentieth century. It was the underlying premise of the book – and, by implication, of the organizers of the event – that elaborating on our differences in dogma and ritual is no longer useful. The current state of the world has put a new urgency on the quest for the unity of all humankind and for harmony with the natural world. Instead of reiterating old dogmas that in the past only served to separate us, the tenor of this conference was our common future. The goal was to find in each of the ancient traditions the most creative and best that we can utilize to change the destructive course of humanity.

Instead of continuing old animosities, the Global Ethics document affirmed, "religions cannot solve the environmental, economic, political, and social problems of Earth." However, religions "can provide what obviously cannot be attained by economic plans, political programs, or legal regulations alone." Churches and religious communities can nurture among their members the compassion needed to save our ailing Earth. They should exhort their followers to engage in ecological action, and they must use their organizing skills to bring together the peoples of this earth, instead of dividing them further. These are also the goals of Transcendental Perspectivism. According to the Document of Global Ethics we need:

> a change in the inner orientation, the whole mentality, the "hearts" of people, and a conversion from a false path to a new orientation for life. Humankind urgently needs social and ecological reforms, but it needs spiritual renewal just as urgently. As religious or spiritual persons we commit ourselves to this task. The spiritual powers of the religions can offer a fundamental sense of trust, a ground of meaning, ultimate standards, and a spiritual home. Of course, religions are credible only when they eliminate those conflicts, which spring from the religions themselves, dismantling mutual arrogance, mistrust, prejudice, and even hostile images, and thus demonstrate respect for the traditions, holy places, feasts, and rituals of people who believe differently.[4]

Many ancient traditions created the symbol of the sacred wheel to express unity within diversity; reinterpreted, this same symbol best expresses a new and urgent sense of common destiny. We see the spokes of the wheel as a multitude of ritual expressions of the Sacred. Different historical situations have created different symbolic expressions and displays. All recognize the sacred hub, which resides at the center, as the powerful focus. Problems arose, however, when religions placed themselves into the center or when they started to define the hub in positive terms. Separation resulted especially when religions claimed that their definition was the only true one. Dogmatism and superior thinking ensued. Such ideologies pitted people and nations against each other in the name of the Sacred. A pyramid of divinely-delegated power soon replaced the sacred wheel. Hierarchy replaced connectedness.

Aristotle compared God with the lover who attracts the beloved. With this, Aristotle did not suggest a movement away from this earth to a transcendent heaven; but that was the interpretation religion chose to believe during the later Christian phase. For Aristotle, the Unmoved Mover was the source of all movement, the efficient and the final cause, all in one, a power that kept the process alive. It was nothing more and nothing less than the principle that guarantees that life is love.

From the human perspective, the truth of the hub is emptiness. Buddhists affirmed this emptiness, and many mystics have experienced it. Ancient Hebrew laws decreed: never name the Unnamable. This emptiness prevents a new dogmatism to take hold. For some, perhaps this emptiness stands for ultimate futility and despair; for others the empty center invites an all-encompassing love. The cosmic response results in an ongoing circle of life. Without needing to define the center, this sense of connectedness alone acts as a powerful force. Recovering a sense of connectedness and interconnectedness is one of the major aims of Perspectivism. We need mature emotional attachment and the ability to love to effectively exercise such interconnectedness.

Traditional Western philosophy (with its focus on reason and rationality) removed emotional attachment from educated discourse. A broad spectrum of critics has rightly exposed this far-reaching fact. Within patriarchal and hierarchical structures, emotions were delegated to the bottom of the heap. In order to achieve a dispassionate middle-way in an ethical judgment the Greeks regarded the influence of emotions as a hindrance. Western philosophers in general dismissed emotive attachment as not worthy of rational consideration – and as feminine, which they considered negative. Reason was supposed to replace emotion. Where reason did not suffice, authoritarianism and naked power stood ready to take its place.

This hostile treatment of emotions resulted in a peculiar situation. Today all necessary data have been collected that are needed to call for an immediate change of the destructive course of humanity on earth. What is lacking is the will to act, not only by the world leaders, but also by the population at large. Emotions motivate us and drive us to act. In antiquity, Aristotle's insistence on prudence as a middle way between two bad passions elevated reason above emotional involvement. Within this conceptual framework, desires and wants were considered at best amoral, at worst inherently evil.

The lack of emotional involvement, which often translates into a lack of a will to live, is frighteningly real and much more widespread than any theoretical exposition can suggest. No philosophical discourse can capture the pain and frustration of many young people today. They grow up in a world without hope, a world without utopia, a world full of cheating and crime and hunger and death, a world without compassion. More teenagers smoke today than only ten years ago. When asked, why, they shrug and may say: "There just isn't anything we can hope for." Searching deeper reveals great despair with the world of adults, the society they are supposed to grow into. They realize the extent to which human beings have damaged the earth, and they don't believe that much can alter the course of destruction. The only escape they can find is emotional detachment in one instance and pleasure for the moment in the next. Since this attitude often fits with the demands of a smoothly functioning consumer society, there exists little incentive to change this cataclysmic direction.

This is perhaps the deepest failure of Western secularism: with its marriage to consumption and presumably endless progress secular society has promoted a passionless reasonability, which leaves our children aimless. Glittering shopping malls have become the temples of Post-Modernity. The only act truly sanctioned, the act that supposedly creates meaning in life, is the consumption of goods. On other actions, those that might be the source of creative joy and alternately the cause for change in society at large, we frown upon as improper and provocative. In our communities we pay little attention to the real needs of our children.

We provide expensive entertainment in video arcades and bowling alleys. These are often costly places business–minded adults have arranged for teenagers to play by the rules of an adult world. When in our own community young people tried to open a self–managed youth club, authorities closed it down quickly. They give code violations and insurance problems as reasons to prevent our youth from developing their ideas. When schools arrange such events they are tightly controlled, often even by police officers. Rock bands must submit their lyrics to an adult supervisor days before the event. All this communicates a sense of powerlessness and authoritarian control.

Many children withdraw from society. In school they learn quickly what's necessary to get by. They play the game and pretend to fit in. But inside they die. Only a few have the courage to revolt. If that revolt ever materializes, people around them react with rejection instead of encouragement. Seldom do they encourage channeling justified anger into fruitful social action and change. They leave frustration to the individual as a totally private expression. Even here consumer society offers legitimate fixes, such as alcohol, cigarettes and other legalized drugs. In spite of the official anti-drug rhetoric, society tolerates and tacitly even sanctions drugs such as alcohol and cigarettes – as long as they do not interfere with work.

How can we get our young generation involved again in the sacred wheel of life? How can we get them passionately dedicated to their well-being and the welfare of all life? Religions have a role to fulfill. Religious congregations are often the only community that young people experience, unfortunately often against their will. Here a spiritual focus toward all being and a complete acceptance of difference must be taught and practiced. Chauvinism, bigotry, and other sectarian phobias must become a thing of the past, especially among those who call themselves religious.

Most of us from the older generation were brought up within the confines of one specific religious creed. To leave the inherited religion behind and gain a larger view of the sacred wheel was often considered a heretical act. This was (and still is) especially true within the mainstream of Christianity, Judaism, and Islam. Yet today's problems demand a new religiosity, one that not only tolerates but also appreciates difference. A new believer needs to emerge who can move with burning heart from one creed to the other and extract the best from all of them. This, in turn, will inspire those within the confines of a specific creed to excel and show the best of their faith. The times of bickering over dogma must finally come to an end. The realization of the boundless variety of the Sacred Hub is at hand.

During the congress of world religions, my son and I wandered through the halls of the Chicago Palmer House Hotel from one lecture to the other, listening to Buddhists and Pagans, to Zoroastrians and Sikhs, to non-denominational Christians and Bahais. My son, about twenty years of age then, remarked: "We are moving from spoke to spoke on the sacred wheel, but we are not just observers. We identify with all of them. We become part of each of these communities, because our hearts are open."

So many academics with their modernist sense of right and wrong go to these conference lectures, performances, and ceremonies, only to find out how they differ intellectually. Often foremost in their minds is how to squeeze out another paper on the disparity between this and that sect. Had we been there with our rational mind alone, we too would have found so much wrong with each individual approach. But since we were there with burning hearts, deeply concerned for the well being of the whole planet, we could participate in their ceremonies with a new sensitivity. We could listen to their lectures with a new mind, a mind that focused not on the differences, but on the passion and beauty of the message, as each offered tools for restoration and repair.

A vision of a new personality emerged from these proceedings. This new person must be able to move between the different creeds and religions and call them all his or her home. All religions, from their perspective, contribute to the beautiful story we call life, and to its preservation and enhancement. This new person takes inspiration from the emptiness of the hub. This person can return to the hub for safety when one of the spokes entangles him or her with the claim of exclusivity and sole truth. Any such claim, from the perspective of the hub, must be seen as idolatry – worthy of deconstruction.

What then is the role of religions in this secular world? Religions can never turn back to a time when one religious faith would align itself with government power and rule over others. The conflicts, wars, and persecutions that resulted from such theocracies were the reason for the secularization process that separated church and state, perhaps forever.

For much of the twentieth century, public education in the West followed the Greek ideal of trust in science and reason. If we could raise the children of the world to apply rational standards in their judgments, goodness would follow. By no means do I advocate here the total abandonment of this noble goal. But we cannot continue to take for granted the modernist definition of rationality (with its base in a traditional concept of scientific truth). As postmodern science allows for a more diverse approach to truth and, by implication, to religious expression, we must develop a new strategy that again allows for value education in public schools without favoring one religion over another. Alongside logic and critical thinking, we must base this new educational model on the teaching and practicing of self-empowerment, emotional intelligence, compassion, and partnership.

The role of all religions, whether their followers meet in churches, synagogues, temples, mosques, private homes, or in nature, will be to give their members a sense of community, tradition, and ritual, while also emphasizing respect for other traditions. We can best achieve this by exposing young people as early as possible to many diverse rituals, by visiting neighboring communities, planning interfaith church outings or inviting groups from different religions to our own meetings, get-togethers, and services. We must abandon the traditional idea of "making converts." Only with mutual acceptance and respect can we approach the much larger goals of saving the planet and of making our environment safe for future generations of human beings, animals, and plants.

In my world religions class, I take students to different religious sites so they can experience first-hand the beauty and sincerity of other faiths. Instead of lecturing about different religions with a sense of detached objectivity, as in the traditional classroom, I expose students to the emotional side of each faith. This gives them the chance to empathize with many traditions in the search for a common spiritual future.

One of the best parables for religious tolerance comes from an old rabbinical story that became the center of a German enlightenment play by Gotthold Ephraim Lessing.[5] In this play, called *Nathan, the Wise*, a father possesses the truth represented by a ring. He passes the ring on to the oldest son who in turn gives it to his son, and so on. The time comes when a father has three sons whom he loves equally. When he is dying he calls each of them separately and gives each a ring. They all believe that they hold the truth.

After the father's death they start quarreling with each other. They end up in a court run by a wise Muslim judge. The judge listens to their story and decides that perhaps none of them has the right ring. Perhaps their father had lost the original and had three fake rings made to please each of his sons. But the judge continues by saying that the true ring also has the power to make the bearer loved by all others. We are asked to appreciate and love each other, so that others may love us in return.

Despite the lack of tolerance often practiced by major religions, we can find evidence for the acceptance of religious diversity in all of them. In the Christian bible, Jesus speaks of the many mansions that can be found in his father's house.[6] I have always taken this as a confirmation of the different religious interpretations possible and the diverse positions we can hold toward the Sacred.

An unambiguous message also comes from the Quuran. Here the prophet explains the division of the human community into factions as a test for people of faith. The prophet encourages responsible and charitable behavior as a way to demonstrate God's love. The Quuran says: "If God had so willed, He would have made all of you one community, (He has not done so) that He may test you in what He has given you; so compete with one another in good works. To God you shall all return and He will tell you (the truth) about that which you have been disputing."[7]

Another example for the kind of attitude needed to promote global religious understanding comes from Mahatma Gandhi. One of his dedicated followers, a Hindu man whose young son had been murdered by Muslims, asked the master what he could do to end the emotional pain and how he could ever learn to forgive. Gandhi told the man that he should go out and adopt one of the many Muslim orphans and raise him as his child, not as a Hindu, but as a Muslim.

Three

PERSPECTIVES
FROM THE EDGE OF CHAOS

> In all chaos there is a cosmos, in all disorder a
> secret order.
>
> Carl Gustav Jung

We live in a chaotic world. Chaos surrounds us. Who would seriously doubt this? When facing chaos, darkness, the unknown, we prefer to recoil, hide away, and turn our face to something familiar.

Frequently, I ask my students to brainstorm: first on order and then on chaos. With order they associate a long line of positive attitudes such as stability, security, direction, trust, even health and long life. Chaos, in turn, stands for fear, darkness, anxiety, loneliness, incoherence, and even death. Seldom do they cross over to see some positive qualities in chaos, such as creativity, fun, and freedom.

Emotions are the chaos within us. In the face of love and goodness exists evil. Sickness and death surround us. Death is the ultimate chaos that we all will have to face someday. What use is there, therefore, in contacting the other? Is not the other only the extended arm of the void? Why should we trust it? In the other we run the chance to lose our hard earned Self.

Odysseus already knew this. When the Sirens called him he asked his colleagues to tie him to the mast of the ship. Self-forgetting, passion, and death are inextricably intertwined.

Who could blame the Greeks when they preferred the light of reason to chaos, and chose rationality? Wasn't reason the voice of the divine? The value a culture puts on order and chaos defines that culture's relationship to the universe and to the natural world. It determines the way people relate to God, nature, animals and each other. Human beings first formulated the story of order and chaos in the oldest mythologies, and then it continued on in religions and, eventually, in science. The story of chaos is central if we want to understand the transformation of our culture into a more cooperative, partnership-oriented one.

Chaos, in Egyptian mythology, occupied a prominent place. The *Book of the Dead* is one of the oldest documents dating between 2000 and 1500 BC. According to that mythology, in the beginning there was Nun, a Chaos-like primal fluid, which like a snake-body lifted itself into being, becoming Atum and Ra, the sun disk and the rising and setting of the sun.[1] Egyptians called Chaos "the father of the gods." It was the creative beginning of everything. Chaos brought forth a line of gods and pharaohs who ruled the destiny of the country for thousands of years. Atum, formless in the beginning and residing within Nun, bore the seed for everything. In later worship, Egyptians considered Atum the father of the human race. Atum, by the effort of his will, rose from the abyss and presided as Ra over the universe. Ra brought forth eight gods. The first human beings grew from his tears and from them came all other living creatures.

Ra at first reigned peacefully over creation. As he aged, however, his divine offspring, Isis, took advantage of his senility and made him reveal his name. By knowing his name, Isis gained magical powers over Ra. From this point on, conflict and strife entered the peaceful heavens of the Egyptians. On orders of Nun, Ra withdrew angrily into a distant heaven and created a new, less-perfect world, in which human beings were condemned to live.

In Greek mythology, chaos played a lesser, more negative role from the beginning. Gaia, the mother goddess of Earth, created the gods and human beings. According to the classical Greek writer Hesiod, Chaos was in the beginning, vast and dark, but Gaia appeared (unrelated to Chaos) and so did Eros. They resided over the formation of all things. In the Greek mind, chaos never had a creative power; instead the Greeks thought of it as an open space, which could be filled with objects. Later still, the idea of disorder was attached to the word Chaos. Some scholars speculate that this was the result of a "false derivation from a word meaning 'to pour'." After this change, Chaos meant the confused, unorganized mass of the elements scattered through space.[2]

From Chaos were born Erebus and Night. Under the reign of Chronos, Night gave birth to a long list of miseries: Doom and Death, from which later came Sleep and Dream. From the same source came the *Fates*, responsible to apportion good and evil at the birth of every child. Night also bore Nemesis, Fraud, Old Age, Incontinence, Sorrow, Forgetfulness and Hunger. Disease, Combat, Murder, Massacres, Lies and Injustices were, according to classical Greek mythology, also the direct creation of Chaos. No wonder the Greeks did everything they could to stay away from this terrible condition.

The whole body of Greek philosophy, which, in turn, has influenced all of Western civilization, represents a persistent attempt to escape and diminish the power of Chaos. For the Greek mind, chaos was a defect, a mistake, an absence of order that had slipped into the world as a result of the dabbling of some lower celestial gods who didn't know any better.

Had the whole universe been the sole creation of the *demiourg*, the master god of Aristotle, chaos would have been non-existent. God, however, endowed us human beings with *ratio*, ordering reason, so we can fix the chaos and provide it with order. In this classical universe, once human beings had achieved total order, they could finally overcome fate, which ruled even the gods of the Greek pantheon. They could know and predict everything. The future would be ours to tell, and this would represent the ultimate triumph of reason.

The Greek faith in the supremacy of reason and order entered into our scientific creed and became the foundation of science. In the mechanical universe of Isaac Newton, the heavenly bodies and the whole physical world followed iron laws of nature. Nature was, as the German philosopher Immanuel Kant expressed, the realm of necessity. Nothing in nature possessed the freedom that human beings enjoyed: the freedom to make choices, the freedom to choose between right and wrong. Here on earth, God gave freedom to human beings, and to them alone, as a special gift.

René Descartes's rationalism, but even Darwinism and the theory of evolution supported this mechanistic view of nature. Scientists considered all of nature as part of a mechanical universe. Human beings alone, because of their ability to make free choices, were set apart. The ability of the human being to experience freedom and make genuine choices became a hotly debated topic in modern philosophy and psychology. Existentialism built the case of humanity on the ability of human beings to make choices. At a time when the sciences, in general, followed the path of relentless materialism, existentialism rescued the human animal from the fate of faceless identification with the rest of the material world. Jean-Paul Sartre's existentialism celebrated the ability to choose death as the ultimate guarantee for human freedom.

Total application of the mechanical universe, however, would condemn the human being to a mere automaton as well. Some influential branches of modern psychology followed precisely that route. The Newtonian worldview left its marks on sociology and psychology. Marxist sociology declared the human being a product of historical forces, while capitalism put more emphasis on the chaotic twists and turns of the marketplace to plot the way of the individual in history. In both models the underlying motives for action were placed on outside forces. The realm of freedom for the individual was increasingly confined to the private sphere. A new individual emerged under the influence of materialism: one that was totally conditioned by external forces. Ivan Petrovich Pavlov's conditioned response system was the perfect application of Newtonian physics to the animal realm and, later, to the human sphere as well. Under the name of behaviorist psychology, the same thinking became popular in the United States as Nick Herbert in *Elemental Mind* points out:

> Behaviorism extended the Newtonian worldview to the realm of living beings, treating dogs as well as human beings as clockwork creatures, whose behavior could be described solely in terms of stimulus/response reaction, without regard to their inner experiences. In this "Newtonian psychology," Pavlov's dog, and by extension Van Pavlov himself and the rest of us, is a mere machine, utterly predictable once experimental psy-

chologists learn the underlying laws of behavior, – animal "laws of motion" corresponding to Newton's physical laws.[3]

Whenever chaos appeared in this Newtonian world, scientists either ignored or eliminated it (since order was always superior to chaos). In the physical sciences, and especially in applied physics, scientists idealized mental models of the real world to such an extent that order seemed evident and workable. The best building was the one with the straightest lines and the most geometrical shapes. The best society was completely engineered from the top down; the best human beings were completely in control of their affairs. Scientists straightened out (by sophisticated and costly behavior modification or chemicals) those who deviated from the norm. Book keepers and bureaucrats, in all their facelessness, became the new ideal.

In the introduction to Ilya Prigogine's ground breaking book *Order Out of Chaos*,[4] Alvin Toffler depicted the world of classical science as "a world in which every event was determined by initial conditions that were, at least in principle, determinable with precision. It was a world in which all the pieces came together like cogs in a cosmic machine."[5] During the nineteenth and most of the twentieth century, the image of a "simple, uniform, mechanical universe" not only shaped the development of science, but influenced most other areas of human development. We even shaped our social orders (the large bureaucracies that governed most modern industrialized nations) like giant machines, their "checks and balances clicking like parts of a clock." The achievements of the technological mind confirmed "the image of the universe as an engineer's giant Tinker toy."[6]

Not surprisingly, the human mind, too, conformed to the same logic that dictates the efficiencies of machines. Human beings often viewed their emotions, disorder, chaos, and the temporal inefficiencies of the creative mind as mental and social aberrations. Well-organized societies installed public systems of education and rehabilitation with a minimal emphasis on the development of the creative mind. Neo-conservative theoretician Allan Bloom, in *The Closing of the American Mind,* even called creativity "a kind of opiate of the masses."[7] Measurability and quantification became the hallmarks of bureaucracies everywhere: all but destroying the soul of education.

In the 1980s, Chaos theory briskly inspired reinterpretations and new avenues in many sciences. For instance, a Jungian psychologist in Switzerland, Joanne Wieland-Burston, extensively researched the application of basic findings of chaos theory in the therapeutic diagnosis of psychological disorders. Wieland-Burston found that "most contemporary Western societies have a negative connotation regarding the idea of Chaos. The denial of the existence of Chaos as a viable aspect of the real world goes hand in hand with our tendency to overestimate order."[8]

In contrast to the traditional sciences, some forward-looking scientists who were influenced by their research into chaotic systems became "more

and more convinced that in nature chaos and order are not irreconcilable con-
tradictions, but that chaos appears as a transitional phase between an old and
a new order. It is revealed as a necessary aspect of all development and
growth."[9]

Wieland-Bursten developed a new approach to psychotherapy utilizing
the chaotic experiences of a patient as a vital component in the healing process. She saw strong emotional experiences, such as the death of a loved one,
the fear involved in coping with sickness, or the boredom that results from an
unfulfilled job as strange-attractors. Scientists use this term in chaotic systems for an attractor that causes a system to deviate from its regular course
and become chaotic. Such strange attractors, often minimal in their initial
impact, become enlarged through feedback loops. When the effects of
strange-attractors reach bifurcation points, they eventually tip the scale of our
life toward one side or the other.

Wieland-Bursten noted that it might be impossible to reach a descrip-
tive model of psychological processes with any absolute precision. Scientists
may explain machines in logical, functional terms, but they can no longer
fully explain (in strictly mechanistic terms) processes of active self-
organization – which modern scientists today not only observe in human beings but also in the physical, chemical, and biological worlds. Contrary to
Freudian psychology, psychologists influenced by chaos theory generally
assert that the logic of the human psyche demands a new, non-linear description.

Similarly, the often chaotic processes of the real world, the dripping of
a water faucet, the turbulent currents of a river, the weather patterns, or the
ups and down of the stock market also required a new description. Mathematicians of chaos found this new description in non-linear mathematics, which
is more suited to describe chaotic processes instead of orderly or static
events.

Fractal geometry and non-linear mathematics provide a new way of
representing chaotic processes of the real world. But does this new
mathematics make those processes of a higher order more understandable,
perhaps even predictable? No inherent principle exists, according to Wieland-Burston, that would make non-linear processes, involving consciousness
and emotions, completely incomprehensible. But because of their non-
linearity and chaos they will never be completely predictable.

To delve into chaos, we need a new understanding – an understanding
that allows and is comfortable with incomplete predictability. This perhaps
means knowing without the ability to control. Traditional scientists aimed for
complete control and manipulation in their understanding of nature. Once
scientists applied these traditional principles of understanding to the human
being, we too became perfect objects of manipulation. For a domineering
man, for instance, a woman who resists submission and stands on her own is
a complete enigma.

In a traditional dominator society, the "mysterious woman" has become proverbial. Sigmund Freud, who believed the therapist needs rational control over his client, found his limits in the young Nora (of whom he wrote extensively). To his great dismay, Freud observed Nora's resistance to an older family friend's sexual advances. This made Nora an interesting case for the therapist, but also a puzzle to understand. Lacking the ability to control, the therapist saw no possible way to heal her. According to Freud, the older man's advances should have flattered the melancholic young woman. Young ladies should react that way, according to the male-centered attitude of that time. Instead, Nora chose the friendship of an older woman from whom she learned the intricacies of womanhood. Against the classical therapist, and his role as a controller and manipulator, Nora found her health in her emancipation as a woman. For this reason, Nora became an icon of modern feminism.[10]

A new understanding of the human psyche, based on the principles of chaos, makes equal use of a patient's rational and irrational parts. This approach to therapy grants the whole other – not just the rational faculties – an emancipated status that a therapist cannot and should not violate. This announces "a paradigm shift" within science, a novel dialogue with nature, as Prigogine asserts. The science of Chaos poses a new challenge to traditional science. An intelligible mixture of chance and necessity marks this revolution in science. According to Prigogine, traditional science's dialogue with nature, though initially extremely successful, eventually yielded the discovery of a silent world.

> This is the paradox of classical science. It revealed to men a dead, a passive nature, a nature that behaves as an automaton that, once programmed, continues to follow the rules inscribed in the program. In this sense the dialogue with nature isolated human beings from nature instead of bringing him closer to it. A triumph of reason turned into a sad truth. It seemed that science debased everything it touched.[11]

Prigogine thought that classical science left a sad heritage: a world in which we could only count one perspective – that of the "rational" human mind. In the end, we only had a domineering perspective of objectivity and system. The mechanical application of scientific principles in sociology and psychology lead to the degradation of the individual in much of the twentieth century. As scientists willingly cooperated with the tyrannical systems on the left and the right, we can hold their scientific indifference at least partially responsible for the dehumanization and totalitarian politics in the East and West.

Chaos theory shows a new perspective. Whenever natural systems encounter an excess of order and sterility, they move themselves toward the edge of chaos. This is true for the simplest logical system played out on a computer screen, as well as for large systems of the material and natural world. Chaos is the creative principle that aids evolution by playfully supplying a continuous storehouse of possibilities. Scientists have found a self-organizing faculty in all chaotic systems. Contrary to Greek and Hebrew myths, chaos does not find order due to an outside force imposing an ordering logos. According to Paul Davies, self-organization presupposes a degree of "global cooperation" of the individual members of a particular system.[12] We find examples of self-organization and global cooperation in many different natural systems such as astronomy, physics, chemistry, and biology. For natural systems to have an intrinsic perspective, the phenomenon of self-organization is essential. Scientists based the theory of quantum animism on the ability of quantum systems to self-organize.

As the Greek myth would have it, nothing useful could ever come from chaos, only misery and death. Under the influence of this classical bend for order, and aided by a similar message of the Judeo-Christian God, Western human beings set out to eliminate chaos and bring order everywhere. In reality this mentality managed to eliminate a great variety of species, which had developed as a result of chaotic self-organization in natural systems. In our ignorance we felt the need to eliminate all those things in nature for which our limited view saw no immediate use. Life on earth would have perished long ago had it been left to the limited imagination of human beings to create order.

The science of chaos adds a new dimension to Perspectivism. Under the old paradigm, we would have had no reason to imagine a perspective of chaos. In the face of a chaotic situation, people had only one direction to go – away from it. Now it makes sense to trust in the value of chaos. We can see disorder and chaos, the unknown, as a friend instead of always as an enemy. Chaos theory breathes new life into the lifeless universe of traditional science.

Though the idea of chaos as a positive and constructive energy has been present since early civilizations, the Western mind only saw its negative aspects. We realize now that those civilizations that lived in harmony with chaos fared better in their interaction with nature. While the West harmed (and possibly irreversibly damaged) the environment and the earth, other so-called primitive cultures lived in greater harmony with nature. Many indigenous cultures, once neglected by Western civilization as savage, can now guide us toward a more environmentally-sound philosophy and a more cooperative way of life.

In a later chapter, I will deal with the dangers inherent in chaos. In the Perspective of Evil, I will consider cases in which a compassionate identification with chaos may be a destructive and self-destroying pursuit. We must therefore study the perspective of chaos with care, under guidance, or, under some conditions, perhaps not at all.

PART II

THE HUMAN PERSPECTIVE

Four

THE QUEST FOR HAPPINESS: PERSPECTIVIST ETHICS, A WAY OUT OF THE CONFUSION?

> When we are happy we are always good, but
> when we are good we are not always happy.
> Oscar Wilde

One of the simplest questions we could ask turns out to be most difficult: How to live a happy and fulfilled life? When the first philosophers asked what the right way to live is, they did not primarily aim for goodness or to please some god; their first concern was happiness. With the passing of the Golden Age, human beings had lost some measure of happiness as well. Proof lies in the Minoan museum on the island of Crete in Heracleon. During most of their history, happy faces filled Minoan art. Playful scenes of human beings and animals flourished. During the last three to five hundred years, the so-called Palace Period, artistic representations of human faces were increasingly more anguished and the elaborate details, so characteristic for early Minoan art, disappeared. The late Palace Period coincides with the complete absorption of the Minoan civilization into mainstream Greek culture. At that time the warrior ethos already strongly influenced Greek culture and therefore, the Greeks developed a dominator way of life. Invading tribes from the north had imported this structure into Greece.

At the dawn of Greek civilization, when the ancient Greeks first found their written voice, much of their poetic literature lamented the loss of peace and harmony. Philosophers, blaming the strife among the gods for their troubles, looked for a rational answer to regain the lost happiness. If we could live in greater harmony with nature, we could recover happiness. To better understand nature and the universe the Greeks developed ontology, the search for the way things are. Plato's forms and Aristotle's universals were supposed to deliver that truth. To live in accordance with that truth would therefore produce a happy life.

This promise fell short in two ways. First, philosophers greatly disagreed about the nature of those universals or forms. Both philosophers insisted the forms should be the same for all. Plato optimistically believed that all those who managed to escape the darkness of the cave and adjust their eyes to see in the bright light would return with the same story. In reality, the stories our prophets told differ vastly and have given cause for much disagreement, fighting, and warfare. Though religions have a similar ethical underpinning, the prophets' stories speak of diversity and difference.

The second problem for philosophers was that few people could agree on what constituted happiness. Once the church fathers worked over the idea of truth they swiftly incorporated it into the paternalistic canon of domination and oppression. Church leaders tabled happiness as a good to have, not in this life, but in the next – in heaven. In the name of an almighty Father God the church instituted morality as a vehicle of control to keep her sheep in line. Philosophers now formulated ethics according to principles given by god or by drawing them from eternal laws in nature. Such disciplinarian ethics had little chance to survive into the modern age.

Eventually, philosophers created a new ethic that went back to the original idea of happiness as the ultimate good. Utilitarian ethics looks at the consequences of an action and determines its value by what is best for the majority of people. We practice such consequential ethics today in the public arena of commerce and politics. Since no stable, underlying values exist to judge our actions, and each action creates its own value system, self-interest, profit, and greed often masquerade as the public good. In politics and commerce, cost-efficiency calculations have replaced ancient principles. The result is widespread relativism, the idea that everything goes. How can Perspectivism navigate a new beginning for happiness to lead out of this confusion?

On a personal level, the tendency of traditional, universal-based ethics encouraged people to be normal. A normal person follows the norm. But we often misuse "normality" in a judgmental and moralistic way. Often, we treat people who are not normal as ill. But what is wrong if a person is not normal, if he or she does not do what other people do? For most of us, normal is still a normative term that we connect with an ought, because many still believe in the old notion that normal is in some way divinely inspired, more natural, or the more reasonable thing to do. This connotation, according to clinical psychologist Bernie Zilbergeld, only "serves to increase our anxiety and bad feelings and therefore makes clear thinking and productive decision making more difficult."[1] Zilbergeld gives a laundry list of does and don'ts that amounts to a minimal ethics worth considering.

Zilbergeld's rule of thumb is simple: "If what you want or do makes your life difficult or sets you and your partner at odds, then there is a problem, regardless of how typical your action may be."[2] Zilbergeld provides a useful list of actions we should try to avoid: If it's illegal, don't do it. If it's driven or compulsive, try to avoid it. If it gets in your way, you may do better looking for different solutions. If it creates problems with your partner, think it over whether you want it.

In human relationships people have problems as a rule. The solution: people must work out their differences, and we can do that through communication. Communication requires sensitivity for others, openness, and empathy. This brings us back to the main requirement of successful Perspectivism. Elaine Rodino, a clinical psychologist, who specializes in therapy for couples, recommends: "Get out of your head and try to understand how he (or she) thinks."[3] The rest is applied communication skills. We can and should practice and teach such skills more often and at all levels of education.

While the quest for a universal ethics as a global set of principles has failed, we have experienced a great revival of professional ethics. Most professions now have a stated set of ethical principles that derive directly from the specific demands of each particular profession. This, again, is Perspectivism in action. Often, in the professions, an ethics board reviews the ethical requirements of the profession. While a review of such professional ethics would be of great interest, for the sake of this book, I will narrow the discussion to one profession, counseling. This profession helps people to connect with themselves and their surroundings and is therefore of special interest for the topic of this book.

A novice counselor must, as a first order of priority, leave personal prejudice and values behind and see the world through the eyes of the client. The counselor needs to develop a second person perspective, or to submerge into the other. In order to do their job "right" counselors must develop a compassionate ear and acquire the skills of empathic listening. This counseling skill can help many of us in other professions and in life. The following story, reported in a counseling book, demonstrates how the lack of true empathy (along with a teacher's insistence on academic accuracy) can stifle and sometimes even crush human communication.

Authors Derald Wing Sue and David Sue, in *Counseling the Culturally Different*, tell the story of a Caucasian female schoolteacher in Oklahoma who had planned an "ethnic minority appreciation day" for her sixth-grade class.[4] The class had a large number of Native American students; therefore, part of the day was devoted to a unit on Native American heritage. An Native American student had designed a bonnet and dress of her tribe. Her fellow students expressed appreciation and admiration for her costume and tribal dance demonstration. However, the teacher was reported to have remained silent. Several days later the student received a low grade for her participation in the activities. The teacher praised the student's dance technique and beautiful costume, but stated critically that the costume was not typical for her tribe, that her dance was not traditional, and that the assignment was graded on "authenticity, not fantasy." The authors continue:

> When the parents heard about the remark they demanded a meeting with the teacher and principal. During the meeting the father expressed anger at "White folks always telling Indians who we are." The teacher's only response was to show the parents an anthropology book with what she claimed to be the typical headgear and costume of the family's tribe.[5]

This story illuminates how the obvious lack of empathy with a living tradition can end in total misunderstanding and insult. This teacher lacked any sensitivity for the still-developing tradition of an active tribe. The French philosopher Jacques Derrida pointed out how much harm we do to living things by freezing their development in concepts and in language. As this story emphasizes, this is especially true for living traditions once anthropologists or other academic disciplines catalogue them. The feedback loop created by such a system and by a teacher who reinforces the "academic truth" is remarkably powerful and, at times, nothing short of genocide.

What can we do to avoid such prejudice? How can we keep our minds open and remain sensitive to the changes that may occur in the other? Solving this question would bring us a big step closer to mutual understanding and peaceful coexistence. It would bring us all closer to happiness.

Sam Keen in *To a Dancing God* talks about bracketing our beliefs, our whole Self, if we truly want to understand the other.[6] Keen calls this "mature awareness." To step beyond ordinary awareness and develop mature awareness, Keen says, we have to give up "idiosyncratic and egocentric perception. . . ." Keen believes that mature awareness is possible only when we have "digested and compensated for the biases and prejudices that are the residue of my personal history."[7] We need to silence the familiar and welcome the strange. Keen believes that each time we approach a strange object, person, or event, we have a tendency to let our present needs, past experience, or expectations for the future determine what we will see. If I am to experience the uniqueness of any datum I must be, according to Keen, "sufficiently aware of my preconceived ideas and characteristic emotional distortions to bracket them long enough to welcome strangeness and novelty into my perceptual world."[8] Keen believes that the discipline of bracketing, compensating, or silencing requires "sophisticated self-knowledge and courageous honesty."[9] But, according to Keen, a sincere counselor cannot get around effective bracketing because "without this discipline each present moment is only the repetition of something already seen or experienced. In order for genuine novelty to emerge, for the unique presence of things, persons or events to take root in me, I must undergo a decentralization of the ego."[10]

The demand to lose our familiar Self is the secret of good counseling. On a larger scale, bracketing our self-interest for the sake of communication with the other is the way to compassionate humanity, the way to become an ethical being. On yet a higher level, going out of our familiar self into the other is the essence of mysticism and shamanism and therefore the central requirement of Perspectivism.

Perspectivist bracketing of our Self does not mean to give it up totally, as some forms of Buddhism may require. In Buddhism, the loss of Self is necessary in order to overcome the cycle of suffering and gain enlightenment. Bracketing as an ethical dimension of Perspectivism, however, means first becoming fully aware of our history and limitations and then putting aside, only temporarily, our Self for the sake of communicating and connecting with the other. The level of this Self-denial may vary depending on the situation and the depth of absorption into the other.

Using bracketing of self-interest as a central quality, the Perspectivist will lead a happier life. Perhaps paradoxically, this avoids using others as mere instruments for our happiness. Without bracketing we are bound to act toward others in a selfish manner, letting our interests prevail at each step. This, in turn, will make the recipient of care suspicious and often unwilling to accept help.

How does bracketing avoid the pitfalls of selfishness? Bracketing sends a signal to the other person that I will attempt to suspend self interest and will, at least for the present task, try to service the other. This signal, when received by others, develops a powerful feedback loop of trust, which often leads to a win-win situation for all participating parties. People are much more willing to give of themselves, give up their self interests, at least for some time, when the partner has given an unmistakable signal of having suspended his or her self interest for the time-being. Eventually this brings self-fulfillment and happiness. Through bracketing our interests, we can truly cooperate with others. We can become good teachers, successful parents, fulfilled partners, and, finally, happy human beings.

We can apply bracketing of self-interest to the larger scale of society and even to a global scale. In modern societies, those on the winning end of the social strata must adopt an ethical philosophy of willing cooperation. Those who carry the power in a given situation must become aware of their responsibility to justice. As Mahatma Gandhi, the great peacemaker of the twentieth century, once said, ". . . the test of orderliness in a country is not the number of millionaires it owns, but the absence of starvation among its masses."[11] Quite contrary to current thinking, Gandhi powerfully asserts, "The rich cannot accumulate wealth without the cooperation of the poor in society." Gandhi exhorts the wealthy in Perspectivist terms to look through the eyes of the dispossessed, if only for a short while. Then they might develop empathy and compassion. The modern empowerment movement has been using these techniques quite effectively, as I will discuss later in this book.

"We should be ashamed," says Gandhi "of resting or having a square meal so long as there is one able-bodied man without work or food." Finally, Gandhi asks the poor, too, to recognize the worth of the wealthy without which society would lack a vital ingredient for progress. Instead of asking – like Karl Marx did – for the elimination of the wealthy through revolution, and instead of creating false hopes for a fictional paradise of total equality, Gandhi encouraged a Perspectivist ethic of mutual compassion and trust. Gandhi says: "All that can legitimately be expected of the wealthy class is that they should hold their riches and talents in trust and use them for the service of the society. To insist on more would be to kill the goose that laid the golden eggs."[12]

When it comes to conflict resolution on a large scale, dominator thinking mostly rules our world community – the hallmark of the old paradigm. Instead of letting law and skilled tactics of non-violent conflict resolution rule our international relations we let them be dictated by power thinking. We allowed conflicts such as the Gulf War to be resolved by force, even while soldiers carried out such force with clinical precision.

What happens on the global scale is mirrored on a micro-scale of individuals and families. Consumerism has produced a passive populous, often incapable of empathy and compassion. The media's only goal is to sell goods and make a profit by selling cheap action and violence to an audience whose attention span has decreased as a result of it. Traditionally, novels and films told stories with the noble goal of allowing an insight into the mind and hearts of others. More recently, commercialized media have often reduced the story to exciting sound bytes and visual snippets that fit conveniently between two commercial messages.

Can we go back to the noblest of Greek aspirations, which claimed that the goodness of the State reflects the nobility and goodness of each individual and vice versa? At the base of our moral decline is the inability of each individual to empathize with the other. On an individual level, this reflects the inability of the State to provide a caring community for each member, especially for our children.

Aristotle believed that a good character is the result of extended moral training. Goodness is not the result of rational deliberation but becomes a compassionate choice under the influence of a supportive community. Religious communities around the world have always understood this habit-forming quality of early character education. During their formative years, most religious congregations teach their children stories of goodness and compassion and encourage positive practice. With the decline of religious influence in the public arena, and the public schools' emphasis on information and skills, we have failed to fill the moral and ethical gap. Our children's habits form and are informed by the shallowness of the commercial media. The media's incessant thirst for ratings has created a powerful feedback loop of increasing mediocrity, mindlessness, and even brutality. When it has become "normal" to feed our need for entertainment with Howard Stern, Jerry Springer shows, and sensational wrestling, we should assist our children in being different from the norm instead of coercing them to comply with it.

The empowerment movement teaches us that an emphasis on the positive can often overcome deviant behavior. From Buddhist ethical practice we might learn that all is nature and all is life. That includes the worst of deviant behavior. Somewhere the seed for hell resides in each of us. Criminalization of deviant behavior resulted from ethical dualism and universal ethics. It divided all actions into right and wrong ones. Ethical rationalism atomized morality and made deviant behavior solely the responsibility of individuals. With their rational mind, they supposedly make informed decisions to commit wrongful acts.

As more and more children at an ever-younger age become perpetrators of violence, we must phrase the communal responsibility for violent acts in a new way. We must use communal efforts to heal, educate, and empower ourselves again as ancient human beings did in tribal societies. Solitary confinements are inhuman inventions of an industrial society that treats human beings as mechanical objects. And today, if confinement doesn't work society assumes the right to lock people up and throw away the keys, or better yet, execute them. How long will it take until this society will call for the execution of children? The United States remains one of the few countries not signing a Human Rights Charter for children, which the United Nations developed some years ago. American lawmakers claimed that several states allow the execution of children younger than this document permitted, and the Federal government had no authority to change these local statutes.

As increasingly younger children pick up guns and shoot their classmates, the call for punishment of these minors (as in the recent case in Michigan, where a six year-old shot another of equal age) becomes louder. All the while child psychologists scramble to figure out at what age level children should know right from wrong. If children have not developed that discrimination, how can we punish them at all? We cannot hold them responsible, but these horrific acts demand answers.

According to cognitive models of moral development, children first need to develop a sense of self in order to make judgments of what benefits or hurts them. Early moral development focuses on the concept of self-interest. According to cognitive thinking, the ideas that "Mommy will punish me" or "How can I earn this or that reward?" supposedly express the earliest stage of moral development. Only much later does this turn into judgment according to intent. Many years later yet, it evolves into judgment according to abstract principles, universal rights, rules, and laws.

According to Perspectivist ethics, cognitive morality is only part of the solution. Long before children learn how to reason, and even before they develop a sense of self, they actively develop empathy on a deep emotional level. A child may even have this basic emotion at birth, as some child psychologists contend. According to psychologist William Damon of Stanford University, "All children are born with a running start on the path to moral development."[13] Empathy, according to Damon, is a key emotion that supports a sense of right and wrong. It "emerges early, and it seems, naturally." According to Carolyn Zahn-Waxler of the National Institute of Mental Health, "Babies cry in response to the wails of other babies, and not just because it's a sound that upsets them. They cry more in response to human cries than to other aversive sounds. Somehow, there is a built-in capacity to respond to the needs of others,"[14] Zahn-Waxler observed: "Babies as young as one year-old try to console others in distress. Toddlers offer their security blanket to a teary-eyed parent or a favorite toy to a distraught sibling, as if understanding that the very object that brings them comfort will do the same for another."[15]

Empathy, as mentioned earlier, is a key element of Perspectivist philosophy. It means, according to Sharon Begley and Claudia Kalb "the ability to respond to another's distress more appropriate to her situation than to your own."[16] But even though we may come equipped with empathy at birth, it does not come automatically. It depends on example and nurturing.

> If a child's sadness is met with stony silence rather than a hug, if her loneliness is met with continued abandonment, then she is in danger of losing her natural empathy. Kids who, as 14-month-olds, exhibit high levels of empathy typically become less empathetic after only six months if they live in homes filled with conflict, and if they seldom feel a mother's love.[17]

In light of these insights, the fatal shooting of the six year old Michigan girl by her classmate appears more to reflect and condemn the environment where this boy was raised than on his cognitive ability to discern right from wrong. As the age of those who commit the most horrific acts of violence in our society grows younger and younger, we should begin mending the fabric of social interconnectedness. While the media quickly blamed the boy's upbringing in a crack-house full of violence and drugs, they said little about the state of the whole community in which the crime took place. Michael Moore, the social critical author of the film *Roger and Me* who lives near that Flint neighborhood, took it upon himself to spread the word about the dismal condition of the ghetto community in which this boy grew up and went to school. The school system itself is impoverished, with no tax base from the surrounding ghettoes able to support it. The neighborhood is so run down that it does not belong to any organized township at all. Like an urban counterpart to a Wild West frontier town, the law is in the hands of the people. But the communal frontier spirit has given way to a selfish and merciless individualism in which each individual feels pitted against the rest. Here, we can best find empathy, consideration for others, cooperation, and community in the lawless circles of thugs and gangs. Drug dealing is the glorified way to make a living; drug taking is the fastest way to kill the pain.

In the last part of this book, I will point out some of the well-tested techniques that we must implement in our schools in order to teach our children the necessary skills for a happy life. We base these skills primarily on the power of empathy and compassion, the power to feel with the other. Under the old paradigm of cognitive objectivity, we placed ethical emphasis on what not to do and how to avoid negative behavior. This turned our educational institutions into prisons. Under the new Perspectivist paradigm, educators first will give emotional support. They must learn to listen and to care.

Teachers must provide daily group interaction. Cooperative (instead of competitive) activities such as music, the arts, drama, etc. create an environment of enjoyment and passion. Instructional efforts will shift away from punitive to positively reinforcing constructive behaviors.

To this end, educators have begun studying the lives of successful people. This emphasis on the positive will profoundly affect the character of our communities and their educational institutions. We can learn and must teach a cooperative and partnership way of life.

Many believe that things have gone so far out of control that we can do nothing. They acknowledge that the world full of injustice and the planet is irreversibly polluted. For them it might do good to remember an old wisdom contained in the Torah. Arthur Waskow in *Proclaim Jubilee* points out that after every period of intense development and work, the Torah suggests rest: rest from physical labor, rest from tilling the land, rest from making money, rest from building houses and apartment complexes, rest from driving a car, and rest from flying airplanes. Give your debtor a rest in paying his debt. Ancient Hebrew Sabbath law laid out this vision of rest.[18]

Waskow summarizes the Sabbath law in the following way: "Even useful institutions must periodically be laid down; the whole rigid pattern of society – with some people on the top, some on the bottom, some assigned to this role and some to that – must also be laid down."[19] This, according to Waskow, would be a sure way to free people up, open their imaginations and nurture their spirits.[20] If human beings would follow this ancient law and voluntarily observe periods of absolute rest, nature could replenish herself easily, before human activities cause irreversible damage.

Based on this biblical wisdom (contained in all three major religions, Christianity, Judaism and Islam), Waskow proposes a bold program of atonement and renewal that would cover three intertwined sicknesses of our generation: economic, environmental, and compassional. Waskow says: "Let us imagine a jubilee program that includes three major structural reforms that can be applied both globally and locally, reforms that churches, synagogues, and temples could initiate, encourage, and implement"[21]

The first reform based on the Torah would recycle investment capital: the billions of dollars that banks, insurance companies, unions, and large religious bodies transfer to the control of giant, longstanding "secure" corporations. Imagine the same money going to decentralized grassroots businesses – especially those that are worker-owned or run by neighborhoods, religious groups, families, or consumer co-ops.

Secondly, we would declare Sabbaticals on research and development. In an agricultural society this meant leaving the land unplanted every four years. What would this mean for a technological society? Perhaps that once every seven years scientists and society as a whole devote a year of reflection. Waskow predicts that such a Sabbatical pause would have profound environmental and cultural effects. He says:

It would slow down the invasion of the web of planetary life, and might encourage reevaluation deep enough to make renewal of the web as important as invading it. It would also teach the society that there are values other than producing, making, doing – indeed that the "producing" values need to be governed by the larger issues of long-term effects on human beings, community, and the earth.[22]

The third structural reform would strengthen local communities through neighborhood celebrations and political empowerment. For nineteen days of the year, people would stay in their neighborhoods, not go shopping, not drive cars, but celebrate their neighborhoods. This five-percent pause would be a major step to cleaning up the environment, the air, and giving a rest to the planet.

Utopian fantasy? Perhaps, but on the long run we fare better to devise voluntary plans of rest instead of letting shortages, brown outs and blackouts, sickness, war and death force us to rest.

How can we bring this powerful message to the people? Once philosophers realized that ethics could not have a rational basis, as the European enlightenment expected, many reverted to telling stories. Stories have the power to create and nourish moral conscience, as Scott Sanders in *The Force of Spirit* pointed out.[23] Stories, according to Sanders, help us "see through the eyes of other people. . . they release us from the confines of self. They nurture compassion and empathy, which are the springs of justice and kindness."[24] This would be truly Perspectivism in action.

The tragic reality today is that commercialism (only a thin disguise for selfishness and greed) holds our stories hostage. The stories our young people hear most often are those told by commercial television, which is an extended arm of the consumer industry. Their purpose is not to nurture compassion but to sell goods. Education in partnership and Perspectivism must reclaim the stories from those powerful sound bytes in order to tell a new story of community, compassion, and justice. If Sanders's claims are true that "Stories do work on us, on our minds and hearts, showing us how we might act, who we might become, and why,"[25] then reclaiming the story must become our most urgent task. For the sake of the happiness of many generations to come, we cannot afford to fail.

Five

THE PARTNERSHIP WAY

> If we free ourselves from the prevailing models
> of reality, it is evident that there is another logi-
> cal alternative: that there can be societies in
> which difference is not necessarily equated with
> inferiority or superiority.
>
> Riane Eisler

At the Goethe University in Frankfurt, Germany, my professors taught me that domination was the price human beings had to pay for becoming self-conscious. My teachers at the famous Frankfurt School had developed an intricate explanation for the almost universal presence of dominance among human beings. Even though they tried to modify dominance by introducing a complex dialectic, they seemed to accept domination, in one form or another, as an almost ontological necessity. Since the rational mind had to be in control, these philosophers, in the tradition of Georg Wilhelm Friedrich Hegel used the mind-body model as the basis for the generalized dominator model. Someone had to be in control, and whoever it was needed to have more reason. If human beings were not ruled by reason, then riots would result, and that would lead to a breakdown of civil society. From Plato to Hegel, domination was part of philosophy and life.

Two discoveries made during the 1980s fundamentally changed my philosophical discourse on domination. Today, I no longer believe that we can necessarily connect domination with the awakening of conscious individuality and self. I believe that such thoughts took root in and stem from the Judeo-Christian fall/redemption thinking so central to these religions. From what we know of the theology of fall and redemption, domination plays an essential role. As Father Matthew Fox pointed out, fall/redemption ideology became prominent in Western civilization and deeply influenced philosophical discourse from the fourth century on.[1]

According to this fall and redemption mindset, human beings are essentially bad. For the Greeks disorder and chaos in nature stemmed from inept actions of lower gods; in Christianity, however, nature's fall from grace is the result of sin. Human nature is evil because of original sin. This ideology entered into Christianity as a result of Augustine's reinterpretation of Plato's works. According to Christian doctrine, Augustine theorized, human beings need an intervention from above to redeem themselves.

In the fall/redemption model, human beings serve a higher power, to which they have to submit, or else be damned. God became the absolute *dominus*. Human beings then patterned their interaction with each other and with animals after this master/servant relationship with God. Eventually we even argued that these patterns were part of the natural process.

Creation spirituality sees domination as one of the causes for injustice and violence, while it teaches that human beings are good by nature. Domination, we now understand, has historical causes, and therefore, we can undo its damage.

Then how did domination develop if not as a natural part of humanity? This is the central question. The research into the development of domination leads us deep into prehistoric times. Archaeologists and anthropologists have positively confirmed that many human societies lived cooperatively for thousands of years before the dominator model took hold.

We can find one of the best-preserved examples of this partnership culture in the Minoan civilization (which centered on the island of Crete). Archeologists and cultural anthropologists interested in the development of domination have focused their research on Minoan art and civilization. The Minoans were one of the longest surviving ancient civilizations in which men and women lived in near equality with each other. In scientific circles, this has become known as the "partnership" model. Riane Eisler, in *The Chalice and the Blade,* concluded that the Minoans did generally not idealize violence. As far as we can tell they seemed to have lived in a highly artistic, pleasurable, and technologically advanced civilization.[2]

In these early societies, according to Eisler, the life-giving powers of women played an essential part. Though they were hierarchically structured their society lacked any rigid ranking of people. In their religious worship these early people celebrated the Mother Goddess as the source of all forms of life.[3]

In her extensive work, Eisler researched the transition from this early partnership model to the still-prevalent dominator model. She found a possible link with the institution of the masculine sky god. A father god in heaven undoubtedly provided a powerful symbol for the justification of male dominance and the dominator model. Eisler explains that during the early Greek period, leaders altered mythology to reflect the dominator culture and the new male dominance. The Greek philosophers tried, but failed, in their attempt to regain the Golden Age by calling on the reasonability of all. Though initially educated by women, the philosophers soon excluded women in their quest to find true harmony in nature. In this exclusion they already reflected the patriarchal tendencies of the new dominator society. Their quest for the universality of reason eventually resulted in the domination of technical rationality over the rest of creation, as we practice so dangerously today.

Eisler's theoretical work of research and discovery convincingly demonstrates that power and domination are not the only, nor the highest of human attainments, but only a temporary deviation. Her research suggests a distinct possibility that true partnership between human beings could exist. No longer a mere utopian dream, we have now documented a realizable goal

in human development. Moreover, Eisler pinpoints the causes of the dominator detour, which has persisted for nearly all of written history.

But perhaps we could argue that these early societies perished precisely
because of their weakness and inefficiency to make room for the new dominator model of society. Does the success of one justify the failure of the
other?

Scientists base the explanation of natural progress solely on the theory
of natural selection. Charles Darwin's natural selection as the exclusive theory to explain progress in nature has been challenged by modern research
influenced by chaos theory and the science of complexity. David Loye, in
Darwin's Lost Theory of Love, points out that on the human level Darwin
emphasized many other factors for cultural evolution, besides his famous
"Survival of the Fittest" concept, which in his later work Darwin used spar-
ingly.[4] Loye believes that many scientists unjustifiably used Darwin's theory
as a neatly tailored explanation to fit the dominator system.

In modern times, Darwin's concept of the survival of the fittest provided the backdrop for a relentless insistence on the dominator principle.
Social scientists used natural selection to justify domination as a fact of survival. Chaos theory exposed Darwin's theory as a selective view, inspired by
the wish to justify domination. The new scientists of Chaos point out that in
biological nature many times cooperative systems survived while competitive
systems perished. This is not only true for single systems, but also for the
harmonic cooperation among systems. The humanity we built on competition
alone may be well on the road to extinction.

On another front, research into the science of complexity concludes that
logical systems, if driven by competitive efficiency as the major characteristics of functional adaptation, succeed less in adapting to new circumstances
than those systems that contain chaos.[5] This, too, confirms the natural need
for cooperation.

Cooperation and communication (for the purpose of cooperation) are
perhaps nature's most powerful constants. To think that the trillions of cells
and neurons that constitute a human body do so because of a cosmic coincidence is unconscionable. Once we accept the premise that we can find life
and the conscious will to exist at all levels (down to the smallest atom), it
becomes obvious that our human bodies serve as a powerful model for cooperative action. Trillions of molecules, cells, and neurons harmonize with each
other to make a human being's existence possible. The brain, too, is a small,
albeit highly developed, part of the complex system that constitutes us. With
these new discoveries we can finally form a theoretical framework to reor-
ganize our understanding of "basic human nature."

By setting ourselves apart from the natural world, we have constructed
an ever-increasing abstraction concerning our position in the universe. By
putting order as a principle above all else, we have denied ourselves our natural heritage of emotional attachment to the ever-evolving natural world. We

constructed a separate mission for ourselves, and we supported this mission by religious and metaphysical fanaticism, which further supported the attempt to justify relentless domination.

In *The Chalice and the Blade,* Riane Eisler develops a picture of a world organized in a partnership way. Under the dominator system, says Eisler, we are socialized from childhood to accept domination as the natural law. Greek dualism located the origin of reason and mind in the Absolute, who for them was the highest principle of order. God, the divine craftsman, created this world in a logical manner. Wherever logic was not evident or missing, it was the result of mistakes made by lower gods or a case of absence of order. The ancient Greeks believed they could discover the logic within things. Wherever it lacked, human beings had the duty to complete it. Human beings were called upon to order the world. This mission became the cornerstones of early Christianity. The Hebrew genesis story powerfully asserts the dominator prototype. A thousand years later science, too, claimed to be the expression of the "ordering mind" that dominates over nature. David Hume, then, equated this mind with the male instead of the female.

Eisler disputes stereotypes of masculinity and femininity rooted in dominator thinking. Eisler's work also challenges the veracity of a linear/upward or straight line upward evolution from barbarism to civilization. The cultural transformation theory proposed by Eisler offers a multi-linear instead of a unilinear view of cultural evolution, with some groups orienting more to what she identifies as the dominator configuration and others more to partnership.

In the dominator model we find rigid top-down control, rigid domination by the male half of humanity over the female half, as well as other rankings of domination, for example masters over slaves as in ancient Greece, race over race, or human beings over nature. This type of organization, according to Eisler, requires a high level of built-in violence to maintain rankings, for example child and wife beating and chronic warfare. In the partnership model we find a more democratic and equitable social organization. An equal partnership exists between the two halves of humanity, and people do not need built-in violence to maintain rigid rankings. We must stress, however, that no society completely orients itself to one or the other. But the degree to which they do molds all relations, from intimate to international, and all social institutions, from the family, education and religion, to politics and economics.

Societies orienting toward the dominator model justify this form of organization with their beliefs, stories and myths. For example, a punitive supreme god is said to be the final judge of an inherently sinful humanity that must be controlled from the top. Societies that orient more to the partnership model have different beliefs, stories and myths. In Eisler's view, human beings have the potential for caring and cruelty, non-violence and violence, mutual respect and unempathic control. But instead of highlighting cruelty, violence, and destruction partnership education emphasizes the human faculty for caring and creativity, Eisler argues that during periods of extreme disequilibrium such as ours human beings can turn chance into choice.

Eisler formulates values based on partnership living. These new values include intuitive thinking and a spiritual relationship with nature as partner. She proposes to practice science in an empathic (not domineering) way and to solve conflicts by dealing effectively with the problem and develop a win/win situation (family model). Eisler sees power in the affiliation with and as empowerment of others. Like in a well-functioning family, members link with each other and develop solidarity. Such a family allows all members to advance themselves without limiting others.

In contrast to the dominator model, which sees love as a complete loss of self, the partnership model describes love as *agape,* which is selfless, non-possessive love. This is the love a mother has for her child, or divine love of the Great Mother for her human children. In contrast to a dominator god, the goddess returns as a symbol of spiritual transformation, of birth and celebration of life. The goddess embodies stereotypical feminine qualities such as caring and nurturing

Eisler wants to turn these ethical principles of partnership into new models for politics and economics in which both women and men can identify their humanity with the values of caring and nurturing. She believes that these values re-assert a social ethos that will redirect the use of natural resources. In this new world, human beings will balance competition, as the highest value in the dominator world, with a new sense of cooperation and care. Love and care will eventually counteract the unyielding individualism so characteristic of our times. Human beings will overcome the relentless conquest of nature and will learn again to live in harmony with nature. Global cooperation will evolve as a free partnership of people where satisfactory emotional relationships will replace our cultural obsession with taking, buying, building, and wasting things. In the current dual economy, care-giving work stereotypically associated with women is generally nearly invisible. A shared economy in which the sexes are in equal positions will eventually replace it. This new economy will no longer underpay and alienate caring and helping labor. Machines and computers will assist in minimizing alienated labor and repetitive tasks.

This truly monumental transformation, Eisler predicts, will bring forth the best in people. As a result a new striving for truth, beauty, and justice will ensue. People will create a pragmatopia as a realizable scenario for partnership instead of a utopia. Perhaps finally it will be possible for humanity to live free of fear of war and global destruction. After developing a rational approach to population growth we will be able to bring birthrates in balance with our resources. We will also develop rational measures to reduce hunger and poverty. People will celebrate cultural diversity, and they will fully accept this as the result of fundamental psychic changes. Having learned to find happiness within themselves and their relationship with others, people will no longer need to rely on the production and consumption of things as a primary source of fulfillment and happiness.

Tremendous social and technological breakthroughs, according to Eisler, will accompany this new age of cooperation. Corporations, for example, will allow for greater worker participation. Putting more emphasis on local production, people will decentralize production and distribution processes and local cooperative units of production and distribution will replace highly centralized hierarchical systems.

Mutual companionship, sexual pleasure, and love will be the primary purpose of bonding. Societies will allow for diverse models of caring relationships, and no longer insist on the traditional heterosexual model as the only one sanctioned by law. This new society, based on partnership principles will put greatest emphasis again on the human child. Public education will include good nutrition, combined with physical and mental exercises. Instead of relying on largely competitive sports, schools might teach advanced yoga and meditation as a standard part of their curriculum. Learning itself will become a lifelong process, which will maximize human flexibility and insure creativity at all stages of life.

Six

THE YEAR THE HORSES CAME: THE ROOTS OF DOMINATION

> Beat. Off beat. Beat. Off beat. This was the
> rhythm of her heart. This was the rise and flow
> of her own blood. This was the Snake Dance of
> Gira done to the beating of the drums.
> Coil forward. Coil sideways. Coil back. Stamp
> your left foot. Stamp your right foot. Be the
> snake. Become the snake.
>
> Mary Mackey

Between approximately 4500 BCE and 1200 BCE, waves of invaders from the steppes of Central Asia spread over Europe and later traveled as far as India – perhaps even to China, as newest discoveries indicate. Due to their common language, these people became known as Aryans (even though we cannot truly assert that they were all from one specific race or tribe, as the German fascists falsely assumed). These Aryans were nomadic and semi-nomadic people who brought with them tamed horses, chariots, and war tools. They ranked themselves hierarchically, lead by a male chieftain. The gods in their heaven followed an equally hierarchical structure.

A male god presided over other gods in the sky. Living as nomads in the Northern steppes, those Aryans brought with them the dominator model and war gods that lived in the sky. The Zoroastrians of Persia eventually believed in a single male god in the sky, whom they called Ahura Mazda. In turn, the ancient Hebrews came to believe in a male supreme being whom they called Yahweh. Like Ahura Mazda, Yahweh was a jealous god who did not tolerate other gods.

We will never know for sure, but those Aryans might have adopted their religious and social hierarchical structures from their observation of the wild herds of horses they tamed. The lead male in a herd of horses has absolute rule. We can easily see that such a hierarchical social model works efficiently for wandering animal herds, and also proved efficient for nomadic people. By using horses to aid in traveling, Aryans could cover a large territory. Once they learned to mount horses and make them obey, they had a distinct advantage over other people. Fighting from horseback, they subdued many groups of people. This made them superior to agricultural tribes who fought on foot and often were not prepared to defend themselves at all. We can see the similar imbalance of power demonstrated again more recently when the Spaniards took to horseback to subdue Native American tribes.

As these militant Aryans migrated to many places of the ancient world, they affected the local, peaceful agrarian societies in profound ways. The new dominator system infected the old earth and life-centered religions like a virus. The agricultural and trading people of Old Europe had little resistance against the new dominator culture.

A group of those Aryan invaders made their way to India. As recent research shows, modern Hinduism assimilated the original Indian tribal religions into the dominant Aryanism. As in other regions, the invading Aryans quickly subdued the earlier civilization in the Hindus valley. The introduction of a caste system put the invaders into the positions of rulers and dominators, while declaring the original inhabitants of the area as the lowest caste.

In Europe, by classical Greek times, only a memory remained of what was then called the Golden Age. It was the memory of a time when life was harmonious, and communication flowed between human beings and the nature gods. Minoan art provides a rich testimony to the Minoan appreciation of beauty, harmony, and play. Their daily life continuously celebrated living in accordance with nature, and unrepressed sexuality was part of this celebration.[1]

In her book *Sacred Pleasure,* Riane Eisler brings forth numerous examples for the way our ancestors revered sexuality as both the source of life as well as a mysterium of sacred power.[2] She says:

> Our ancestors celebrated sex not only in relation to birth and procreation, but as the mysterious – and in that sense, magical – source of both pleasure and life. In other words, I am proposing that prehistoric erotic myths and rites were not only expressions of our ancestors' joy and gratitude for the Goddess's gift of life, but also expressions of joy and gratitude for the Goddess's gift of love and pleasure – particularly for that most intense of physical pleasures, the pleasure of sex.[3]

As artworks from these times and regions testify, rich cultures flourished for thousands of years – long before the ancient Greeks and Romans laid the foundations of our current civilization. These prehistoric people lived in advanced city-like settlements, and developed a high standard of living. Free and open sexuality constituted a large part of their daily lives. They worshipped primarily earth-connected goddesses and gods. The Minoan civilization and the Etruscans in Italy provide two well-documented examples of societies that showed no marked difference in the social treatment of men and women.[4]

In contrast to these animistic beginnings, the new male-centered religions favored highly-stratified social models. Nomadic people perhaps needed an all-powerful portable sky god, allowing them to follow their large herds of animals and still worship effectively. Similarly, one strong man who demonstrated absolute power could easily rule a nomadic tribe. As the dominator idea spread, this stratified monistic model became popular because it neatly reflected the power structure of the status quo.

Between 1400 and 800 BCE, Zoroastrianism developed in the area of Persia. The prophet Zoroaster founded a religion that instituted a monotheistic male god in the sky. Zoroaster was the son of an old priest family, who most likely directly descended from those Aryan nomads who had settled in the same area. Zoroaster turned against polytheistic nomads whom he called "the perpetrators of lies." But some major features of the lost religion remained part of Zoroastrianism. Zoroaster's god, Ahura Mazda, initially presided over other gods (mazdas) in his heaven, but Ahura Mazda was the most powerful one. The other gods did not deserve worship and sacrifice, and eventually they were forgotten. Human beings first conceived monotheism.[5]

When the ancient Hebrews were released from Babylonian captivity, they brought with them the monistic idea of a most-powerful male god, whom they called Yahweh. Other less powerful gods initially accompanied the Hebrew god as well, however, they were eliminated when Moses brought forth the Ten Commandments. Only one God was to rule Israel. Early Hebrew religion continuously attempted to discredit and eradicate its polytheistic roots. For example, they condemned the snake, which by many early religions was considered a mysterious and even holy animal.

In the Greek polytheistic culture, some of the ritual practices of the Golden Age survived the massive Dorian invasion. Greek mythology adopted Zeus, a male god, as the head of the pantheon of many gods. With Zeus, a militant attitude became popular in the Greek heaven and in Greek culture. Gentler ritual practices of the earlier culture survived in popular festivals such as the Eleusinian Mysteries. With their origins in Minoan culture, this cult was devoted to creativity, fertility, sexual pleasures, regeneration and rebirth. Many of the early Greek philosophers were educated by and remained in contact with female priestesses, from whom they learned the mysteries of nature and of the gods. Pythagoras founded a community to which men and women were equally accepted. Plato still allowed women to become members of his academy and was an advocate for the education of women at least among the ruling class. Education for women in those days did generally not exist any more. According to Eisler's careful documentation, as male domination took a firmer hold, Greek mythology systematically changed to reflect the new reality.

Plato divided human nature into two. The part, in which reason ruled, was declared the higher, more valuable part, made by the highest God. This was also the realm in which we could make true predictions. As long as actions were guided by reason, we could predict and carry them out in a responsible fashion. This was also the realm equated with true masculinity. The other part, which housed emotions and sexual desires, Plato considered part of the lower faculties. This was equated with women.

With the new emphasis on reason, Plato degraded sexuality as a necessary expression only for the lower classes, and for soldiers, in organized intervals only. In his *Republic,* the ruling philosophical elite had to abstain from sex altogether since sexuality was an activity of the lowest part of the soul. Fabricated by lower celestial gods, sexual desires, as all emotions, were considered a mistake. The body itself had no distinction at all in Platonism. It originated from the formless Void, unbounded empty space, that was synonymous with chaos. The material world for Plato was a bad copy of the eternal world of ideas and forms.

When Saint Augustine incorporated Platonism into Christianity, the Platonic ranking of sexuality as a low and degrading activity became the norm. Augustinian thought found human beings badly deficient. This deficiency was the reason why we need love. By ourselves we are utterly incomplete. Unable to blame lower gods for human weakness, Augustine instead introduced the idea of original sin into Christianity. The original fall resulted in human incompleteness and frailty. Because of this defect, human beings had to go out to find the other; contacting the other was no longer a celebration, but a need to escape isolation and imperfection.

Following the hierarchical ranking that entered into Christianity through Greek Platonism and Hebrew sources, Augustine established an acceptable ranking for objects of love as well. The love of God, a solely spiritual love, ranked highest; the love of flesh, which included all sexual activity, ranked lowest and was often considered sinful. Though the Church generally sanctified human bonding in the sacrament of marriage, the sexual act, especially its natural expression of pleasure, remained low in the Christian hierarchy of values even within the bond of marriage. We only have to consider the number of virgin saints in Catholicism and how it celebrates women for their abstinence. Few married women ever attained saintly status. Saint Paul's edict declared it sinful to even have pleasurable thoughts. This added to the general condemnation of all sexual desires.

During the Reformation, Greek rationalism – now with more emphasis on Aristotelian ideals – exerted another negative influence on the Christian position toward sexuality and the human body. Pietism and Protestant ethics did their part to completely exclude sexuality from those activities that they considered worthy to save our soul. They believed the mind represented the rational, worthier part of the human being, while the body is full of lust. Eventually they considered all pleasurable activities outside of the reach of the divine and the sacred.

Platonic dualism and Aristotelian rationalism, when combined with Christian otherworldliness and the prevailing attitude of sinfulness and guilt, produced a culture intensely hostile to sexuality and pleasure. A feel-good atmosphere, promoted by popular culture today, is the only remainder of a once-sacred activity designated to celebrate the great mystery of life and the divine.

We replaced the direct experience of pleasure and pain – these two eminent vehicles of life that promote our continuation – with abstract notions that carry the meaning, but not the experiential powers, of these original energies. When René Descartes declared that animals don't feel pain because they don't know pain, he managed to disconnect pain from its existential root. If we assume, as Descartes and the Enlightenment did, that human beings only know pleasure and pain when they become intellectually aware of it, then pleasure and pain turn into language. But every action that is only known through concepts and words loses its authenticity and ultimately becomes technique.

The dualistic separation between direct experience and the notion of that experience in language prepared the way for a secular society that promotes shallow and empty sexual practices. They are shallow and empty because they have been robbed of the mystery that connects them to the sacred and divine web of life. A return to an invocation of the sacred and the divine in sexual matters does not imply an otherworldly meaning of sexuality. It implies the interwovenness of the divine into this world, which dualistic religions both reject and deny.

Christianity generally reinforced the need for the subjugation of women and the dominance of males. This became obvious during the colonization by Christian missionaries of some Native American tribes. Among some Canadian tribes, women led the agricultural development while men hunted. Since agriculture provided a major part of the tribes income the role of men almost completely diminished. When the Christian missionaries arrived women ran some native tribes and men were only tolerated. If a woman wanted to get rid of a man, she just had to place his belongings in front of the home. In returning from the hunt (which had become almost irrelevant in regards to supplying food for the family) the man had to move back to his mother. If she refused him, he had to "disappear" in the woods. During colonization, in order to make these women good Christians, the Jesuit priest had to break their spirits and make them subservient to men.[6]

Male dominated societies, unaware of the daily chores of female labor, even today refuse to adequately compensate women for their daily work. Women still cannot accumulate social security benefits for their work of raising children. One of my sons was born in Finland. We were amazed to find out that the government supplies a housekeeper to each woman after childbirth almost free of charge. The temporary maid would do everything in the house the mother would usually do while the husband worked. The mother had the complete freedom to care for the new child. The government offered this help to everyone for several weeks after childbirth: a most sensible arrangement, and yet how inconceivable in America.

In the United States, women working at home are not allowed sick days, nor do they generally receive any other monetary rewards for their work as mothers. After a divorce, women are usually worse off, while men generally do financially better.

The economic reality of the 1980s and 1990s, with both husband and wife engaged in the work place, often demanded a greater contribution in regards to the housework from the husband. But more frequently this has not happened. Women are left to both keep the home running and contribute to the family income.

How can Perspectivism help us to understand and appreciate ourselves again as physical and sexual beings ready to nurture and care for the other?

First, we must relearn to respect ourselves as part of the natural world. Though consumer culture appears to glorify physicality, this is a false emphasis. Respect for our bodies means realizing the shortcomings of human reason in the face of the combined wisdom of the natural world. It means listening to nature and to our bodies as much and as often as we use judgment guided by the rules of logic and reason. Neither perspective is more valuable than the other. The mind is not a kind of divine implant that will single-handedly solve all our problems and guide us out of this "valley of tears." Relearning the perspective of our bodies means the abrogation of all false dualisms and the full recognition of our selves as part of the natural world. This recognition will have to penetrate our educational system, our culture, and our lives. Where it runs counter to religious and cultural norms, these norms will eventually have to change and adjust. The alternative is unnatural and ultimately will mean the self-inflicted destruction of the human race.

For the first time in the history of humanity we can envision a future marked by less necessary labor (if we define labor as the alienated work we perform for the sake of profit). Because of human inventiveness, through technology and automation, we can finally reinvent our humanity and fill our lives with more creativity and more fun. We must understand ourselves again as part of the web of life that continues on in cycles of creation and destruction. We must gain a new understanding of pleasure as the fullest expression of life, not as a sinful afterthought. Only then we can recover a sacred appreciation of something that we will try to understand on ever-deeper levels, but never perhaps in its completeness.

In order to meaningfully plan for a better future it may help to look into the past, into a time before the dominator principle took over human development. Lacking historical documents, we can only imagine what such a past might have been like. In her historic novel, *The Year the Horses Came,* Mary Mackey gave a sensitive account of the life of early people that lived in the villages and forests of Old Europe.[7] Mackey's narration follows the general impressions accumulated by anthropological discoveries and by visiting the ruins of the earliest European settlements. We may also cite the oral accounts that made their way into the folk songs, legends, and fairy tales of Europe. Mackey also draws on customs and rituals of currently surviving primal groups and uses some of the rituals found among Native Americans.

We can use Mackey's book to visualize the cataclysm that the arrival of the Northern horse people caused to the way of life in Old Europe. Her rich cultural details and her vivid descriptions of customs and rituals focus on the change that took place in sexual *mores* once the invaders brought their male centered, domination-oriented sexuality and their particular way of life with them.

Journeying through vast areas of Old Europe, Marrah, the youthful heroine of Mackey's novel, experiences the hospitality and peacefulness of the people that inhabit these regions. Stavan, her traveling companion and later lover, is a member of the Hansi people, one of the many worrying tribes that roam the great savannas, or the "sea of grass" in the North. On a journey to search for the city of gold, before meeting Marrah, Stavan lost his companions, who were also warriors from the Hansi tribe. He washed ashore in Brittany, in a village of those peace-loving Xori people. Marrah rescues and nourishes him. As Stavan recovers, he learns the ways of cooperation and peace. In turn, he tells his new friend Marrah about the way of life of the Hansi people. Compared to her tribe, the Hansi people appear to be hostile and dangerous. Marrah feels she has to inform her people of the impending threat.

Following the command of the Goddess, Marrah now goes on a long journey to tell her people about the destructive ways of the horse people. The reader learns from the contrast of the two ways of life, the partnership and the dominator way. We can have little doubt that the horse people will be victorious in the end. The lasting influence of the dominator culture of those "six-legged" horse people still marks our civilization today.

The domineering Hansi people valued property above all and often traveled great distances to find gold and other valuable metals, mostly to add to the elaborate funeral gifts of their deceased chieftains. Their deceased move on to a different place where they continue their struggle and enjoy ruling powers. The Hansi do not believe in reincarnation.

Male deities, such as the god Han, rule the sky. Strong males also are the leaders down here on earth. They frequently fight to prove their superiority. Hansi people sacrifice large numbers of animals, especially when a great chieftain dies. The Hansi commonly use physical punishment with children, especially boys. They believe this prepares them for a tough life as warriors. Adults, especially men, hardly ever show affection, not even to children. They believe they are meant to rule over others. From observing horses and wolf packs they have learned to rule and to obey. Their religion, too, teaches that the gods created the powerful to rule and the weak to follow subserviently. By taming wolves as dogs and horses for domestic use, they learned the value of property. Knowing the value of property, they commonly steel other tribes' belongings, especially horses and women. Warriors keep women, especially those stolen from other tribes, as concubines for their private pleasure.

Among the Hansi, shamans enjoy great power that often balances the physical power of the tribal leaders. But only men can be shamans. The shamans are powerful and feared; they perform rituals for sick people, but do not nurse them. They know the occult, communicate with spirits, and predict the future. A man purchases a woman from her father. She has no voice in sexual matters. Men see women as property, just like horses.

In contrast, the customs, habits, and values of the Xori people express peacefulness and harmony with each other and nature, based on natural partnership and reverence for the earth.

The Xori people seldom venture far away from their homes. They love their people and the land they live on. When someone dies they believe that he or she returns into the womb of the Goddess, and eventually will be reborn. Through the earth, where they lay their dead, the living stay in contact with the dead.

The sun is the daughter of Mother Earth. They believe that animal sacrifice hurts Mother Earth, and therefore they do not allow it. Even when they kill an animal for food, the Xori people ask the animal for forgiveness.

Xori people treasure their children as sacred gifts. They would never harm them. Adults, males and females, show children that they love them by hugging them often. They value physical contact as a sign of affection and seldom allow corporeal punishment. In dancing circles the Xori people celebrate their oneness with the Goddess and with an all-knowing over-mind.

The Goddess Earth asks that people live together in love and harmony. The Xori choose men and women equally as shamans and healers. A shaman's main occupation is nursing sick people. On rare occasions a shaman is also able to go into trance, talk to spirits and see the future.

A mother raises her child. An uncle or another close male relative is assigned as paternal guardian, because the natural father was often not identified. A natural father's role was fairly inconsequential, since the Xori did not necessarily connect sexuality with fatherhood.

Sex is always consensual. Women and men are allowed to "share joy" with other partners even after marriage. In yearly events, such as the snake festival or carnival, the Xori allow sexual intimacy with many partners, and this becomes a public ritual.

Once those Hansi warriors had taken over the peaceful Xori tribes, their ancient way of life all but disappeared.

Seven

CHASING AMY: OUR SEXUAL SELVES

> Understand that sexuality is as wide as the sea.
> Understand that your morality is not law. Un-
> derstand that we are you. Understand that if we
> decide to have sex whether safe, safer, or unsafe,
> it is our decision and you have no rights in our
> lovemaking.
>
> Derek Jarman

When our old morals become outdated, when the ideals they promote become unachievable, and their essence has proven irrelevant, people go on to
search for new ones. Unwilling to give up their customary power and supported by those whose interests they served, the old morals drone on for
some time. Institutions that favor them are often themselves on the verge of
losing their influence and meaning, but they, too, resist change. We see this
most evidently when we consider the current upheaval in sexual mores in our
society that began during the sexual revolution of the 1960s.

On the surface, the recent film *Chasing Amy*[1] is about a bunch of confused young people in search for their identity. The main characters most
remarkably do not adhere to any conventional norms (not that none exist at
all in the film). Human beings tend to pattern the norms of their peers until
they develop their own. Perhaps, because of the absence of a meaningful sex
education and the total lack of guidance and positive role modeling from the
older generation, these young people search for guidance within themselves.

The young heroine of the movie has built her identity through sexual
experimentation. In a sexual relationship she hopes to find closeness, trust,
friendship, tenderness, caring, and compassion. Early on, she failed to experience this in encounters with men, so she turned to female partners for
fulfillment. Searching and insecure about her sexuality, she considers herself
bisexual, like so many experimenting youth today. Sensitive to brute advances by the males in her life, who in the past had degraded her into an object, she found that her female friends treated her more caringly.

When an equally caring male comes along, she attempts an intimate relationship with him, which is her true goal. But instead of accepting her for
the person she is right now, her male friend gets hung up in her past. Not that
he condemns her for her past actions, as a moralist of the old school would
do, but he feels inadequate in comparison to her experience. In school he has
learned that competition is the name of the game. The lessons he learned in
competitive sports he applies now to life. For him and his friends sex is cu-
mulative action that has little to do with a qualitative experience of relation-

ship. Her past, her experience, and the balance of pleasure and pain she has gone through, taught her the hard way that casual relationships, especially of the non-committal group type, hurt in the long run and are not worth the pleasure of the moment. He believes that he will be on equal footing with her only after he has had group sex with her and his friend. The difference in their expectations and his lack of insight into her wishes and pain cause the relationship to break up. A cautious approach and a compassionate friendship could have brought both of them together and led to a lasting relationship.

In all its confusion, the movie mourns the lack of compassion in relationships. It does not condemn any expression of sexual content per se as long as the participating partners are mature enough to understand the actions and their consequences. Sexuality and sexual expression is most deeply connected to our ability to empathize with the other. The lack of compassion experienced by so many children in our society directly causes the breakdown of our moral and social fabric. Children are killing children. The news stories chase each other while the rest of society chases for the shadows of an illusionary Amy.

What if men and women are fundamentally different in their expectations, especially in matters of sex? More and more research points in that direction. Socio-biologists and socio-psychologists have accumulated a large body of evidence in support of this. What if men are from Mars and women are from Venus? Only a compassionate upbringing and an education that focuses on communication and empathy will help.

Family, schools, and society must work together to bring forth this noble goal. Unfortunately, a dominator society tends to reinforce the natural tendency in males to toughness and callousness. In ancient times, the male might have needed this attitude to defend against enemies. Societies that were dedicated to the spirit of war (such as the Spartans) took young male children away from their mothers at an early age in order to raise them as warriors and combatants. Until recently, the separation of boys and girls (in public schools in most of the Western world) had similar effects.

Armies, in the past, had to break the compassionate spirit of young men on their way to becoming soldiers. The compassion they had learned as children or even had come equipped with from nature was contrary to the military spirit of fighting and winning. Today's armies are changing. Soldiers no longer primarily train to personally face the enemy in combat. They train to be technocrats, working a machine designed to kill. Today's soldier trains to push buttons and execute commands. In the age of clinical strikes and precision bombing, war loses its dirty face. Little cameras mounted on top of the laser-guided missiles transmit the images of destruction, but they hardly ever show the close-up images of the desperate faces of death that characterized images of the war in Vietnam. In our collective mind we can deal with blown up factories, even if they housed a couple of hundred people or produced infant formula.

The dominator culture that still surrounds us connects sex with violence. Already the Greek High God was a violent god who occasionally raped. Even the Hebrew God did not seem terribly upset when, in war, a couple of thousand virgins were sold into slavery. Even though Christ preached the feminine virtues of care, love, and forgiveness, among the Christian rulers of the Holy Roman Empire his gospel fell on deaf ears. The Christian church generally enforced an anti-sexual attitude for the lower class, while the ruling class, the clergy often included, selectively reserved for itself the privileges of sexual promiscuity. As the feudal system that bestowed those privileges by birth onto the upper class, disappeared, a class system of merit and money replaced it. Status and money allowed more access to women whose beauty, obedience, and sexuality were sold. This was true for the prince of the feudal past, for the political and academic elite of the recent past, and it continues to be true for the economic and political elite of today. This remains one of the hidden reasons for the glass ceiling that prevents many capable women to access powerful positions in today's political and economic climate.

How can we envision a new society that is guided more by compassion and less by what we see as conventional and "normal?" How can we make even the practice of law more compassionate?

Much depends on family and community structures to foster compassion in girls and in boys. Our educational system must abandon its fixation on information and numbers, and find a new focus on individual care. Above all, educators must rethink their dichotomous approach to values. Compassion, as a value, is part of all religions. But it must not necessarily be derived from religious sources. Compassion is a natural part of life. Therefore educating in the ways of compassion does not have to fall under the law of separation of church and state. Teachers can and must provide exercises in compassionate action, conflict resolution, and group interaction as part of every curriculum in both public and private schools. We must declare the teaching of compassion a priority issue in our civic society if we truly believe in democracy, partnership, and equality. Scientific research, too, must include a compassionate outlook as so many feminist scholars theorize.

René Descartes mistakenly separated emotions from reason. This left our schools lacking any education in emotional intelligence. As I will point out in a later chapter, we must declare emotional intelligence public health issue number one. Herein lies the solution to teen pregnancies, teen suicides, children shooting children, and many other ills that plague our lives and, more, those of our children.

We took a giant step in teaching compassion to men, when at the end of the 1960s, men were allowed to fully take part in the process of birth. As a father, I was among the first group of Chicago parents who took the Lamaze training of natural childbirth. Our group had to take legal action to force access to the delivery room. The hospitals fought this not only for insurance reasons. Male gynecologists feared they would lose their dual role as modern patriarchs and powerful medical technicians. They saw this as an unwanted intrusion into their territory and possible loss of revenues.

For me, an active involvement in the birth of my five children was a life altering experience, to say the least. During the intense period of female labor, when the new life asserts its own right and gets ready to separate from the protective womb, the male can intimately experience life's frailty and female strength. The father trains to coach the woman, guiding her through this difficult period. His reward is a deep and profound sense of connectedness. During the transition period, which only lasts a few seconds (when the child's head passes through the birth canal) my wife regularly passed out. I could see it in her eyes. My efforts encouraged her and brought her back to the task of pushing our child fully out into the world. She later told me that in that transitory moment, her mind was a thousand miles away. Afterwards, she believed that this moment had lasted forever.

Male and female partners alike can enjoy this moment of connectedness in the birth of a child. The midwives who assisted in the birth of our children must also have found great satisfaction to assist in this incredible miracle of life. In the process of birth and in child-rearing the essential question we should always ask is "What works best for the child?" For the male partner to experience this moment is a precious privilege.

As sexual mores change, so do the norms that govern human relationships and family. In the cycle of life, one of the main reasons for human beings to bond for long periods is so we can raise our children. But I believe it was mostly for religious reasons that the bond of heterosexual monogamy became the norm in Western society. It will remain the norm for many years in the future as well, but in times of change and rethinking of old attitudes we need to remain open to other unions. Perhaps some other unions could work equally well in bringing up children in a caring and compassionate way. Perhaps in the future, we need to rethink the concept of monogamy as the only union we call family. Currently, the law only sanctions a monogamous union. In spite of much criticism, the law today considers a monogamous union alone legal and adequate to raise children. Bernard Shaw once critically remarked that confusing monogamy with morality has done more to destroy the conscience of the human race than any other error.

How did it develop that in our secular world the Judeo–Christian institution of monogamy became the indisputable law of the land? Should not the overriding question here as well be what works best for our children? Today we can hardly doubt that the nuclear family is failing. With both parents involved in the working world, children are often left alone and deprived. Educational institutions were supposed to pick up what parents could no longer achieve. But they fail precisely in teaching compassion and in providing a safe place to practice compassion. With their main focus on excellence and competitiveness, our schools poorly substitute the loving and caring environment that our children need to fully develop.

Consider the case of a three-year-old girl in Tennessee who the state took away from her mother because officials found a multiple-parent group unfit to raise her. In a show about multiple partners relating to each other, MTV interviewed the girl's "family," consisting of three adults – two of them female and one male. The judge who decided to take away the child did not consider whether this group of adults could nurture the child. All that mattered was that this family did not fit the traditional mold. In the eyes of the state, three adults cannot be considered a loving unit in which to bring up a child. This was reason enough to charge them with child abuse.

Other mammals, especially our closest evolutionary relatives, often practice polygamy. Scientists observed that this practice has the potential to turn into an "evolutionary arms race" between the sexes. This in turn can lead to violence and rape. Such destructive sexual behavior exists among orangutans. But in spite of prevailing monogamy, sexual violence and rape are epidemic among human beings as well. According to some scientists, a peculiar set of genes, called imprinted genes, guarantees this kind of non-cooperative behavior in human beings and other mammals.[2] This again would suggest that violence and domination are an inevitable part of human existence.

Archeological evidence, however, points in a different direction. Much suggests that our primal ancestors practiced cooperation instead of competition and domination. Our ancestors, before they left the continent of Africa and central Europe to venture into more hostile climates, lived in communal arrangements based on a cooperative group spirit, similar to those found among baboons and chimpanzees. They all needed each other for food, survival, and extended care for their offspring. Human beings, in those early groups, did not necessarily connect sexual activity with the conception of a child. Human beings realized this much later, when in domesticating and raising animals they became aware of the connection between sex and breeding.

In comparison to other larger animals, human beings were neither strong nor fast. Their advantage lay in their wits and intelligence. Lacking strength, speed, and size, early human beings survived because their brains helped them develop a keen sense of what worked. After leaving the fertile grounds of the African continent and venturing into more hostile climate in the Northern parts of Europe, human beings had to develop new strategies for survival. They often accomplished this by observing and imitating the animals that had lived in those regions long before human beings ever set foot there. Among the tribal people living in the harsh North, a strict hierarchical model worked more efficiently as a social tool than an egalitarian communal structure. Whereas in the communal settlements of the milder regions people lived mainly from picking berries and hunting small animals, in the hostile North the possession of animals became a necessity. With the training and possession of animals came a culture of adding wealth through breeding. They extended this to the breeding of children and the possession of women as commodities. With the advent of monotheism, a jealous chieftain became the absolute ruler in heaven and the dominating male became his delegate on earth. When monogamy finally became the rule, the dominator model had already become an intrinsic part of family life. As such it was applied to the family structure

Eventually, the dominator culture from the north, after taming horses, made use of the wheel for long distance traveling and forcefully expanded south. Perhaps the gold the Mother people had accumulated lured the domineering tribes as Mary Mackey suggests. Whatever the reasons, those domineering tribes expanded and overran the egalitarian tribes in the south. Women, who had until then enjoyed equal partnership in the joys, pleasures, and daily adventures of life, were not readily willing to give up their equality and subject themselves to male domination.

Was monogamy the price men paid for the willing subjugation of women? For the privilege of having nearly unlimited access to one woman, men gave up the ancient practice of having access to many. Consensual sexuality, which the mother people practiced as a gift of the goddess and often as intrinsic part of public rituals, turned into a battleground of the male's fight for scarce resources and possessions. In the dominator culture, men would spend a lot of energy competing with each other for access to women. The institution of marriage and monogamy became a practical solution. The energies that eligible males used to spend for female access they now could spend in other, more useful, activities. From a social perspective, monogamy was the tool to accomplish this goal. As long as the male was guaranteed unlimited access to his female partner, regardless of her wishes, needs, and desires, monogamy allowed the male time for work and warfare. This would also provide an explanation for the nearly unanimous rejection of homosexuality in monogamous cultures.

Since men and women undoubtedly differ in their needs for sexual pleasure and these needs change continuously in the cycles of life, human beings could only base an egalitarian union on a cooperative relationship. But since men are from Mars and women are from Venus, human beings lost equality in gender relationships and male domination became the firm rule in the monogamous family.

Eight

MEN ARE FROM MARS, WOMEN ARE FROM VENUS

> Not only do men and women communicate differently but they think, feel, perceive, react, respond, love, need, and appreciate differently. They almost seem to be from different planets, speaking different languages and needing different nourishment.
>
> John Gray

A few years into my marriage of now almost thirty years, I wrote a play. I called it *Holiday In*. The major scenes of the story took place in a hotel room, a Holiday Inn. The play depicts three stages in married life from the perspective of a man:

The early stages of the honeymoon and planning for the first child.

The third stage of years of unrest, the feeling of being trapped.

A mature couple is reminiscing about the ups and downs of their marriage. My plan was to make a statement about my male expectations of married life. I based the story on my fantasies and my experiences in a young marriage.

In this first part, the young couple spends a weekend in a hotel. While the husband lounges around the hotel pool, the wife is upstairs in their suite taking her temperature. She determines that this is an opportune time for conception. Excited, she summons her husband from the pool and asks him to have sex immediately. Even though he finds her request strange he complies. During the following night the husband gets up and goes into the bathroom to masturbate. His young wife notices this, and it upsets her. She wants to know why he has the need to masturbate with her lying next to him. In the ensuing discussion, they reveal their mutually different concepts of what constitutes good sex.

The woman's thoughts never stray far from contemplating the results of the intercourse, the conception of a child. She has planned their sexual activities by the calendar in order to insure that the whole course of pregnancy and birth occurs at an optimal time for her and the child. She would not want to carry the baby through the summer, as it would be too hot and cumbersome. A birth in the middle of winter might have a different set of problems: driving to the hospital in a snowstorm, car problems, cold rooms, etc. In her view, conception would be best during fall. This way, she would carry the baby during winter, be heaviest during the early spring months and deliver in late spring or early summer.

The man meets the woman's plan with misunderstanding and disbelief. He counters with a plan of his own, focusing totally on the pleasure of the sexual act, which he views as a kind of Russian roulette. In order to optimize the number of sexual encounters with his wife before a pregnancy would occur, the male proposes to have sex at first only during the totally safe days of the monthly cycle. Then each month they would add one day on each end of the cycle until they have sex every day of the month, or nearly so. In this random fashion, nature would take its course, and she could conceive a child. The couple eventually agrees to follow her course of action, which quite obviously is the more rational and useful plan.

As men and women, we have different sexual expectations and interests. From early on in our marriage I suspected this, but had never been told so by anybody, neither teacher, nor parent, nor anyone else. Nothing had prepared me for the differences I could expect in living together with a woman I hardly knew. A partnership marriage is Perspectivism in action. Often, only an open sensitivity could let me in on where my wife was coming from. When early feminist theories tried to cover up and ignore the difference between men and women, especially in sexual matters, I was silent and thought to myself that my experience was different. First socio-biologists, then evolutionary psychologists have taken a second look at the differences in gender behavior and found reason to believe that, in many ways, nature comes before nurture.

A psychological experiment from the early 1960s became the standard example to prove that most gender behavior results from nurture instead of nature. Only recently, long-range results overturned this case, and they now stand to prove the opposite of the earlier assumption: we now know that our natural makeup, especially in regard to our gender identity, plays a decisive role. In the above case, during circumcision the doctor accidentally severed the genitals of one of a couple of twin boys. A leading psychologist was called in for consultation. He decided to raise the boy as a girl, believing this would be the better choice for someone without male organs. During the growing years, doctors performed numerous physiological and psychological procedures to insure that this "girl" received all the nurturing support that would insure her to grow up as a proper girl. Scientists claimed the experiment as a full success and many psychology texts used it as a standard support for nurture over nature. Well after puberty, however, the "girl" accidentally found out about her true identity. Instead of being angry, "she" experienced relief to find out who she/he was. The young man, now almost twenty, initiated every necessary change to switch his identity back into that of a male, which he always had suspected that he was. The young man finally had found peace and contentment now that he had reclaimed his original gender.[1]

Who we are results from a careful dialogue with our natural makeup. If social forces overpower these gentle beginnings, the results cause confusion and, in some cases, desperation. In a society that condones only heterosexual relationships, teenagers who find themselves attracted to the same gender, for instance, experience a high level of insecurity and anxiety. A proportionally high rate of suicide among homosexual teens is the unacceptable result. Perspectivist instruction and sensitivity exercises can help here, too, to increase the level of awareness, empathy, and acceptance.

In the old nature versus nurture debate, some scientists today are carefully reevaluating whether a genetically set difference between men and women, especially in their emotional setup, exists. Marc Breedlove, a behavioral endocrinologist at the University of California at Berkeley, pioneered the study of defining how hormones can help to build sexually different nervous systems. Breedlove affirms, "there is plenty of room to influence sex differences" but he also states: "Yes, we are born with predispositions, but it's society that amplifies them, exaggerates them. I believe that – except for the sex difference in aggression. Those differences are too massive to be explained simply by society."[2]

Much scientific research has focused on this difference in aggression. In *The Gender Blur: Where Does Biology End and Society Take Over?* Deborah Blum gives a laundry list of statistical evidence to support the case of male aggressiveness. For every fifteen robberies committed by men, a woman commits only one. Men are drawn to guns: twice as many male thieves use guns in robberies when compared to female thieves. Three-fourths of males use guns in domestic murders while only 50 percent of women do, even though the "pro-firearms" lobby advertises guns as "the great equalizers." In conflicts in which a woman kills a man, the man started the fight more often than not. In a fight in which a woman died, she instigated it only 12.5 percent of the time. From this Blum concludes: "Males are more aggressive, not only in humans but among almost all species on earth. Male chimpanzees, for instance, declare war on neighboring troops, and one of their strategies is a warning strike: they kill females and infants to terrorize and intimidate."[3]

Scientists say that socio-biological reasons exist for this aggressive nature. Says Blum:

> In terms of simple reproductive genetics, it's an advantage of males to be aggressive: you can muscle your way into dominance, winning more sexual encounters, more offspring, more genetic future. For the female – especially in a species like ours, with time for just one successful pregnancy a year – what's the genetic advantage of brawling?[4]

In the world today, however, with its over-population and considering the still real threat of nuclear extinction, we can no longer view aggressiveness as a genetic advantage or necessity. For many thousand years, under the influence of a dominator principle, culture has reinforced aggression in males. Many males are gentle and non-aggressive human beings. Others, who have a tendency to aggression, have decided (for a variety of reasons: cultural, moral, practical, and religious) to be caring, cooperative, and gentle.

In the past and still today, we frequently explain male aggression as natural – hardwired into the male's psyche. Perspectivism tells a different story. Nothing in my psyche is hardwired. We learn everything and therefore we can change, even if those changes are not easy to make and sometimes would take many generations to learn. Even our genes have the ability to learn and to change. Our subconscious mind results from our acquired knowledge, even if this is not immediately available to my conscious mind. Today we have ways to change our "inborn" behavior if we choose. With the help of modern techniques developed by neurolinguistic programming, Perspectivism can show us the way.

On a cognitive level we can make an obvious start in terms of improving relationships by learning more about other people and the other gender's ways of communication. In *Men are from Mars, Women are from Venus*, author John Gray provides a practical guide and an effective tool for learning Perspectivist communication.[5] Gray's invaluable advice: "When you remember that your partner is as different from you as someone from another planet, you can relax and cooperate with the differences instead of resisting or trying to change them."[6]

Gray regularly conducts successful relationship seminars. For his book, he interviewed more than twenty five thousand individuals in order to "define in positive terms how men and women are different." He promises that, for the faithful reader and practitioner, as he or she explores these differences, "walls of resentment and mistrust" will melt down. Gray's promise does not conservatively return to traditional values and patterns, which were often marred by hierarchical domination and submission. His vision, instead, leaps boldly into a future characterized by trust in communication, or a Perspectivist search for the other. According to Gray, "to improve relationships between the sexes it is necessary to create an understanding of our differences that raises self-esteem and personal dignity while inspiring mutual trust, personal responsibility, increased cooperation, and greater love."[7]

Some of the major differences discussed by Gray are these: men offer solutions and often invalidate women's feelings. Women give unsolicited advice and direction. Men are motivated when they feel needed. Women are motivated when they feel cherished. Men and women speak and stop communicating for entirely different reasons. Men and women have entirely different needs for intimacy. Men need a kind of love that is trusting, accepting, and appreciative. Women need a love that is caring, understanding, and respectful.

Anyone who would like to improve his or her relationship should read Gray's book. An appended version could also deal with nontraditional families and homosexual relationships. Partners of the same sex also need to work on understanding each other. We might assume that understanding among same sex partners would naturally be less complicated since both are "from the same planet," to use Gray's metaphor. But often this is not the case. Traditional upbringing of both partners in a heterosexual and hierarchically structured world did not prepare them at all for their union. Much of the communication work between same sex partners, therefore, has to focus on undoing the traditional patterns of a dominator relationship that suggests that one of the partners must play a subservient role instead of building a relationship on equal terms.

Natural differences and deep emotional expectations must become part of our educational programs instead of leaving them to mere accidental discovery. But students cannot achieve this knowledge on a cognitive level alone; they must experience it in order for it to be effective and lasting. In traditional educational settings administrators often see group interaction, role-playing, and creative dramatics as superfluous and less meaningful than conventional instruction in the basics though these are vital tools for Perspectivist practice and life. Artistic expression that involves both the mind and the emotions is an invaluable tool to practice cross gender communication.

In the future, virtual reality might also play a role in improving Perspectivist sensibilities. We could use the total submersion into the world of the other that virtual reality offers as a tool to teach and practice compassion.

Nine

HEALING THE BODY AND THE MIND

> I realized that the subject of healing and the mind stretches beyond medicine into issues about what we value in society and who we are as human beings. As patients, we are more than lonely, isolated flecks of matter; we are members of families, communities, and cultures. As this awareness finds its way into hospitals, operating rooms, clinics, and doctors' offices, perhaps it will spread further as well. Healing begins with caring. So does civilization.
>
> Bill Moyers

If the experience of counseling can supply an ethics for Perspectivist philosophy, progressive branches of neuroscience and the healing profession can provide a new ontology. Newest research in these fields can provide insights into the intricate connection between body and mind. For some of the most advanced professionals in medical research, the gap between mind and body has all but disappeared.

The connection and interaction between mind and body in healing is evident. When our body is sick, we do not feel well in our mind either. The physical well-being of our body quite obviously affects our mental energies and our state of mind. But is the reverse also true? Does our mental state affect our physical well-being?

Until recently, Western medicine would have answered this question with "no," though any cautious practitioner must have had an awareness of such a connection. As a result of the dualistic worldview, Western medicine generally treated the body separate from the mind. Within the prevalent Newtonian paradigm, scientists considered the body a machine. They treated a sickness of the body with mechanical and chemical intervention. One inanimate substance responds in a predictable manner to the intervention of another such substance, just as if the two substances were combined in a test tube. The mind, at least in theory, played no role in this process. In traditional practice, scientific methodology all but demands the exclusion of the mind's influence when testing new drugs. Scientists use blind tests and placebos as tools to verify the effectiveness of a drug.

In tribal medicine the influence of the mind on the body has never been in doubt. Still today, we can find some religious people practicing shamanistic methods of healing, which we traditionally find in primal and tribal medicine. Spiritual practices, too, can influence the body's well-being. Statistics have proven that people with faith live longer.[1] We have also established the effectiveness of prayer as a form of healing.[2] From the perspective of Western medicine, people still generally dismiss these practices as primitive superstitions or illusions that hardly warrant serious scientific consideration.[3]

As Western medicine came in touch with medical practices in Eastern cultures, such as China, Japan, and India, medical experts conducted some isolated studies. These pioneers of a more holistic approach to medicine were honest enough to realize the occasionally surprising effectiveness of these ancient ways. Are these methods always working? I believe not; but neither does chemical medicine. In many cases, when doctors prescribe pills, the side effects are worse than the sickness. According to some experts, a high percentage of Western-style interventions are inefficient or even deadly.

One difference between Western scientific medicine and the Eastern art of healing seemed to be the preferential place of the mind. In Eastern medicine, as in tribal shamanism, the mind plays a large part in harmonizing and healing the body. Only in the past few decades have scientists more seriously attempted to understand these ancient ways and to establish a scientific underpinning for how the mind influences the body in the process of healing. The Fetzer Institute in Kalamazoo, Michigan, sponsored a series of scientific studies in regard to the mind-body connection in medicine. As of today, these studies culminated in two publications: *Mind Body Medicine*[4] edited by Daniel Goleman and Joel Gurin and *Healing and the Mind* [5] by Bill Moyer. The book *Healing and the Mind* is also the basis for a successful television series. Both works contain a wealth of information collected with both scientific method and anecdotal experiences. The publications generally support the idea that the mind plays a vital role in healing the body.

The research of Candice Pert, a Visiting Professor at the Center for Molecular and Behavioral Neuroscience at Rutgers University, interests us in our attempt to understand the mind-body connection and the philosophy of Perspectivism.[6] Her research supports the idea that consciousness does not only center in the human brain, but is present in all cells of the human body. Should the medical and scientific community fully accept her research, the old dualistic paradigm would have to yield forever to a new unity of mind and body. We would have to fully accept consciousness as an integral part of the living world. In addition, research on other fronts suggests that we can find consciousness not only in so-called living things, but also in all parts of the natural world.

We cannot, at least as of now, observe pure consciousness under a microscope. We cannot survey consciousness like other material substances. But we can observe the effects of consciousness and the way mind travels throughout the body.

It has been known for some time that thoughts and emotions travel within the brain via electrical and chemical impulses. We release observable electrical impulses and chemicals in our brains when areas of the brain are active. We call these chemicals endorphins. Endorphins bear some similarity to psychoactive drugs such as opium or heroin. The human brain produces such endorphins to create emotional states. New research has shown that the human body has these endorphins in the immune system and in every cell.

Endorphins or neuropeptides, as scientists also call them, operate a communications network throughout the entire body. Scientists have found millions of receptors for these messenger molecules on the surface of every cell. According to Pert: "These neuropeptides and their receptors are the bio-chemical correlates of emotions. . . . they appear to mediate intercellular communication throughout the brain and body."[7]

When the philosopher René Descartes excluded mind or consciousness from the sphere of scientific research he made, according to Pert, a deal with the Roman Catholic Church:

> He got to study science as we know it, and left the soul, the mind, the emotions, and the consciousness to the realm of the church. It's incredible how far Western science has come with that reductionist paradigm. But, unfortunately, more and more things don't quite fit into that paradigm. What's happening now may have to do with the integration of mind and matter.[8]

Pert works from the premise that "the mind is not just in the brain, but that the mind is part of a communications network throughout the brain and body."[9] On this basis we can now establish a theory that contains the interrelation between mind and body. This theory, according to Pert, explains, "how physiology can affect mental functioning on a moment to moment, hour-by-hour, day-to-day basis," and how the mind can influence the body in healing itself. Even though Pert concedes, "the killer experiment that will link mind to matter, and peptides and receptors to emotion, has not yet been done," as a scientist, she confidently believes that her research is on the right track. Contrary to Descartes and traditional science, Pert is sure that all the emotions are not in the head. "The chemicals that mediate emotion and the receptors for those chemicals are found in almost every cell in the body. In fact, even one celled animals have these peptides."[10]

Emotions, which Greek philosophers considered a defect, the making of lower celestial gods, or the bronze part of the human soul, provide the link between mind and body. As Western human beings advanced down the road of dualistic separation between mind and body, they subscribed wholeheartedly to the Aristotelian vision of a wholly rational human being. But we slowly lost our most vital link to the natural and material world. Ultimately we lost our link to our bodies.

Feminists proposed the lack of emotional attachment as one of the decisive critiques of our male culture. Some feminist scientists projected the need to reintroduce emotions into science. As victims of oppressed emotions in an oppressive male–dominated culture they knew the importance of emotional attachment and sensitivity. Women know their need for emotional sensitivity in the most female of all experiences, the bearing and birthing of children.

The closest I myself, as a male, ever came to feeling the presence of a child in the womb was when I was cuddled up one night to the bulging stomach of my wife in bed. Half asleep, I could feel the little creature inside her change position. A little hand or foot was pressing against the soft uterine wall, and through her our baby touched me.

Assisting my wife in natural childbirth for our five children, I became intensely sensitized to the emotional needs of this most precious gift of life that nature perpetuates on a physiological, biological plane. When in the late 1960s, we had to fight through court to attain my presence in the birthing room, I realized how incredibly insensitive the traditional Western way of child bearing and child birthing had become to the needs and requirements of nature. The male doctor's overemphasis on mechanical intervention and machines directly resulted from the mechanical worldview that was the heart and brain of the old paradigm. The traditional doctor, an authoritarian father figure, perceived the presence of the real father at birth as interference, more like a nuisance. In a conventional birth, doctors used chemicals to dull and desensitize the mind of the birthing mother to the activities so vital for the continuation of life. If the slightest need arose, the anesthesiologist stood by to administer a knockout dose so the doctor could fulfill his task in supreme command over nature.

The new ways of birthing and the methods of natural childbirth, worked out by pioneers such as Dr. Frédérick Leboyer and Dr. Fernand Lamaze, were immensely more sensitive to the voice of nature. In exercise classes for both the husband and wife, we learned about techniques that enabled a woman to stay in tune with her body by using ancient breathing and relaxation techniques (many gleaned from the Eastern practice of Yoga). An intense pain frequently occurs during the transition period. This is the moment when the head of the child passes through the birthing canal. This pain can be excruciating, bringing the woman to the threshold of the unconscious. But ultimately she must prevail. Her ability to control the pain and remain in charge infinitely increases through the conscious coaching of the partner, whose role finds its fulfillment in those short few moments, when mind merges with mind and brings forth the new life in joint agony and hope.

How different the role of the husband and father becomes when doctors allow him to partake in these precious moments! Compare this to a traditional father who had to wait outside in the lobby or went to a pub until the newborn arrived.

This new art of childbirth unites the father with the miracle of life from the beginning, instead of leaving him out in the cold, caring for the monetary welfare of the family, more than for connectedness and love. In this "reinvention of natural childbirth" we have taken our first step in putting more trust in the ancient wisdom of our bodies and of nature. This provides a powerful example for the rest of technology. Many times, when human knowledge and ingenuity fail, the best course of action may be doing less and letting nature take its course.

Pert and other practitioners in the new tradition of "emotional science" have no shame in speaking about the wisdom of the body and the accumulated wisdom of nature. The central fault of the machine paradigm, the seduction of quick fixes, has become evident on all levels of Western life: fast food, fast drugs, fast happiness, painless childbirth, and painless education.

The separation of the mind from the body had perhaps its deepest and most damaging effect in the way we educate our children. Being in tune with our body is the first requirement for natural childbirth and for natural healing to take place, but Western education has put little emphasis on the emotional education of children. We leave emotional training almost entirely to the home, but there, television and video games often replace dialogue and social interaction.

Studies of the Chinese practices of Tai Chi and other ancient arts of healing have shown that it often takes ten, twenty, even thirty years to perfect a person's integration of mind and body. In our public schools, we train the mind as if it was an empty hard drive that we have to fill with information. Those philosophers who influenced our culture most profoundly called the mind a *tabula rasa*, an empty slate. And not only the empiricists, but the rationalist, too, followed the Aristotelian contempt for emotions. Many believe that raw emotions link us to the beasts. Georg Wilhelm Friedrich Hegel feared that an emotional state of the masses would cause Bacchantic riots that we have to avoid at any price. Most political philosophers feared anarchy, even though anarchy in its origin means the state of non-domination. In terms of emotions, it means granting equal right to the development of a natural emotional state.

A few renowned educators have pointed out the importance of emotions for the development of a child. Rudolf Steiner and the Waldorf Schools come to mind. John Dewey's emphasis on creativity and art granted a priority status to the emotional development of a child during his or her growing years. But in general, the Western world has shunned emotions. Becoming adult means being in charge of our emotions to such an extent, that they become all but invisible. Only in the most private sphere of the home do we still permit emotions – for women more readily than for men.

Modern research stresses the importance of a person's emotional life in regard to longevity.[11] The company of others has a profound influence on the length of a person's life as well. This influence is more evident in women. Society generally socializes them to express their emotions with more ease than men. Scientists have found a considerable and measurable increase in life span when women live in the company of other women and when men live in the company of women, but predictably less so when men live with other men or alone.

In our search for the reality of the other, for the origin of mind and the connection between mind and body, a new picture emerges: the mind provides the way for nature to become aware. Through mind, nature conceives of itself from the inside out. Mind is not just a human prerogative. We can find mind at all levels of the natural world, even though so far we have only brought evidence for the presence of mind in living things.

In later chapters we will follow this inside out view, the view of the shamans, the view of Perspectivism down to the level of the so-called inanimate nature. If today we still fall short of a definite proof, we at least will collect evidence for the possibility of such a view, the possibility for the presence of consciousness at all levels of the natural world. This alone makes Perspectivism a complete philosophy and viable alternative to the old objectivist philosophy that has left the world as a soulless machine.

Ten

MISSION OR MISSION IMPOSSIBLE: REDISCOVERING COMMUNITY?

> One has but to observe a community of beavers at work in a stream to understand the loss in his sagacity, balance, co-operation, competence, and purpose which Man has suffered since he rose up on his hind legs. He began to chatter and he developed Reason, Thought, and Imagination, qualities, which would get the smartest group of rabbits or orioles in the world into inextricable trouble overnight.
>
> James Thurber

Futurist Jeremy Rifkin, in *Choosing Our Future*, developed a model of a future society organized around the concepts of service and community.[1] This type of society, Rifkin believes, will eventually replace our current individualistic, atomistic, and alienated one – a utopian world well worth considering:

> The year is 2045. Life for most Americans is quite different from what it was half a century ago. Perhaps the greatest visible change is the diminishing role of the economic marketplace in day-to-day affairs. Now that we are deep into the Information Age most of the world's goods and services are produced in nearly workerless factories and marketed by virtual companies run by a small team of entrepreneurs and highly trained professionals. Sophisticated computers, robots, and state-of-the-art telecommunications technologies have replaced the "worker" of the industrial era. Less than 20 percent of the adult population works full time.[2]

In Rifkin's utopian society the majority of people spend their time and energy doing community service work in not-for-profit organizations. For their volunteer work they receive vouchers to buy goods and services as they wish. A new ethos centering on service to others and community has replaced the old emphasis on selfishness and greed. "Their projects run the gamut from helping take care of children and the elderly to working in preventive health programs, local art galleries, park maintenance, history projects, adult education, community gardens, and neighborhood sports teams as well as religious and political activities."[3]

Since, according to Rifkin, "caring tasks that require intimate relationships between people are far too complex and difficult to be attended to by high-tech software,"[4] automation and computers would least likely replace these kinds of service jobs.

Rifkin projects a monumental change in values as humanity moves from industrial production to information processing. Like the partnership model developed by Riane Eisler, Rifkin also envisions a future that stresses personal transformation, community participation, and global responsibility. He says:

> The older market system reinforced a materialist vision glorifying production and efficiency as the chief means of advancing happiness. As long as people's primary identification was with the market economy, the vision of unlimited personal consumption continued to influence most people's behavior. Americans thought of themselves first and foremost as "consumers," not as neighbors and citizens.[5]

Is it only a nice utopia that Americans will reinvent a communitarian spirit? Where does Rifkin believe all this change will come from? Which forces will bring it about? The new communitarian spirit will evolve, according to Rifkin, "as a necessary antidote to the increasingly impersonal interaction generated by new computer and telecommunications technologies."[6]

Though it would seem desirable to follow Rifkin's dream, is his projection based on past experience? When keeping an analytical eye on human civilizational development in the past, can we rightly assume that such a monumental shift in values will take place to contradict our existing conditions?

Our future will be inundated and overwhelmed by technological advances, but can we assume that such an extreme alienation will automatically turn into its opposite? Will human beings have the strength to emerge with an all new value system and ethics when we already feel powerless to resist the encroaching forces of technological anonymity? What clues can we gather from a rational analysis of our civilizational past, in order to predict a more benign future? Or, is human civilization doomed?

If former President Clinton was right, rediscovering our communities is one of the most burning tasks facing Americans. That is the only guarantee to keep the American dream alive. In a speech to supporters he said:

> I ask you to join in a re-United States. We need to empower our people so they can take more responsibility for their own lives in a world that is ever smaller, where everyone counts. . . . We need a new spirit of community, a sense that we are all in this together, or the American Dream will continue to wither.

Our destiny is bound up with the destiny of every other American.[7]

Based on the philosophy of Transcendental Perspectivism with its roots in chaos theory, shamanism, and partnership thinking, I will develop a social theory that can provide a rational underpinning for the kind of value change that we need in order to avert disaster. Much of what I will discuss we can already observe in current trends, theories, and actions. In Transcendental Perspectivism, these diverse and unrelated trends converge and can provide a focus for a new social theory that will lead humanity into the third millennium and beyond.

Ever since human beings began reflecting on their social positions and structures, people have realized the importance of forming groups and communities. The impulse to live in groups and communities preceded our historical awareness. The sociologist Emile Durkheim noted that from ancient times human beings have derived a sense of cosmic totality from the experience of the village community. Durkheim believed that concepts such as order and organization, the relationship of the whole and to its part, the idea of force and law were derived from the lived experience of a community and not from abstract philosophical speculation.

The Greek philosopher Aristotle believed that the trend of human beings to group together, to live in communities, was one of the most basic characteristics that made us human. Aristotle called it one of the essential characteristics of a human being. The human being was a *Zoon Politikon*, a political animal. Western civilization views those who live in isolation as loners; we see hermits as aberrations. In the past people often deemed the person who would chose this lifestyle as an outlaw. Living in increasingly organized and complex societies became the goal of civilization.

Aristotle also coined the idea of teleology, which became a key concept in early social theory. He thought societies, just as everything else in this world, develop toward a pre-defined goal, a *telos*. This goal epitomized the perfected ideal of everything, in the case of a society, the perfect society.

Teleology was Aristotle's answer to the question: "Why do things change?" Under the influence of Christianity, Aristotle's teleology was applied to society as a whole. During the enlightenment, Aristotelian teleology emerged as a unilinear theory of civilizational development. This new theory completely replaced the ancient pagan idea of a circular recurrence of events that patterned after the cycles of nature. The German philosopher Johann Gottfried von Herder believed that humanity's natural purpose would lead us progressively toward perfection. Voltaire, too, believed that enlightenment and reason would result in an upward progress that would lead to an increasingly perfect society.

Unilinear theories supported an optimistic view of history. The idea was that history, almost with necessity, moved toward a higher, more perfect and fulfilled stage. From our advanced stage, we could recognize other less-developed stages of historical development. The superior position of our civilization gave us the right, even the duty to bring other, less-advanced people up to our standards. Greek classical thinking neatly merged with the Judaic belief in the special mission of God's chosen people. Early Christian philosophers incorporated Greek teleology deeply into Christian eschatology. Such ideas lead to extreme ethnocentrism and a dogmatic belief in the rightness of our culture and cause. Still today, a good measure of such thinking presents itself in the policies and fantasies of the Christian Right in America and similar groups around the world.

Unilinear theories first fell victim to nineteenth-century philosophical pessimism. Ancient cyclical theories reappeared but now with a distinct downward, pessimistic turn. Friedrich Nietzsche's contemporaries found little hope in his eternal reoccurrence of history in grand cycles. The German historian Oswald Spengler adopted Nietzsche's historical negativism, emphasizing more the decline of civilization than the eventual rebirth of a new one.

The early twentieth century saw the bloom of two new social theories. The industrialized countries of the Western world experienced a dramatic increase in the need for bureaucratic administration. As the centralized power of the states grew ever larger, central authorities took over and administered more and more segments of the formerly private sphere. Max Weber, the German Protestant sociologist, became the mastermind behind a rational defense of an ever-increasing administration in the modern world. Many saw Weber's sociology of a rational course in social engineering as a triumph over a haphazard, accidental approach that they attributed to a free market system.

At the same time the other half of the world, under the spell of Marxism, also experimented for over half a century with social engineering. Today we commonly assume that Marxism with its ties to a strict and rational planning process did not work. Though Marxists predicted that social progress would occur through the dialectic of historical forces, once in power, traditional communist regimes held on to it in a unilateral way and abolished all resistance within their sphere of influence. Communist leadership, once established, violated its own historical principle of permanent revolution as the motor for progress and justice. Once in power, Marxism performed as just another unilinear force – expecting progress by preventing change.

For a multitude of other reasons, however, unilinear social theories have not survived the scrutiny, criticism, and confusion of twentieth century social science. Modern research did not verify earlier assumptions. What we often saw as progress, a more scrutinizing research into history uncovered as a bending of historical facts in order to make them fit ideological and ethnocentric assumptions.

At the end of the twentieth century the remnants of social theory bring together many different perspectives – all of them having a better or worse history of acceptance and success. In these postmodern theories, notable absence of a single evolutionary process or pattern exists: "There is for instance no attempt to define progress or evolution in terms of laissez-faire, survival-of-the-fittest doctrine, or some invisible hand of fate. Nor, conversely, is there any attempt to fasten on so-called telic, rational, conscious change as the single motive of evolution."[8]

Today we view evolutionary social processes as indefinable. Perhaps in no other field have the principles of the new science of Chaos had as much influence as on modern social theory. System theory takes a new structural look at human societies. From the view of system theory, societies are complex, adaptive systems. Scientists have also observed, in computer simulated models as well as in nature, that such complex systems move themselves to the edge of chaos in order to rejuvenate themselves and achieve a better chance in the ongoing evolutionary game. Scientists have properly termed this process deterministic chaos. They have found that such chaotic systems are not absolutely random, but inherently self-organizing and creative. But even though groups of scientists in several locations are working on computer models to simulate cultural evolution, until now, the motivator of cultural evolution remained unknown.

Roger Lewin, in *Complexity,* wonders whether discrete levels of social organization are common to all of cultural evolution, similar to the classes and species in the animal world, to which "the evolving cultural system is inexorably drawn."[9] If so, then perhaps a new telic model is in the making? But, as of now, Lewin concludes: "History is full of examples of social groups achieving a higher level of organization, and then falling back. This is what happened at Chaco. And, until recent times, every society that has achieved level four – the state – has eventually collapsed."[10]

Scientists at the Santa Fe Institute where Lewin works have intensified their search for some "universal principles, fundamental rules that shape all complex adaptive systems."[11] Could collective, synergistic behavior and community creation be one of these universal principles? Preliminary evidence in biology and even in physics suggests that at all levels individuals under some specific conditions come together to perform tasks they could not perform by themselves. A stunning example comes from the murky world of one-cell organisms.

At the threshold of what we generally call life, at the level where chemistry meets biology, one-celled organisms called dictyostelium live alone and isolated for most of their existence. As individual particles they do not even qualify as "alive." Like a virus, they have hardly an existence of their own. As much as scientists can tell, each of these tiny particles is identical with the other. But a strange mutation occurs when a qualified number of these creatures experience a deficiency in food and space. Scientists have observed how they suddenly group together to cooperate in a formerly unknown way. Collectively, they form one large multi-celled organism with head, tail, and digestive system. Each cell takes over a specific function within the new organism. They evidently group together to achieve goals that they could not achieve by themselves. In the case of the dictyostelium, the new body enables this collection of individual cells to move to new feeding grounds. They accomplish this in several metamorphic stages:

> After several hours, the Dictyostelium slug goes through another change. The back end catches up with the tip, and the slug turns into a blob. The blob stretches upward a second time, and now some amoeba produce rigid bundles of cellulose. They die in the process, but their sacrifice allows the blob to become a slender stalk. Perched atop the stalk is a globe, bulging with living amoebas, each of which covers itself in a cellulose coat and becomes a dormant spore. In this form the colony will wait until something – a drop of rainwater, a passing worm, the foot of a bird – picks up the spores and takes them to a bacteria-rich place where they can emerge from their shells and start their lives over.[12]

Today scientists have no idea what makes some cells become tail, others head, and yet others, digestive organs. Scientists cannot find any observable DNA in the original units. As far as science can say, they are identical. Yet, at the moment of unification they "know" or perhaps even "choose" their places. Scientists have speculated much about this phenomenon. Is there a hidden variable, something that has evaded the observing scientist?

What if these tiny organisms do have an inside-out view, similar to the way other living creatures do? What if at that level already some rudimentary mind exists that makes decisions about whether to become a head or a tail? What if the individual entities already at this stage have a sense of the cooperative power that enhances each individual's chance of survival? Is this a plausible alternative? I will investigate this question in more detail in the third section of this book, which I have devoted to the problem of consciousness and mind on the material level.

In nature, it appears autonomous individuals at times collaborate in a synergistic way, when natural conditions make such collaboration advantageous and necessary. Once they achieve this cooperation, development in natural systems levels off and remains static, at least for some time. We can observe such plateaus in evolutionary development at all natural levels. They have been called forms, universal categories, class, or species depending on the cognitive frame and the theory behind it.

What are the energies behind synergistic behavior? What natural power orchestrates such community formation? Is it possible that one day an organized colony of these amoebas, did not disperse again after they had found new feeding grounds, but stayed together as one organism, forming the new beginning of a higher form of life? Remarkably, scientists have noticed that dictyostelium are similar to the cells that make up the human system. Millions of other bacteria and microbes have not become part of our complex system. Why is it that these community creating dictyostelia have become part of the success story of life? Could this collective orchestration be the tool with which nature proceeds and climbs up the evolutionary ladder to ever-new plateaus?

We have observed the phenomenon of collective orchestration at different stages in the evolutionary development. We should not confuse such collective orchestration with procreation, the ordinary process of maintaining the chain of life, which we achieve through cell division or sexual intercourse. Instead, collective orchestration tends to produce not more of the same but a new and higher level of life, an entirely different phenomenon. While it appears on many levels of the natural world on a daily basis, collective orchestration rarely occurs as a dimensional quantum leap. Scientists have observed it at the quantum level and when photons "cooperate" to create a laser beam. Others interpret collective orchestration of microtubules in the brain as the seat for conscious thought.[13] Conscious activity and thinking center around the brain's neural networks. Collective orchestration could help explain the mysterious "life" found by cosmologists in the self-organizing processes of galaxies and stars.

Collective orchestration is also a well-known occurrence among insects. When a new hive forms, bees join together in a swarm. They leave the old habitat and collect around the queen, often hanging from a tree. The collective slapping of the bees wings produces a temperature in the center of the blob that differs from the temperature of each individual bee. This is the optimal temperature for the queen to conceive new life.

Could collective orchestration also drive human collaboration? Could the same collective orchestration cause human beings to form communities? Is there a subconscious awareness that through collective orchestration the whole human race will reach a level of realization, a new dimension of awareness, which we cannot reach individually? If so, nurturing human communities could be one of the most burning missions of humanity on earth.

PART III

THE ANIMAL PERSPECTIVE

Eleven

ANIMALS: OUR TEACHERS AND HEALERS, OUR BROTHERS AND SISTERS

> She had been watching the wolves for two days,
> trying to discern which of their sounds and
> movements expressed goodwill and friendship.
> Most animals had such signals. The little arctic
> ground squirrels flicked their tails sideways to
> notify others of their kind that they were
> friendly. By imitating this signal with her fore-
> fingers, Miyax had lured many a squirrel to her
> hand. If she could discover such a gesture for
> the wolves she would be able to make friends
> with them and share their food.
>
> Julie of the Wolves

In recent decades, human beings have recognized the value of being near and with animals. Given the rate of extinction of a large number of species on a daily basis, this recognition may come too late for many animals. What human beings in ancient and prehistoric times learned by observing and imitating animals, has been all but forgotten, even among those scholars who have made that specific part of human development their field of interest.

Imitation is one of the most powerful learning tools in nature. Animals first observe, and then imitate others as an elementary road to communication, the way to contact and be with the other. The intelligence of the human brain allows us to replace direct imitation as a way to communicate with symbolic representations of objects. These only need to be real and present in the mind of the communicators. We can fairly assume that communication is a basic quality of all life; in the human world, however, symbolic signs (such as words and language) have largely replaced sounds, odors, and gestures as means to communicate.

Long before human beings learned symbolic language they also communicated with each other and with other animals on a direct and perhaps non-symbolic basis. The countless rituals involving animals and animal masks that primal societies use even today can testify to this. Art works from prehistoric societies such as the Minoans often contain animal scenes and representations of human beings intermingling with animals. Mythological stories talk about the friendship, but also about the rivalry and hostility between human beings and animals. In one of the most sensitive scenes in early literature, the giant Cyclops, after he had lost his one eye to the cunning

Odysseus, finds comfort and sympathy from his flock of sheep. A whale saves Jonas in the Bible. He survives in the whale's stomach for three days.

These works of art and stories make it apparent that people often looked to animals as their friends and teachers, but the trend in Western civilization moved in the opposite direction. Here people frequently viewed animals as inadequate and often even as dispensable creatures. This attitude at the core of Western civilization dominates philosophy and religion as Peter Singer pointed out in *Animal Liberation*[1].

Even though Singer and many others have strongly criticized our handling of animals prompting Singer to propose a new ethics in the treatment of animals the attitude of neglect and disrespect of animals often still prevails among modern people. Only slowly a change appears on the horizon. This contrasts with the attitudes of reverence toward animals found among most primal people, a frame of mind that we can still find among native people in the Americas today. Native Americans frequently refer to animals as their brothers and sisters. In their mythologies they used animals, more often than gods and spirits, to explain the secrets of nature and the meaning of life.

Informed by a hierarchical sense of superiority over animals as lesser creatures, Western civilization from its beginning had a negative attitude toward them. This pejorative evaluation of animals began in early Hebrew history as a rejection of the pagan reverence for animals as holy and divine. Early Mediterranean civilizations revered the snake and the bull as holy animals of procreation and earthly power. Overpowering both animals, the bull and the snake, became a fixation in early Western religions. Still, in modern times, the fight of the matador overcoming the bull and humiliating him publicly recalls that early resentment. Human beings had to demonstrate their superiority over the bull just as in early Jesuit writing men had to appear superior to women in regard to the newly subjugated native tribes in North America. Similarly turning the snake, this sacred animal of the mother Goddess, into an incarnation of evil, demonized the snake. The merciless killing of snakes in Europe may have even caused the rampant advance and spreading of the plague at the end of the Middle Ages. As we know today, rodents spread the plague and rodents are the natural prey of snakes.

The Hindu religion still considers the snake holy. Worshippers realize the benefits of having snakes in and around human habitats. They view the poisonous aspects of snakes as a demonstration of the superb power of these animals instead of their danger to humanity, as depicted in Western culture.

The people of the Christian Middle Ages divided all animals into good and beneficial animals on one hand and bad or evil ones on the other. In an agricultural society, farmers considered animals beneficial if they were useful to farm work. Easily tamed animals that human beings could benefit from were often revered as an incarnation of holiness, even of Christ. Animals that resisted taming and use by human beings or animals like the fox that preyed on livestock were considered sly and an incarnation of evil. Medieval European biology mirrored the dualistic medieval world informed by Christian/Platonic philosophy. Some animals represented fallen nature or Satan, while others were the kin of Christ. Medieval Europeans saw the goat as patient and submissive. They viewed our closest kin, the large apes and chimpanzees, as also having a fallen nature. Medieval sideshows often exhibited the Orangutan caged and in chains, this demonstrated sinful nature and never let human beings forget the wide rift between themselves and the natural world. Medieval human beings looked at such animals to learn the meaning of falling away from the grace of God.

When science later began to take more interest in animals, it was even more in the interest of their usefulness to human beings. Perhaps as the result of the global influence of Western culture, this attitude toward animals today is almost universal. We may find one rare exception in some Asian countries, where, since ancient times, cows, elephants, and snakes have enjoyed a protected or sacred status. Not until quite recently did we have any widespread concern for animals for their own sake, as Perspectivist philosophy would strongly suggest. In most parts of the world, human beings still measure animals by their value for human exploitation.

In *Shooting Elephants in Zimbabwe*, Ken Simonsen writes about the commercialization of wildlife management in that African country:

> Outside of the parks, wild animals are regarded as akin to maize and tobacco; they can be "harvested," "cropped," or "culled" like any commercial commodity. Following this agricultural metaphor, wildlife can be regarded as a sustainable crop; in this way, animals can and should pay their own way.[2]

But underneath this commercial attitude toward wildlife Simonsen finds an even more disturbing anthropocentric attitude. According to Simonsen, we have "a presumption about nature that is profoundly anthropocentric. Wildlife has only extrinsic value; it should be used for human benefit . . . the elephant should be used for its meat, hide, and ivory. It should be valued for its contribution to tourism 'in the service of man.'"[3]

While Asians often still revere the elephant as a sacred, Africans, according to Simonsen, generally regard the elephant as "a mountain of meat." This extreme anthropocentric view of much of African politics signals the deep rift that exists between ancient African tribalism and modern political demands that resulted from extended periods of colonial exploitation and cultural indoctrination.

From early on, Western human beings were convinced of their superiority over the animal world. Human beings received their souls and earthly mission directly from God. The rest of the world was free to exploit, neglect, and even demonize. René Descartes declared animals as little machines whose screams we can ignore – since they have no concept of pain, they do not feel pain. With this statement, he opened the doors for relentless scientific research on animals in the name of progress, for human beings' sake. In the name of science, animals became the victims of an ever-advancing humanity.

During the industrial revolution, human beings wrote the next episode of expansion and animal neglect. Agricultural society still had multiple uses for animals. Human beings took in, harnessed, and exploited animals due to their usefulness as willing agricultural slaves. Often when they had outlived their usefulness as workers they were eaten. Spurred by new inventions, however, the needs and demands of the industrial revolution replaced working animals with motors and machines. With increasing frequency, we raised animals for food only. The stench of the gigantic slaughterhouses of the twentieth century went hand in hand with the expansion of factories and cities. Perhaps only in retrospect can we appreciate the dehumanizing aspect of both.

At the end of the twentieth century, a new sensitivity toward "animals as brothers and sisters," to use the Native American metaphor, was taking hold. We have best expressed this changing attitude by reintroducing the wolf in the national parks of the American West. Research showed that in recent years the majority of people favor such a move, even though "the mythical image of the big, bad wolf is still haunting."[4] William Robinson, professor of biology at Northern Michigan University, expressed this new sensibility. Robinson said: "The old way we learned was that there were good animals and bad animals. And it was part of our job as humans on earth to get rid of the bad ones and foster the good ones . . . . Now we look at the world as a community of life in which each species has a role to play."[5]

Others concur with this view by acknowledging that the return of the gray wolf plays a much larger metaphorical role in our relationship to wild animals. René Askin, founder of *The Wolf Fund*, said: "I really think this battle is about ecosystems and our willingness to make room for wild creatures like wolves and grizzly bears more than it is about wolves or reintroducing wolves."[6]

In the meantime, research into the behavior and the minds of our animal brothers and sisters has taken on new Perspectivist dimensions. New scientific tools have made it possible to communicate with animals in a previously unheard of way. Researchers have learned how to use specific tools of animal communication to relate to animals, instead of imposing on them our human specific tools. Scholars such as Dian Fossey pioneered this new research. Trained and equipped as a sophisticated scientist, Fossey eventually devoted her whole life to living with apes in the wild and learning as much as possible about them from their perspective.

Some impressive contributions at the *Science of Consciousness* Conference, held biannually at the University of Arizona in Tucson, came from scholars who had worked with animals in such intense communication relationships. For example, in her lecture on "Communication and Cognition in

Dolphins," Diane Reiss spoke about the incredible sophistication she observed in communicating with dolphins, while Irene Pepperberg testified to a bird's ability to learn well over one-thousand signs and to distinguish between abstract symbols and colors.

While some scientists may dismiss this kind of intense research as cute (and at best only a deeper level of anthropomorphizing), these insights have a significant value to us. When Aristotle defined "humanness" as the ability to reason, he set the difference between human beings and the rest of the animal world that we followed for nearly two thousand years. Charles Darwin showed how human beings evolved from the rest of the animal kingdom. As Darwin's theories gradually became popular, most people accepted the idea that our bodies had evolved from animal species. However, we still often question and even dismiss the concept that our social behavior, especially our moral judgment was also influenced by and evolved from animal behavior. Christian, Judaic, and Islamic religions and cultures teach that God directly created the whole human being, including human moral behavior (expressed by conscience and soul), and God continuously guides us.

According to this view, moral considerations guide human behavior and only human behavior. This leaves no room for moral behavior among so-called wild animals, whose behavior supposedly always follows mere function. When biologists in the past occasionally observed a kind of moral decision-making among domesticated and caged animals they usually assumed it was either automatic behavior or the result of mindless imitation of human beings. Behaviorist psychology confirmed this set of beliefs that left no possibility for a decision making process in animals, and, ultimately, even denied it for human beings. For example, recently, a female ape in a Chicago zoo gently picked up and cradled a human child that had fallen into her cage. She guarded the child until she could turn him over safely to the human attendant. The news reports generally stated that the animal learned such caring behavior by observing human beings. Stories of animals in the wild taking care of and raising human babies have always been looked upon as peculiar exceptions.

Some modern scholars have taken a more careful look at the behavior of wild animals. They began to tell a different story. They have observed quite complex ethical behaviors among primates that include collaborative and altruistic behavior, and peacemaking and purposeful behavior (such as the exclusion from the community for those who violate the group's rules repeatedly). Frans B. M. De Waal, a professor of psychology at Emory University, found that "in primate societies, peacemaking is as natural as war."[7] De Waal continues, "reconciliation is an essential trait of many social animals, because of the need continually to repair and reaffirm their relationship, as well as to keep peace within their societies."[8]

In observing animal behavior, scientists have tried to avoid being accused of so-called anthropomorphizing (using human concepts to describe and explain animal behavior). In "Peacemaking Among Primates," Kim A. McDonald says that in the nineteenth century, "Darwin and many other scientists freely attributed emotions to animals. But with the rise at the turn of the century of the hard sciences and positivism, Western scientists became increasingly reductionist."[9] Scientists, according to Anne Bekoff, a biologist at the University of Colorado, "began looking at animals as stimulus-response machines."[10]

Today scientists are again reversing this trend, as more of them find it useful and accurate to describe some animal traits in humanistic terms. They have an interest in the cognitive abilities of animals when compared to human beings. According to the old school, such abilities in animals exist minimally, if at all. The problem with traditional theory, however, is that the theory often dictated the outcome of the description, as de Waal observed.[11] Ethology, the study of animal behavior, says de Waal, must establish a careful description before it can reach a provisional theory. Such a description should not assume to be "objective," because the human perspective often masquerades as such objectivity.

McDonald illustrates what she means by assuming the perspective of the animal when she cites an example of Gordon Burghardt's studies as a psychology professor at the University of Tennessee. Burghardt reports that hognose snakes, when confronted with predators, "stop breathing, bleed from their mouths, and flip on their backs with their tongues hanging out."[12] Scientists used to believe that the reaction of the snake was due to fright. By measuring the time it took for the snake "to recover" Burghardt showed that "the snakes were consciously deceiving their predators." If fright would have been the cause, the presence of danger should not have influenced the recovery time. The snake, however, prolonged "playing dead" if the predator remained in the presence of the snake. Burghardt then tested whether the snake would react to the predator's gaze – either staring directly at the snake versus looking away. Again, the experiments showed that the snake played dead longer if the eye of the predator was focused on the snake then when the predator looked away. This work showed the snake to be aware of the attacker and to be engaged in a game of hide and seek. Burghardt said he first got the idea of setting up this research by imagining himself in place of the snake. "Imagining himself as the snake, he asked how he would assess the potential danger of a predator."[13]

If we want to gain a better understanding of animals, ethology must assume such a Perspectivist view, observing and describing animal behavior from their perspective. A theory resulting from such ethology will have an awareness of its own shortcomings and of the shortcomings of all theory. It can neither afford to imbed itself in ideological frames, as the traditional theory so easily did, nor can this Perspectivist theory ever assume to have spoken the last word. All animals are their own agents of change. They learn, adapt, and make decisions on their own behalf. Often these decisions are not so different from the practical and moral ones human beings make. If new observations of animal behavior, therefore, disprove old theories, we must carefully assess whether the old theories need updating, because the observed subject itself may have changed.

Twelve

HORSE WHISPERING

> If you want the horse to do something, you be-
> gin by letting the horse know that it's okay to be
> a horse, not your version of what you think you
> need. It's about understanding who you are and
> respecting your place with one another. To have
> that kind of acceptance requires a certain degree
> of spirituality.
>
> Robert Redford

Human beings have spent much time and energy to teach and train animals. We have done this mostly with the purpose of making animals fit our human environment and, most of all, using them for our human needs. We started training and taming animals some thirteen thousand years ago, when, accord-ing to available records, we first used dogs to aid in hunting. Paul Shephard, in *The Others: How Animals Made Us Human,* reflects about the multiple uses of animals in human history. During that extended period of human co-habitation with animals, an animal's pet function was not always separated from its usefulness. According to Shephard, animals were used as sources of manure, milk, meat, and skins. Often they also served as sacrificial offerings and symbolic and aesthetic objects.

> In the past a tiny bullock might be cared for with familial
> warmth and attachment in the household, exchanged as cur-
> rency, kept as a fertilizer machine, admired for its strength and
> beauty, or sacrificed on an altar and then eaten, all the while
> talked to, touched, and loved as a member of the family. Do-
> mestic animals have gradually become surrogate companions,
> siblings, lovers, victims, workers, parents, competitors, deities,
> oracles, enemies, kinfolk, caretaker-guards, and so on.[1]

As a result of the Industrial Revolution, animals have largely outlived their usefulness as working machines. They acquired a new place in the heart of an urban society as pets, often to overcome the loneliness of urban life. Perhaps recognizing the loss of nature, modern human beings adopted ani-mals in increasingly larger numbers. More recently, pets have taken "a new leap into institutional respectability" when they became "part of the pharma-cology of medicine."[2]

As part of a new "integrated treatment," medical doctors have stressed the usefulness of animals as companions. Shephard says:

In the presence of pets, those who suffer from Alzheimer's disease and autism are inclined to speak. Incarcerated, incompetent, handicapped outpatients, plain folks who are just getting old, impoverished or stressed executives and their lonely children – all are happier and live longer in the regular presence of friendly animals. There is also less suicide and aggression among the criminally insane, greater calming among the bereaved, quicker rehabilitation among alcoholics, improved self-esteem among the elderly, increased longevity among cardiac patients and cancer victims, improved emotional states among disturbed children, better morale among the blind and deaf, more cheer among the mentally and physically handicapped, faster learning among the retarded, solace for the terminally ill – and general facilitation of social relationships. Hearing dogs accompany the deaf, guide dogs lead the blind, hospice pets give unqualified cheer, animals help retarded children, and monkeys have "hands" for the handicapped.[3]

As this list indicates, the usefulness of animals for people is endless. An animal's ability "to fit" into the ever-more complicated world of human beings is astounding, to say the least. This ability alone should earn animals a much greater degree of respect from human beings, as it testifies to their immense evolutionary adaptability and collective wisdom of survival.

In *Adams Task,* Vicky Hearne, a renowned animal trainer and accomplished author, faces the question of whether animals can think.[4] "In 1993," says Hearne, "*Time* magazine announced that anthropomorphism is no longer a sin, that it's okay to say that animals think, hope, are puzzled, have expectations, are disappointed, even, for some, make their own little plans in a time scheme of their own."[5] Hearne contends that much of what animals will accomplish in their lives depends on the trainer. Hearne says: "If a very serious dog and a very serious trainer handler are lucky enough to walk in a serious world together, then there is, say, no biting problem. In a different world with a different handler, that's a different dog, and someone has to haul out either some doggie Prozac or the sodium Phenobarbital."[6]

In the final analysis, according to Hearne, "skepticism about animal minds is a kind of panic, whether the authority endorses or refutes anthropomorphism on the one hand, mechanomorphism on the other."[7] The purpose of her book, Hearne says, is philosophical. She wants to find "an accurate way of talking about our relationship with domestic animals." While working for years with dogs and horse trainers in the field, Hearne discovered a peculiar philosophy in that world. Based in experience, this philosophy is "a rich and ever changing web" – away from the lecture halls of *academia*. "These philosophies remember and speak to their sources in the thought of the past and are, unlike the general run of philosophies, continually tested and either reaffirmed or revised, since the world of the genuinely good dog or horse trainer is one in which reality is quite clearly, as Wallace Stevens had it, 'an activity of the most august imagination.' "[8]

For much of her professional career, Hearne says, she lived in two separate worlds, drawn from the kennel and the tack room back into university libraries, laboratories, and classrooms. "The result was that for some years I uneasily inhabited at least two worlds of discourse, each using a group of languages that were intertranslatable – dog trainers can talk to horse trainers, and philosophers can talk to linguists and psychologists, but dog trainers and philosophers can't make much sense of each other."[9]

Through her peculiar background Hearne had learned to live in both of these worlds. This enabled her, as she says, to understand, perhaps in a completely new way, the implications of Ludwig Wittgenstein's remark: "To imagine a language is to imagine a form of life."[10]

Hearne's book studies the language, and therefore, the mind of animals. As human beings introduce animals (through training) into a sophisticated human world, we can study communication patterns between them and us. In the trainers' language, according to Hearne, there exists: "the notion that animals are capable not only of activities requiring 'IQ' – a rather arid conception – but also of a complex and delicate (though not infallible) moral understanding that is so inextricably a function of their relationship with human beings that it may well be said to constitute those relationships.[11]

Hearne debunks outdated, but still popular, notions of animals acting mechanically and on instinct alone. She shows that animals have a sense of self, a mind, and a differentiated will to choose. If we accept this notion we must also accept that animals can communicate, and that they have a language.

One last example that demonstrates how we can apply Perspectivism in our relationship to animals is found in the recent film *The Horse Whisperer*, produced and directed by Robert Redford. In this film, a horse is badly injured in a terrible accident involving a truck. The horse is all but useless, his body maimed and his mind disturbed. No one can get near him. The owner of the horse, a little girl, was injured as well and lost a leg in the accident. When the parents of the girl follow the advice of the doctor and decide to "put down" the horse, the girl asks them cynically if she should be killed, too. The mother decides to go a different route. She reads up on horse training and comes across the concept of horse whispering. This is a compassionate way of training a horse in which the trainer enters into a dialogue with the horse instead of using the traditional method of breaking the horse to make him obey. Fear exists in the heart of every horse, says Nicholas Evans, because a million years before human beings developed, horses grazed the vast empty planes. They were:

living by voices only they could hear. They first came to know man as the hunted knows the hunter. For long before he used horses for his labors he killed them for meat. The alliance with man would forever be fragile for the fear he had struck in their hearts was too deep to be dislodged.[12]

Under the influence of the dominator culture, the assertion of human domination marked the standard method of training horses. After a rider breaks a young horse it follows every command as an obedient machine. The term "push button horse" is a colloquial expression still used today for a well-trained horse. There have always been those other type of trainers who could see deep into the heart of a horse and empathize with his fear and his pain. Says Evans: "Since that Neolithic moment when a horse was first haltered there were those among men who understood this. They could see into the creature's soul and soothe the wounds they found there, the secrets uttered softly into troubled ears. These men were known as the whisperers."[13]

Horse whispering as a gentle art of training horses accepts the horse as a partner. According to Redford, the term "horse whispering" is "a kind of euphemism for a state of being, a relationship between a human and a horse."[14] Horse whispering, says Redford,

is simply a way to be with horses that sends a message of understanding and compassion. Instead of beating a horse into submission, or using punishment as a tool, it's a way of developing trust and understanding. If you want the horse to do something, you begin by letting the horse know that it's okay to be a horse, not your version of what you think you need. It's about understanding who you are and respecting your place with one another. To have that kind of acceptance requires a certain degree of spirituality.[15]

Stan Allen is an animal trainer at the Split Mountain Horse Training Facility in Teasdale, Utah. Horse whispering, according to Allen, is:

a powerful, effective method used to train horses that is gentle to both the trainer and the horse. It has been discovered that people and horses learn in much the same way. A strong bond of trust, control, and compassion must be developed between the trainer and the horse. Based on these simple principles, the Horse Whispering training philosophy has been remarkably successful.[16]

In all of human history astounding bonds have occurred between human beings and animals, whenever human beings took their relationship with animals seriously and accepted them as equal partners. Supposedly necessary to feed mass society, gigantic slaughterhouses, dominate the world today. We raise animals in misery, as they live in facilities that recall the worst concentration camps. Every day we wipe out hundreds of species of animals by our activities.

We need to develop a new compassion for our animal brothers and sisters who populated this earth long before us. Their fate is our fate. Their demise will eventually be ours. Giving their silent suffering a voice is the duty of all compassionate human beings.

PART IV

INANIMATE NATURE

Thirteen

WHERE DOES MIND ORIGINATE? PLOTTING OUT A NEW SCIENCE OF AWARENESS

> Metaphysics abstracts the mind from the senses, and the poetic faculty must submerge the whole mind in the senses. Metaphysics soars up to universals, and the poetic faculty must plunge deep into particulars.
>
> Giambattista Vico

When the Greeks divided the world into living and non-living things they assumed material things that did not move by themselves were inanimate and without a soul. We still maintain this distinction today in our academic divisions of organic and inorganic chemistry, even though scientists acknowledge the complexity and obscurity involved in distinguishing life from non-life. Today we have the tools to probe into the smallest particles that make up those so-called inorganic objects. The Greeks lacked such tools. When they observed a rock and found that it did not move, they called it inanimate. With water they had greater difficulties: on the surface it seemed inanimate, but left to itself for a few days it grew life. Frogs appeared out of nowhere. This quality contributed to water's mythical character. The Greeks had no way to observe the seeds of life that were already present in water at the microscopic level. They did not know the technology of scaling. Through discoveries of the science of chaos, today's scientists have recognized the importance of scale. When observing something, scale makes all the difference.

For example, let us assume we are in a police helicopter observing rush hour traffic. The cars on the expressway roll evenly at a speed of 30 miles per hour, bumper-to-bumper. We can predict that it will take a specific amount of time to move from point A to point B. We can statistically describe the traffic situation beneath us. From our current height, we can hardly discern individual cars, though our previous knowledge helps us to fill in the details. For a space traveler who is not familiar with individual cars moving in a line, this may appear like two giant snakes of light moving in opposite directions. But we know better because we are familiar with the scale.

Imagine we have been pursuing a criminal, and he observes the police helicopter from below. He knows we watch him from above. He suddenly breaks out onto the road's shoulder and speeds away. Any statistical prediction we might have had ceases to be valid. Our prediction of the light pattern cannot cover individual behavior. It only covers the average of all participants. But by knowing the context of the event, we can adjust our measuring device to the individual event, and make new predictions.

Lets scale-back even further from the event – too far to see the individual car speeding away. Our original measurements are valid again for the lane as a whole and for all cars moving in the lane. If we do not have knowledge concerning the potential for individual behavior, we will assume that our predictions are valid for all events.

In the new language of chaos theory, we call this process scaling. Scaling means that the distance from an observed event determines the amount of information we can gather from that event. The further away we are, the less information we have.

Let me give another example: I was sitting at the rim of the Grand Canyon, gazing over the vast beauty. Gorges, ravines, rifts, and valleys stretched out before my eyes. The scenery was breathtakingly majestic. Here, nature did not seem to need a human being to appreciate her. She seemed fulfilled in her eternal stillness. Looking down, I could see no sign of any human beings. But I held a two-way radio in my hand. It beeped, and I heard the voice of one of my sons. I knew they were hiking down in the canyon. Over the air, they gave me a precise description of their location. I could make out the side of a slope they just had climbed. I could give them details of the landscape on the other side. From my perspective, I had the overview; from where they were, they could not see across the cliff. After they had signed off, nature resumed her silence. I only heard the rustling of the summer breeze. Not a sign of a conscious mind down there, yet I had the knowledge. I knew my sons were down there in the midst of all that silence. This is scaling.

Scaling limits the information about what happens as we move deeper and deeper into the smallest particles of nature. Events in the quantum world are much further removed from us than my sons were from me at the rim of the Grand Canyon. We do not have a radio connection with the quantum world, even though it exists deep within all of us. To try to recognize details is about as difficult as seeing an orange on Mars from Earth with a naked eye. Everything we know about this miniature world is second hand, brought to us by means of conjecture, and only sometimes by means of traceable results. But if we want to make an informed decision whether we can find some form of life at the quantum level, we have to probe into that mysterious world, as many scientists have done during the course of the twentieth century. Working with quantum effects and quantum mechanics has become so popular during that century we may someday call this the century of the quantum. At the same time, most scientists today will readily admit that something is missing in our picture of the quantum world, that at its deepest levels our standard model does not add up.

Most notably, scientists have not brought the results of the other great and successful theory of the twentieth century, general relativity, into agreement with the workings of the quantum world. Quantum theory remains incomplete as long as it fails to account for the phenomena of life, mind and consciousness. Theories that assume some level of awareness at the level of the quantum have alternately been called "panpsychism," "panexperientialism," and "quantum animism." I will show here that in order to complete the philosophy of Transcendental Perspectivism we must follow these theoretical beginnings. We must begin to assume that awareness and life do not start at the level of one-cell creatures, animals, or even only with human beings, but that a rudimentary level of awareness exists at the deepest level of the material world.

In this chapter, to quote the famous physicist Richard Feynman, "we will go down the drain, into a blind alley from which nobody has yet escaped." In spite of Feynman's warning not to make images of the weird world of quanta, numerous scientists have tried to develop a picture of the quantum world that includes mind and consciousness as key players.

The idea of locating consciousness within materia is not new. In *The Spirit of Materia*, the French nuclear physicist Jean Charon identified electrons as the most likely carriers of mind and spirit.[1] Charon claimed that the basic building blocks of *materia* and spirit directly connect on a material level. As an extension to Albert Einstein's theory of relativity, which, according to Charon, left no room for spirit in the universe, Charon proposed a "Complex Theory of Relativity," which includes the possibility of consciousness.

According to the traditional mechanistic view of the universe, the laws of nature run like clockwork, governing the world and all events in it. These laws causally determine and therefore predict everything. This view, according to Charon, failed to address spiritual phenomena, driving out the last of whatever spirit remained from mythical times. According to Charon, only after the more flexible quantum theory replaced the mechanical worldview were we able to rethink the position of consciousness or spirit in the composition of the universe. Quantum theory replaced the stringent logical order proposed by the strict geometrization inherent in traditional science with a new order of probability.

Charon claimed that another space-time complements the space-time of our immediate experience. In that complementary space-time the coordinates are reversed. Every electron is an entity with its bulk existing in that other space-time. Charon used the image of an ocean and the airspace above it to explain his speculation. The ocean corresponds to our world. The airspace above the ocean reflects this other reality, the realm of spirit. Each electron, according to Charon, lives in the airspace above the ocean and only touches the surface of the ocean at one point. This single point is the only appearance of an electron in this world. This other space is a spiritual world where information is stored by the infinite multitude of electrons. Each electron, according to Charon:

represents an autonomous individuality, which has its very
own space-time. This space-time differs from ours substan-
tially. Each electron forms a separate micro-universe. Its time
is cyclical, which allows it to recollect all past events of the
space it consists of. All events within this micro-universe develop with increasing negentropy. All this is evidence for our
conclusion that the electron contains a spiritual space-time.[2]

According to Charon, electrons have the ability to form systems with
other electrons without any external help, and they can develop hierarchical
orders of ever-higher complexity through increased information.[3] He claimed
that his research into the physics of elementary particles showed that electrons have the ability to store information. They have a system of remembering and retrieving such information, and they communicate and cooperate with other electrons to create and operate complex systems.[4] This
creation and operation of systems counteracts, according to Charon, the en-
tropic decay that otherwise rules the material world. Negentropy is the ability
of mind, according to Charon, to overcome the disintegration of *materia* by
systematic organization.[5] Similar to the binary model of storing information
that computers use, Charon suggests that the negative or positive spin within
each electron constitutes the mechanism of electrons to store information.[6]
The exchange of information between electrons, said Charon, is connected
with the electric magnetic properties of electrons. Contrary to the functional
character of computer chips, however, electrons have the freedom to enter
into relations with other electrons. The free exchange of information and affection between the elementary particles of *materia*, Charon said, is similar
to the exchange of affection human beings experience as love. According to
Charon, elementary particles, not unlike human beings in love, experience a
telepathic communication that transcends words and other forms of exchang-
ing information.

When Charon's book was first published in 1979, scientists had not yet
discovered the science of chaos. Charon had little support for his thesis of a
self-organizing tendency among elementary particles. Chaos theory put self-
organization in the center of the discussion as a common property of chaotic
systems, which includes the systems of smallest particle. Today the idea of a
self-organizing quantum world does not seem so far fetched. In *The Life of
the Cosmos* Lee Smolin, a physics professor at Pennsylvania State University, tried to connect self-organizational processes observed on the large scale
of galaxies with those observed on the quantum scale.[7] He asks, "Is it not
possible that self-organization through processes analogous to natural selection is, indeed, the missing element without which we have so far been unable to construct a quantum theory of cosmology?[8]

James Culbertson, another pioneer of basic mind research, also believed
that mind and matter are linked at the most fundamental level. Mind perme-

ates all of nature, according to Culbertson. In his model, "mind is completely accounted for by movements of matter. Matter is all there is, but Culbertsonian matter is, by its very nature, everywhere sentient, possessed of an invisible inner life."[9]

Culbertson advanced the study of consciousness by focusing on one of the central features of the human mind: its sense of unity and wholeness. Culbertson wondered how isolated atoms comprise a unified mind. He resolves this isolation dilemma by describing Democritean atoms not as unconnected particles in space, but as interacting world lines in Einsteinean space-time. The arena in which the material world, in Einstein's view, performs its tricks is:

> not space or time but a union of the two – space-time, in which time is treated as a fourth dimension on a par with the three spatial dimensions. In this lofty space-time view every event that has ever happened or will ever happen is located somewhere in the block universe of space-time. Visualizing the world as a four-dimensional solid, Einstein took a godlike view of things; his space-time picture is a kind of snapshot of eternity.[10]

In developing the idea of a block universe, Culbertson followed Einstein's theory of relativity, which predicted that time and space inescapably intertwine. Time forms a fourth dimension in addition to the three dimensions of space. Culbertson now asked where in this block universe consciousness could be found. As particles move through space-time they leave a world line behind. We can visualize each event as a world line. As bodies and events meet, the world lines intermingle with each other. For Culbertson, these world lines and their entanglements represent the presence of consciousness. They resemble threads in a fabric, but the patterns in this four-dimensional fabric are alive. They are elements of sentient life. "Culbertson breaks the Democritean isolation of lonely atoms by picturing these particles' space-time paths as threads in an elaborate tapestry – a tapestry in which the universe's entire history from the beginning to the end is woven."[11]

But how can the phenomenon of a unified mind (such as our own) develop out of the multitude of individual minds – out of a world "permeated at all levels with a carnival of tiny minds?" We have not yet answered this question. The Greek philosopher Democritus held that individual unrelated atoms composed matter. If we assume this materialist position, as many traditional scientists do, the presence of mind is obscure. As to the occurrence of mind, we have four options:

(1) A divine power implanted mind only in creatures of a higher order, such as human beings. Most religions adopt this traditional dualistic assumption.

(2) Mind does not exist at all, but is just an illusion. We operate as automatons according to eternal laws, and the universe is one giant machine. Some psychologists adopted this traditional materialistic assumption.

(3) Mind comes into play at a later point in evolution as a result of increased formal complexity. This model is proposed by the science of complexity.

(4) Mind is present at all levels. It exists in rudimentary form and is present in the smallest particles, even in the quanta that form space and time.

Perspectivism adopts this last option: mind is present at all levels as a property of the quantum world. Present at even the smallest scale, it follows that mind is present everywhere. Mind is the flip side of *materia*. No *materia* exists without mind. If *materia* appears to be mindless, scaling is the cause: we are not close enough or lack the instruments to observe the presence of mind.

The idea that mind and the material world are connected reaches back to the animistic beliefs of our ancestors. It has also been part of philosophical thinking even in the Western tradition. We can find animistic tendencies in Platonism. We can find them again in aesthetic theories of the Renaissance. Pantheistic philosophies assumed that a god or spirit's presence existed within the objects of the natural world. The smallest particles, which the philosopher Gottfried Wilhelm Leibniz called monads, are not dead entities – even though Leibniz needed God to establish their communicative harmony. Leibniz thought of monads as "true individuals."

More recently, the idea that some kind of consciousness exists at all levels of the natural world found its strongest defender in the American philosopher Whitehead. His process philosophy centers on the idea that the basic elements of the natural world are not little dead objects, but fluctuating world processes. These basic entities form relationships with each other in order to create higher units of awareness. We call this philosophical position panpsychism or panexperientialism. Both of these positions enjoy repute and some scientists defend them, namely Stuart Hameroff and David Chalmers.

Not too long ago, scientists in the Western tradition believed that only human beings are endowed with consciousness and mind. Today, few would defend this position any longer. But how would we ever know whether mind is present in any given object? Philosophers have spent much time debating whether a squirrel thinks or a bat has a mind. More recently, the physicist Roger Penrose put a camcorder in front of a mirror watching itself in the mirror. Can we call this video camera conscious? Intuitively, we know that the camera has no conscious experience from the inside even though it might link to a computer that runs a software program that pretends it has an inside view. How can we know that what we observe is consciousness? The only "absolute" example we have is our mind, as the philosopher René Descartes in his *cogito ergo sum* so cleverly deduced.

In *Elemental Mind: Human Consciousness and the New Physics,*[12] the physicist Nick Herbert researched the scientific evidence for the presence of mind within matter.[13] Herbert called this central feature of mind an inside/out view: he starts out with a critique of the Turing test, which he says bases the question whether a machine is conscious or not on the gullibility of human beings. A Turing machine is an imaginary apparatus, a kind of a super computer, named so after its inventor Alan Turing. It can potentially carry out every possible calculation that can be expressed in binary code. The result of such calculations would be a universal distinction of those things that we can logically express as algorithms and those that we cannot. A universal Turing machine is, as of now, still only a theoretical machine – though every computer, as it solves algorithmic, mechanical problems, is a small Turing machine, in a sense. A universal Turing machine is something incomparably larger; in the wildest of imaginations it would be as large as the entire universe.

The purpose of this machine: to probe the extent of what we can possibly calculate. If, in effect, every event in the universe were the result of every prior event (so that all events are irrevocably connected by a definite and calculable sequence of causes and effects) then it would only be a question of size, a quantitative question, before we could calculate all future events. The future would become predictable and knowable. This concept descends from "Laplace's demon," an all-knowing machine in a mechanical universe. In some way we could understand the human brain as such an all-knowing Turing machine. The goal of this thought experiment was the attempt to understand knowing as algorithmic. The rest was then a question of size, so it was thought. Needles to say, scientists still debate this question fiercely.

In *The Emperor's New Mind*, Roger Penrose proposed to investigate the presence of mind by its functions.[14] He concluded that we cannot understand some operations of the mind algorithmically. An algorithm solves a problem in a step-by-step procedure, especially an established, recursive computational procedure for solving a problem in a finite number of steps.

Both machines and carbon-based minds can perform algorithmic operations. The Turing test is based on a kind of functionalist philosophy, a philosophy that comes to conclusions by checking the results of an operation. But such a test appears useless when it comes to verifying the presence of mind. If we could assume that machines could do some mathematical calculations, but more complex calculations could only be done by mind, then we could devise a Turing test that could produce positive results when checking for the presence of mind. However, the opposite is the case. Machines are much better than any natural carbon based mind we know in computing algorithm. We cannot use this to test for the presence of mind. Penrose concludes, we can characterize mind by the ability to perform non-algorithmic computations, such as aesthetic judgments.

Herbert tries to secure a foundation for the presence of mind in a different way. He believes that an investigation of the presence of mind from the outside, from the perspective of the observer, is fruitless. The true test, according to Herbert, comes from within. The question, according to Herbert now is: does a machine or a thing "feel" its own existence?

Against all functional tests that judge the presence of mind by observable actions, Herbert insists, "consciousness seems not to be concerned so much with what an entity does as with what it experiences while it is doing it."[15] Such conscious experiences result in what we sentient beings generally conceive of as "insides." According to Herbert, objects that do not have such an inside might as well be called dead things.[16]

Herbert proposed that scientists should try to find a direct way to connect with the mind in other objects and verify their presence from within. I call this the Perspectivist or shamanistic way.

Herbert pursues this second route on a distinctly technological level. He asks: how close are we to building a mind link – a direct connection between one consciousness and another, a kind of computer interface among minds – carbon based or other? As of now, this idea is the stuff for science fiction stories. Optimistically, Herbert theorizes: "The sharing of another person's inner life, not by inference, empathy, or analogy but by merging of the two insides into a new type of co-conscious experience, would constitute powerful evidence for the presence of inner experience in that other being, no matter what that being's outward behavior might be."[17]

Are such mind links possible? Not in the near future, says Herbert, but the idea is intriguing and worth pondering. Since shamanistic experiences of mind linking are generally private non-testable events, Herbert would prefer a technical solution. A technology-based mind link, according to Herbert, "would solve the problem of other minds in the simplest possible way by making the presence and contents of other minds publicly available in a manner as direct and undeniable as the presence and contents of your own mind." Mind link, according to Herbert, would become a purely physical connection between cooperating minds, available and open to anyone, "as public as the telephone."[18] Could we then use this to contact minds in the rest of the material world?

According to Herbert, we are far from inventing such an interface machine that could connect mind with mind. The reason for this technological shortcoming is, according to Herbert, not so much found in our technological inability, but in our lack of understanding of what mind is. Not only do we not understand what mind is; we don't even have an adequate theory to give mind a proper place within a materialist, scientific worldview. Mind has not been the center of research because of its traditional connection with dualistic philosophies and metaphysics. To make progress, Herbert proposed first to establish a good theory of consciousness. This is, incidentally, an ongoing task at the biannual Tucson Conferences on Consciousness Studies at the University of Arizona in Tucson.

Hameroff, an anesthesiologist and co-organizer of the international and interdisciplinary conferences "Toward a Science of Consciousness" at the University of Arizona, spent much emphasis on researching the presence of mind at the quantum level.[19] While assuming a panpsychic position Hameroff speculates that higher-level consciousness might have developed during the Cambrian revolution. Reflecting on the evolutionary advantage of consciousness, Hameroff says, "One possible advantage of consciousness for natural selection is the ability to make choices." He quotes Erwin Schroedinger, who once said: "If we grant our ancestors even a tiny fraction of free will, consciousness, and culture we humans experience, the increase in [life's] complexity on Earth over the last several million years becomes easier to explain: life is the product not only of blind forces but also of selection in the sense that organisms choose."[20]

Hameroff says, "Generally, intelligent behavior can enhance a species' survivability and enhance the opportunity for mutation to avoid extinction." He asserts:

> purposeful behavior occurred in unicellular eukariotic ancestors of modern organisms such as Paramecia and Euglena, which perform rather complex adaptive movements. Paramecia swim in a graceful, gliding fashion via coordinated actions of hundreds of MT–based cilia on their outer surface. In this way they seek and find food, avoid obstacles and predators, and identify and couple with mates to exchange genetic material. Some studies suggest Paramecia can learn (e.g. they escape more quickly from capillary tubes with each subsequent attempt, Gelber, 1958). Having no synapses or neural networks, Paramecia and similar organisms rely on their cytoskeleton for sensation, locomotion, and information processing.[21]

From this Hameroff concludes, "The cytoskeleton organizes intelligent behavior in eukariotic cells." A level of consciousness in one-cell organisms is at least plausible, but without a good theory of what consciousness is we will have a hard time making any progress.

At the Tucson conference, scientists have begun to map out the human brain. Herbert called this a "mind geography." But for Herbert, this is not just a map of the human brain, but a map of all the possible and known centers of consciousness in the universe. The physical sciences have mapped out the universe in great detail, but we have no such map for the presence of mind. In order to establish criteria for a suitable theory of consciousness, we would have to ask: which minds besides our own inhabit the physical world? Is the Earth perhaps a living organism with a mind, which we might contact someday? We have no idea how this could be done, but we do know that shamans in many civilizations, at times even in pre-enlightenment Christian communities, believed it possible to communicate with natural powers. With his "Gaia principle" the scientist James Lovelock developed a kind of scientific theses centered on Earth as a living system. Other scientists have suggested that we can find self-organizing processes at the cosmic level of galaxies. But does self-organization necessarily include consciousness or awareness?

Herbert suggests a checklist for the development of a theory of mind:

(1) A good theory of consciousness should give an explanation for such ordinary experiences as sleep, coma, and similar occasions where the sensation of conscious awareness has ceased to exist while the organism that usually has the awareness still operates.

(2) How does the mind distinguish between colors, tastes, etc.?

(3) How do we pay attention to one thing and not to another?

(4) How and why do we conceive ourselves as one?

(5) Personality: "A good mind model should generate a theory of personality – both human and robotic – based not on external behavior, but on the structure of the material (or spiritual) processes that support the inner experiences that form personality and character."[22]

(6) Free will: this philosophical question marks the dividing line between atomistic/mechanical theory and dualistic/philosophical theory. Somehow, we would have to prove the connection between mental and willful acts and the laws of physics. Our immediate experience tells us that we are free agents, at least in some cases. If the Self were not in charge of its behavior no legal system in the world would have the right to punish an offender. "Do willful acts violate the laws of physics?"[23]

(7) Death: a theory of consciousness, according to Herbert, would be incomplete if it could not resolve "on scientific rather than religious or philosophical grounds the important question of what happens to the mind when the body ceases to exist as one conscious whole."[24]

(8) What is the survival value of consciousness? At what point on the evolutionary scale did consciousness emerge?

A good theory of consciousness will have to take a new look at the traditional theory of evolution. If mind is not implanted from the outside, but has been present in *materia* from the beginning, then we would have to consider Charles Darwin's theory of evolution an incomplete theory. It only takes advantage of the possibilities of volition and selective choices at higher levels of nature, not from the smallest entities upward. What if, at the scale of the smallest particles, the time spans for choices that determine evolutionary development are so long, that they exist completely outside of our frame of reference? Perhaps at the level of the smallest particles, selection happens on a scale of a few billion (or even many billions) of years. In this case, we would have another scaling problem, not of space, but of time. The physicist and science writer Paul Davies concedes that at the quantum level not all particles are identical – even though we generally assume this for conventional computation. Classical physics assumed time symmetry as well, which meant that a particle should take approximately as long to create as it takes to disintegrate. For short-lived particles such as kaons, however, science has shown that it takes a million times longer to decay than to begin life. These particles appear to cling to existence.[25] Neutrons seem to have an intrinsic sense of time.[26] Even though we should not assume that the same kind of conscious mind as ours exists at the micro level, perhaps a rudimentary kind of mind exists – characterized as an inside-out view, connected with some sense of preferred state.

Perspectivist philosophy assumes awareness at the smallest quanta of reality. Without the presence of an inside-out view, we have no reason to talk about a perspective. If mostly dead *materia* composes the universe, and conscious mind only developed at a high level of complexity, perhaps we should only concern ourselves with human beings. While researching consciousness at the human level is a significant part of Perspectivism, as a comprehensive philosophy the search for mind must not end here. If we could apply Perspectivism to all levels of so-called material nature, we could somehow close the experiential gap. Panpsychism, panexperientialism, and quantum animism offer solutions to the problem and need further investigation. We can no longer justify a stringent division between living and dead things.

In the face of the impending ecological crisis, we must realize the utmost importance of the perspectives of animals, trees, and plants (and even the perspective of Earth and all her resources). Ignoring these perspectives will bring about the extinction of the human race. If we continue on in ignorance, we will not find the compassion that we need to change the destructive course, a course that is based on the outdated model of human beings against nature. This is the urgent mission of mind and awareness research. We must prove, with the method of science, that consciousness exists at all levels, and that this sentient awareness is our kin and wants to cooperate with us and survive. This is true in spite of some parts of nature (such as many viruses and bacteria) often being adversarial to our existence. Nature balances cooperation and competition in favor of cooperation. Otherwise we would not exist at all. Only if we continue to consciously realize this delicate balance can we generate the compassion needed for the ecological revolution and the gigantic shift in values that we require to ensure our survival.

Fourteen

PANEXPERIENTIALISM, PANPSYCHISM, AND QUANTUM ANIMISM

> We live between two worlds; we soar in the at-
> mosphere; we creep upon the soil; we have the
> aspirations of creators and the propensities of
> quadrupeds. There can be but one explanation of
> this fact. We are passing from the animal into a
> higher form, and the drama of this planet is in its
> second act.
>
> W. Winwood Reade

The essential mystery of quantum mechanics lies in quantum particles behav-
ing in strange ways. They behave like waves when not observed, and instantaneously they behave like particles when observed. Somehow the act of observation alters the nature of the quantum.

Scientists do not have only one description of an electron or a photon,
but two. This discrepancy causes quantum weirdness. We need both descriptions, even though both seem to describe a different object. When observed,
we can adequately describe these elementary particles, even though we can
never define both the location and the momentum at the same time. If we
observe location, then we cannot obtain a measurement for momentum. If
our goal is to measure momentum, the location becomes fuzzy and inaccu-
rate. If an observer makes a measurement of a quantum as it moves from
point A to point B, then looks away, then looks back again and takes another
measurement, both times it will appear as a particle. But if that observer
wants to describe what happens in between, the mathematically correct description is that of a wave. We must remember, however, that when we use
our every day experience of observing, we cannot apply this to the quantum
world. No human eye has ever seen a quantum particle because they are too
small. Observing a quantum particle means using an apparatus to measure it.

In their mathematical representation, elementary particles exist everywhere and nowhere at the same time. Scientists call this fact non-locality.
Non-locality is another weird characteristic of the quantum world that we
have verified experimentally. The principle of locality dominates the physical
world of our observation. Objects exist either here or there. It also means that
any interaction of two objects has to traverse the space in between these two
objects. The speed of this interaction cannot be faster than the speed of light.
Albert Einstein established this with his theory of relativity.

In the quantum world, this fact does not seem to hold true. Two quantum objects, once they have been in contact with each other, may be separated by light years. Yet, if one of the two objects reacts to being measured or observed, the other one, even though light years apart, instantaneously "knows" of the intrusion and reacts by exhibiting a complementary reaction. This fact has been called "inseparability of the quantum object." The physicist John Stuart Bell experimentally verified this beyond any doubt in 1964.

These unsolved mysteries of the quantum world have given rise to numerous speculations. In regard to our discussion about the origin of mind, scientists have made conjectures based on these characteristics. The quintessential wholeness of the quantum world corresponds with the commonplace experience of the unity of our mind. Unlike physical objects, our thoughts seem to have a non-local character. We can traverse unlimited distances and time in our mind, apparently instantaneously. Our mind has the ability to make physical things move, at least within our body.

Based on these speculations, Nick Herbert developed the concept of quantum animism. Herbert argues that our brains' material conditions strongly influence our actions. Are physical acts perhaps likewise shaped by the "innerlife" of invisible beings? Herbert asks: "Are the laws of quantum theory a public reflection of innumerable private experiences? The notion that behind every physical process lies an invisible mental experience might be called the hypotheses of 'quantum animism.' "[1]

Herbert's quantum animism differs from traditional animism in that it avoids assuming a dualistic model of mind and matter. Traditional dualism assumes that some kind of spirit inhabits a body and makes it move, a ghost in the machine. Herbert's quantum animism presents the idea that every natural system has an inner life, a conscious center, from which it directs and observes its action. "A system's possibility wave represents the range of action – or realm of possibility – open to the conscious being inside that system. Every quantum wave is the potential home of some form of consciousness, and vice versa: where there is a will there is a wave."[2]

During the early 1990s the debate about the origin of consciousness gained a new forum in biannual meetings on consciousness at the University of Arizona. As a result of this new interdisciplinary emphasis, the University of Arizona and the University of Copenhagen in Denmark established consciousness research centers. A bi-monthly publication, the *Journal for Consciousness Studies*, published by Virginia Commonwealth University, keeps track of new developments in consciousness research.[3] Contributions to Tucson I (1994), Tucson II (1996), Tucson III (1998), and Tucson IV (2000) showed the immense depths of the subject, as well as the need for an interdisciplinary approach. In a novel way, consciousness research unites members from the empirical sciences with philosophers, humanists, mystics and nearly all other disciplines of academia. Remarkably, the department of anesthesiology at the University of Arizona at Tucson organized and founded the event. Many of the participants hold a primary interest in the little-known interplay of chemicals and the mind.

Stuart Hameroff, Head of the Department of Anesthesiology in Tucson, is one of the leading experts in mind research. In 1994, he became widely known when he began collaborating with Roger Penrose who had become interested in Hameroff's concept of microtubulas as the seat of consciousness.

According to traditional science, insentient entities compose the brain. This theory dates back to the Cartesian division of mind and matter and survives to this day as the primary model of the mind. This theory, however, does not adequately explain the emergence of mental activities and consciousness. Hameroff uses the concept of quantum uncertainty to speculate about the origins of consciousness.

Hameroff refers to the philosopher Alfred North Whitehead who explained that "occasions of experience" comprise the universe at its smallest level. According to Whitehead, at the smallest level *materia* does not consist of small little concrete blocks as traditional science assumes. Instead everything is in constant process and flux. With this, Whitehead became an early critic of the mechanical universe, before quantum physics provided an empirical and theoretical basis. In *Science and the Modern World*, Whitehead emphatically states that we did not have to wait for quantum theory to find out that the theory of materialistic mechanism, as he called it, was logically indefensible.[4] Instead of analyzing nature as a material structure of ever-increasing complexity that eventually evolves (more or less accidentally) into life, Whitehead assumed individuality and organism at all levels of nature, down to the smallest constituencies.

Whitehead refers to the German philosopher Gottfried Wilhelm Leibniz who first developed the idea of a monad as the smallest entity of the natural world. But Leibniz believed that these monads had no innate energy to relate to each other. He said they were "windowless." Therefore, Leibniz had to resort to a divine power to insure relations of the monads among each other in the cosmic game of building structures of higher complexity. For Whitehead, however, these monads are not without relation, or windowless, as they were for Leibniz. Leibniz, according to Whitehead, failed to grant his monads concrete internal and external relations. By giving these monads the possibility for engaging into relationships with each other (by opening up the windows of the monads, so to speak), by making them subjects instead of mere objects, Whitehead avoided the need for a Divine Being in assembling intelligent nature. Long before chaos theory empirically verified a self-organizing quality of natural systems, nature for Whitehead did not accidentally assemble mindless particles, but he saw it as a self-organizing system of ever-higher complexity. This Whiteheadean view is essential for a theoretical understanding of mind as part of nature and for the full completion of Perspectivist philosophy. With this recognition, Whitehead became one of the most influential philosophers for the foundation of Perspectivism as a philosophical model of the world

In Whitehead's world, mind is an organic part of the growth process of ever-more complex events that comprise the natural world. The "beautiful mathematics," which Albert Einstein assumed to underlie the natural world, is, according to Whitehead, filled with individual subjective events. They are eternal objects in their purity. Beautiful mathematics is absolute being. According to Whitehead, it is the most aesthetic of all creations. It is involved in all processes, the basis of the natural world.

Mind, in this Whiteheadean world, is not a mysterious spirit added to the world from the outside through divine intervention, as it was for Leibniz. Mind grows organically from within to ever-higher complexity in the hierarchy of living things. We could also call this panpsychic concept continualism, an incremental increase of conscious awareness. Mental awareness grows with increasing complexity until within the human brain it has come to inhabit one of the most complex structures in the known universe.

Whitehead's process-oriented philosophy further insists on the natural harmony of all living things. In the Cartesian view, a world of insentient objects surrounds the isolated human subject. This sad and hostile world model provided the foundation for not only modern science, but also for twentieth-century existentialism. An unknowable world of things surrounded the transcendental Self. This Self assumed freedom and chose its own subjectivity. Perspectivism instead sees the human Self as part of a long chain of subjects with decision-making processes at all levels.

Materialists and dualists both assume that the physical world is devoid of experience. Whitehead called this empty reality a "vacuous actuality." This means that the material world is comprised of empty or mindless objects. This, according to Whitehead, is a basic mistake and a wrong assumption. Many contemporary physicists and philosophers agree. In his article "Panexperientialist Physicalism and the Mind-Body Problem,"[5] David R. Griffin provides some reasons why this position of traditional materialism is no longer tenable. The rejection of materialism is based on the following reasons:

The idea of vacuous actualities is counterintuitive. We know from our experience that "experiencing actualities" exist, "but we have no experiential knowledge that a vacuous actuality is even possible."[6]

The materialist concept that the basic units of nature have no consciousness has no basis in science, but instead was originally based on theology. The mechanical view of nature resulted from theological speculations and René Descartes's concessions to a powerful church.

Science abstracts from the things it discusses. As Whitehead pointed out: "Physics ignores what anything is in itself."

Our sensory perceptions do not tell us that things are by themselves. Our senses present to us things in space with spatially defined properties. From experiencing ourselves we know that this is not all we are.

Things that appear devoid of self-motion or spontaneity (such as rocks and planets) are not individuals, but large clusters, or aggregational societies, thereof. Quantum physics shows us the falsity of the assumption that atoms are like billiard balls, only smaller. (This point separates quantum animism from traditional or "naïve" animism, which assumed that rocks and mountains have consciousness.)[7]

Since the dualistic position that produced the mind-body problem failed to give any reasonable explanation of how mind emerges out of unconscious matter, we are more justified to "postulate with at least bare intelligibility that [experience] is a fundamental feature of the universe."[8]

Griffin then suggests several reasons why we can justifiably affirm pan-experientialism: First, our conscious experience is fully natural and interacts with other parts of the natural world. Second, in ourselves, we can observe how natural individuals are within themselves and how they appear to others.

Science has provided positive support to the idea that all individuals embody spontaneity and experience. Leading ethologists have suggested purposeful behavior at least down to the level of bees. Hameroff, according to Griffin, went many steps further, when he collected evidence suggestive of the idea that single cell organisms such as amoebae and paramecia, have a primitive type of consciousness. According to Hameroff, "going all the way down, quantum physics, as already mentioned, has shown entities at this level not to be analogous with billiard balls, and as Seager has stressed, quantum theory implies that the behavior of the elementary units of nature can only be explained by attributing to elementary particles something analogous to our own mentality."[9]

Our most immediate experience of nature is the experience of our bodies from within. Panexperientialism offers a solution to the mind-body problem. Whatever the name, panexperientialism, panpsychism, or quantum animism, the idea that some inner awareness exists at all levels is obviously gaining momentum and is finding scientific support. It is an essential ingredient of Transcendental Perspectivism as a viable philosophy.

PART FIVE

INFINITY: THE SUPER PERSPECTIVE
OF THE ABSOLUTE

Fifteen

NUMINOUS AND MYSTICAL EXPERIENCES

> What does mysticism really mean? It means the
> way to attain knowledge. It's close to philoso-
> phy, except in philosophy you go horizontally
> while in mysticism you go vertically.
>
> Elie Wiesel

> Mysticism and exaggeration go together. A mys-
> tic must not fear ridicule if he is to push all the
> way to the limits of humility or the limits of de-
> light.
>
> Milan Kundera

"Verily, in the beginning this world was Brahman, the limitless One – limitless to the east, limitless to the north. . .limitless in every direction. Incomprehensible is that supreme Soul, unlimited, unborn not to be reasoned about,
unthinkable. . . ." So it says in the Maitri-Upanishad, one of the oldest written
documents of humankind."[1] In spite of the awesome distance, since ancient
times, human beings have fancied to make contact with the Great Spirit and
assume the perspective of the absolute, the limitless one. We have called
such experiences numinous or "mystical."

Imagine the unimaginable. Imagine the whole world like a giant movie
screen. You are a tiny particle on the screen, one speck of dust among un-
counted others – a drop of water in an ocean. Through some strange power
you have been singled out and invited to sit in the projection booth of this
gigantic theater. In a cosmic swoop, something hurls you into the center of
creation. Your consciousness finds itself inside the hub of the sacred wheel –
from which everything emanates. What would you experience? What would
you see?

Oneness with spirits or God has been a goal of shamanistic religions.
Prophets described it and poets wrote about it, while mystics reported their
unspeakable experiences.

Johann Wolfgang von Goethe's *Faust* is one such story. Goethe, one of
the most sensible artists of all times, described an experience of oneness with
the creative energy at the ground of all being. To experience that immediacy,
Goethe's Faust promises to give his soul to the devil. Throughout Faust's
life, a savage fire for an absolute experience burned inside of him. To fulfill
this desire, he entered a pact with the devil. Thanks to Mephistopheles,
Goethe's character of the devil, the rejuvenated Faust experienced all the

pleasures of youth, but nothing sufficed. Unsatisfied and unhappy, he moved from enjoyment to enjoyment – to no avail.

The mature Faust (in *Faust Part II*) again urges Mephistopheles to fulfill his promise. From sensuous and sexual pleasures, Faust turns to occult powers for the satisfaction of his dreams. He drags Mephistopheles into a dark gallery, away from the enjoyment of the crowds. Faust commands his servant not to use any more tricks, but to conjure up the classical forms of antiquity where he expects to find Platonic perfection and truth. To accomplish this, "a lofty mystery" is revealed to Faust. Mephistopheles tells him that Faust will have to descend to a secret and terrifying place where he will meet the primordial Mothers. It embarrasses to speak of them, says the poet Goethe. These are strange goddesses, he says "to men unknown, – Whom we are loath to name or own."[2]

On his mystical way to the Mothers, Faust must leave the world behind. He will see nothing in the vast Void, he will hear no footsteps, and there will be no firm ground upon which to rest his feet. But Faust (and with him, the poet) has no fear. With dialectical fervency he explores the emptiness: "In your Nothingness I hope to find my All."[3]

For good reasons Goethe is known in his German homeland as the Great Pagan (*der grosse Heide*). In his poetic search for union with nature and God, he was dissatisfied with the serenity and lack of symbols that characterized the Protestantism of his youth. Early, Goethe was drawn to Catholicism. Here he found a symbolic closeness to the Earth and to material things. The divine was not as abstracted as it often was in Protestantism. He could experience the divine in the symbolic representation of God: in colorful art works, music, saints, and most of all in the sacraments of bread and wine. Goethe, a romantic at heart, always loved this earthy connection with the divine that Catholicism offered.

At the height of his creative development, Goethe went one step further – away from Christianity – when he rediscovered the classical beauty of Greek art and the unspeakable mysteries of the Eleusinian cult. Beauty for him was spiritual and religious experience, not an abstract play with forms. He saw the world beautified in a Platonic way through a reflection of divine beauty within the world of objects. Even as a scientist Goethe preserved this idealistic, organic view of the world. The world of things was permeated by a spiritual energy. In aesthetic re-creation, in art, this world becomes divine.

The poet Goethe intuited a self-organizing harmony at work in nature. Nature does not need human or divine intervention to order it. Humanness, in particular, is part of nature and therefore does not need divine intervention in order to harmonize with nature. For the mature Goethe, harmony is not a result of a divine plan of redemption; it is not a Christian thought. He gains this insight by going back to classical Greece and even further, to the Eleusinian mysteries and ancient Egypt. An original pagan insight permeates Goethe's mature work: the recognition of a great harmony that holds this world in balance. In the beginning there was a balance between Chaos and Order, a self-ordering chaos (the Yin and Yang, as the ancient Chinese expressed it). In the beginning, says the Egyptian Book of the Dead, chaos created itself like a snake body out of nothingness.

Comparing Goethe with the philosopher Georg Wilhelm Friedrich Hegel, we can see the similarity and the difference between the philosopher and the artist in the way they both described the descent into the Absolute. From the standpoint of logic, such a descent is fruitless because, from the perspective of the logical mind absolute Being and absolute Nothing are identical, as Hegel expressed. In both cases, all distinction ceases to exist. Logically, only distinction and differentiation makes something real. Union with the divine (*unio mystica*) happens in aesthetic creation. The reality of the Absolute appears in the creative act. Practical mysticism is capable of reaching and meeting the divine in poetic union with nature. The trip into Nothingness does not exactly yield positive, rational results, but it assures the continuation of the dream, which is ultimately Faust's salvation. But perhaps only the poet's expectation assures results.

If we find the "All in the Void" because we expect it, what difference does it make? Subjectivity becomes objectivity, objective truth in the experience of and for the subject. What ultimately will count is the effect of such experience. According to ancient pagan wisdom we can only know "the All, yet None, yet One" in the depth of creative practice.

Though most Western religions have traditionally discouraged their followers from attempting direct experiences of the divine, a large body of evidence exists for such occurrences. Let's take a closer look now into what we know today about mystical practices.

Ninian Smart, in *World Views: Cross-Cultural Explorations of Human Beliefs,* explores the experiential dimension of human belief.[4] On the way to an encounter with the Absolute, two routes are possible: one leads away from the Self into the other, the second way seeks the Absolute by submersion into the Self. When people think of the cosmos as the work of a great god, says Smart, "it is perhaps partly because they reason that the cosmos must have come from somewhere, and its beauties and design suggest a Creator of vast intelligence."[5] The Bible, the Quuran, the Bhagavad-Gita, all are filled with references to meetings with God. "Indeed, if we look in the Song of the Lord (the Gita) we find there the most dramatic account of how Arjuna, the hero of the narrative, is confronted by the Lord in all his many-formed glistening power, like a very personal nuclear explosion."[6]

This kind of encounter with God has been called a *numinous* experience, derived from the Latin word *numen* for spirit. To facilitate such *numinous* experiences, architects in the Middle Ages built gigantic cathedrals that defied gravity and poked high into the sky. Artists such as Beethoven and Schubert wrote their spiritual music, and preachers let the spirit take over their thunderous sermons. According to Smart, we can also get a sense of the *numinous* "outside the cathedral, church or temple – in nature. Religious thinkers and believers have long heard the 'voice of God' in the wind on the tips of the soaring mountains, for instance, or in the churning of the ocean."[7]

It was such an experience that thrust the Roman soldier Saul from his horse and altered his life forever. From that point on, he changed his name to Paul and became a fervent defender of the young Christian faith. As evinced by many such occurrences in a variety of religions, these encounters do not lend themselves to one specific creed or time alone. Many people, even today, report such personal experiences. Often they have profound effects and may change a person's life forever. Sometimes they are associated with near death experiences as reported in several recent publications. Often they occur during extended illnesses, but sometimes no special cause or event can be found. Often, they occur to people who have no specific religious background either. It can take people years to come to terms with these powerful experiences, especially when all their surroundings tell them that what they have experienced should not have happened to them at all, that what happened to them is somehow weird, or even borders on insanity.

Before she immigrated to the United States, Elizabeth Kuebler Ross, a Swiss psychologist, wrote about near-death experiences from a purely clinical, academic point of view. While she was a scholar in Europe she wrote in the accepted distant and objective language of the conventional academician – anything else would have been unthinkable for a European scholar. At the time of her early writings her peers would have considered it heretical to mention any after-death experiences. Her move to the United States liberated her. She now could report her experiences with dying people in a completely new and more honest way. Even then, her more orthodox colleagues quickly dismissed her.

We will take a look now at two events: one that I have experienced myself and another one that the Danish industrialist and philosopher Jens Jacobsen reported to me.

Sixteen

HOLOTROPIC STATES OF CONSCIOUSNESS AND MYSTICAL ENCOUNTERS: TWO CASE HISTORIES

> The mystical life is the centre of all that I do and all that I think and all that I write. . . . I have always considered myself a voice of what I believe to be a greater renaissance – the revolt of the soul against the intellect.
>
> W. B. Yeats

In his book *The Cosmic Game*, Stanislav Grof wrote about the phenomena of transpersonal encounters.[1] He reports about numerous cases, both from his experience and from his practice as a psychiatrist. His interest in transpersonal experiences began, says Grof, when shortly after his graduation he took part in an LSD experiment. After that incident, his interest awoke more or less accidentally, and the famous psychiatrist went on a long search. He conducted a series of in-depth studies of the kind of experiences in which the human mind transgresses the narrow boundaries of the self. Such experiences, Grof contends, sharply oppose traditional Western science. But even though Western psychiatry, according to Grof, often "interprets such visionary experiences as manifestations of serious mental diseases," we must note that such "powerful personal experiences" were "at the cradle of all great religions of the world."[2]

These experiences, according to Grof, reveal the existence of sacred dimensions of reality. They inspired and provided the vital source of all religious movements. As examples Grof mentions the vision of Gautama Buddha meditating under the Bo tree, Mohammed's miraculous journey during which he encountered the archangel Gabriel, Moses' encounter with Yahweh in the burning bush, or Jesus' journey with Satan into the underworld – to name a few.

According to Grof, these images of reality are part of the great tradition of "perennial philosophy." They could easily be dismissed as "irrational, ungrounded, and 'unscientific'." Grof asserts, however, "when we take a closer look, we will see that rigid adherence to the current Western scientific worldview that leads to such judgments should not be confused with true science. In the last several decades, the understanding of reality expounded by mainstream science has been subjected to many critical challenges and its basic assumptions are being seriously questioned."[3]

The metaphysical insights described in his book are, says Grof, "certainly in an irreconcilable conflict with science as we have known it in the past." But at the same time, he contends "they are actually surprisingly compatible with many revolutionary advances of the recent decades that are usually referred to as the new or emerging paradigm."[4]

In observing such extraordinary events, which he calls "boundary transgression," Grof distinguishes between two different types of "non-ordinary states of consciousness." Consciousness, Grof says, "can be profoundly changed by a variety of pathological conditions – by cerebral traumas, by intoxication with poisonous substances, by infections, or by degenerative and circulatory processes in the brain."[5] While such conditions, according to Grof, often cause impaired mental functioning which cause "trivial deliria" or "organic psychoses" that leaves people disoriented and amnesic, the type of experience we will focus on produces, what Grof calls, a "holotropic" state of consciousness. Such states, according to Grof, are "oriented toward wholeness" or "moving in the direction of wholeness." Grof says that holotropic states work by causing:

> dramatic perceptual changes in all sensory areas, intense and often unusual emotions, and profound alterations in the thought processes and behavior. They can also be accompanied by a variety of psychosomatic manifestations. The emotions associated with these states cover a very wide range from ecstatic raptures and "peace that passes all understanding" to hellish episodes of abysmal terror, guilt, and despair.[6]

I was born at the height of World-War-II and grew up during the traumatic years of post-war Germany. As a child, I experienced a series of fainting spells that might have shaped my later sensitivity. During those formative years, Meinrad, a close childhood friend, was my constant companion. His father was a deeply psychic and mysterious man. He was a musician, political activist, and graphologist. As long as I remember, Meinrad believed in his powers of telepathy and, to some extent, clairvoyance. Meinrad was convinced that, on rare occasions, strange spirits possessed him.

At one occasion, we both were young men in our early twenties, Meinrad invited me to his house to listen to music. For many hours we listened to Pink Floyd music. I remember meditating into the source of the music for an extended time period. I had my eyes closed when Meinrad began to speak. He described his old age in vivid colors. He said how it horrified him to think that he would ever become old. Then I suddenly found myself in Meinrad's mind; I saw the images in his mind and felt his pain. I saw an old man in worn clothes, bent over by pain on a country road. To my horror, I recognized Meinrad, and I was joining in his vision of himself some ten (perhaps twenty) years later.

Quite forcefully, I had to tear myself away from that vision. Gathering all my energy, I left Meinrad's place. I fled from it. For over a year, visions of death haunted and terrified me. The mere noise of a car driving by could make me tremble; I thought it would be my end. Streetcars and trains had an even more terrifying impact. Just about ten years after that episode, Meinrad died from a drug overdose somewhere in Frankfurt. I had gone on to study in America, perhaps subconsciously fleeing from him. I had to get distance between him and me.

Another experience, many years later, resembles even more closely the holotropic state-of-mind described by Grof. During a theater festival in Poland in 1976, I had an experience, which I first reported about in my book *The Dice-Playing God.*[7] I based the narration of the book on notes from my diary, which I had kept meticulously while events unfolded around me. I wrote:

> The following events took place in the days immediately following the Polish festival. I remained for some days in the city waiting for transportation back home to Finland. The day after the events reported in chapter nine, my mind was healed and united. The intense feeling of having to take notice of every moment had left me, but I was aware and sensitive to my environment. I wrote into my diary:

> Somewhat aimlessly I wandered through the halls of the empty club. Only a few days earlier it had been filled with bodies. I thought how unimportant these halls were now, since the festival was over and nothing was left to do. I ended up in the large room used as a dancing space. It had been filled with disco music and sweating bodies. An intense silence surrounded me now. I enjoyed it for a while and observed my silent breathing. Then I moved carefully into the room as if not to disturb it in its rest. In the dusk of the room I sat down on one of the chairs placed in long lines along the sides. As soon as I sat down the room suddenly seemed not to be sleeping, but that it had observed me from the first moment I entered. I had no feeling of fear, but a feeling of warmth, because somehow I knew that this space would not hurt me or take advantage of me. I sat back, and I opened myself up, and I felt the room respond.

> The room seemed to invite me to take a closer look. For a moment the idea disquieted me, because I had just found out how horrible the compulsion for a detailed description of the world could be and how it could take over one's whole being.

"But no," the room whispered, "just look! I am not as empty as you might assume."

The room sounded wiser than I would have expected. I even had the feeling that the room was smiling. So I looked and I tried to remember every detail. But now the urge to take notice was not so forceful anymore. I no longer had the feeling that I might miss something that would make my report less authentic. After all, yesterday I decided that my report about the festival was over, and whatever the room now had to offer, was only a little addition – more for me personally than for anybody else to read. So I didn't try hard to remember every detail, but I absorbed it all inside of me.

There were white long curtains. They swayed slowly in the wind of the open windows, through which a last shimmer of the dying day poured in. Opposite me in the corner was a long table. It had been set up to hold the sound equipment. It was covered with a white tablecloth that gave it a festive look. The table stood on a small platform, and a decorative frame surrounded the whole scene, making it look like a little chapel. In the back, a cast-iron staircase led up to the high ceiling, where a small door seemed to lead into nowhere.

After I looked at all of this sufficiently, I noticed that the room seemed content to be observed in this manner. It totally lost its shyness and invited me to further observations. So I agreed, and my eyes wandered now more attentively and looked more into the depth. They now gazed more willingly through the space, and stopped only when they became aware of a large mirror on the wall to the left. Its upper frame was drawn in Gothic lines. The mirror was placed in such a way that from the place I was sitting I could not see its content. But before I was able to ask the room for permission to move to another place, because I suspected that the mirror would tell me more secrets of the room, I felt movement in the room. I interrupted my curiosity to let it speak:

"Watch, I will show you what I have observed many times. Though each time different, each time it is interesting again. Hide as well as you can and I will . . ."

Before it finished speaking a young man entered the room with loud steps. He stopped for a moment, then went straight across the room to an open door from which a bright light poured forth. He looked for a while, then turned around and left the same way he had entered. I was surprised and amused, and I wanted to ask the room, what this whole thing was supposed to mean.

"Quiet," said the room, "we don't have time now to speak about it. Perhaps later. Just watch!"

And I saw a young girl entering. She was dressed in a short skirt and carrying a handbag. She crossed the room, and I held my breath wondering whether she would find her way to the illuminated door. But she stopped halfway through turned around and stood in front of the dark mirror. Though it was quite dark now, she stared into it and shaped her hair for a while. Then she stretched her body and touched her rounded breasts with her hands. Suddenly, she turned away and left the room the same way she had come in.

"See," said the room, "she looks but she doesn't see, because in everything she only sees her own image."

Now I became somewhat impatient, and I collected all my courage and asked the room:

"Will you allow me to change my position, so I can have a look into the mirror myself? I know well that you are conceited, too, and you surround yourself with mirrors in which you can see yourself and your own image again and again."

"You certainly may," said the room, and I felt again that it smiled.

Not to disturb the silence I walked quietly across the room toward the mirror, curiously awaiting what I would see. How surprised was I when I took a look into the mirror to see a second mirror, straight across the room and identical to the one in front of me, in which the first mirror was totally reflected. This gave the room a depth that I never expected. When building this arrangement the architects must have taken great care to put the two huge mirrors exactly opposite each other. From the place I was sitting I observed a perfect reflection of the two mirrors extending into infinity.

Of course, I wanted to know immediately what was in the next room, and in the next, and so on.

"I will grant you a look," said the room. "What do you see, when you look right into the center of all the rooms which are open in front of you, yet closed at the same time?"

"I see nothing but a black point, deeper and blacker than everything I have ever seen."

"You see," said the room, and I had the impression that its voice was trembling, "that is the depth I try to hide with every moment, because no one can bear it. But this I will tell you for your consolation: before you will reach this depth, there is much light, because every room behind the one you are in now is only a fraction darker then the preceding one. After you have transgressed each room slowly and with grace, your sight will have gotten used to the darkness long before you enter the darkest room. Then you will accept the darkness like a brother with open arms. But woe to those, who pass through the rooms in fast descent and fall into the darkness like into the open mouth of a beast and die . . . . But I see that I have frightened you with my last remarks, and if you want so I will make them unsaid, because as you have seen there are many possibilities."

By now I had descended so far into the depth of the rooms, that even the last remark was not able to call me back. But I was to experience the goodness of the room, for it took me by my shoulders and shook me. Then it moved my head forcefully away from the mirrors, and brought me back to reality.

Ever since I had this experience I have been trying to make sense of it and somehow incorporate it into the meaning I have constructed for my life. This, I believe, is one of our most basic human needs, to make sense out of events that occur to us. If we would ever lose this urge completely, I believe that humanity would have lost an essential part of itself. Perhaps this is what Socrates meant when he said that the unexamined life is not worth living. When something strange occurs we cannot easily put it aside and declare it as not valid, even though our current scientific knowledge suggests we should. If an event does not fit into our cognitive worldview we tend to dismiss it as nothing but a hallucination, a deception of the senses, or an illusion.

But when we persist in our search, we often find fellow human beings who have had similar experiences and lived through similar anguish. Finally we begin to realize that our experiences are not totally unique. Many others have had similar experiences. Some only reluctantly talk about it for fear of being ridiculed, others have written about it in encrypted form – by way of poetry or fiction.

More recently, I met a person who had been deeply influenced by a mystical experience that he had as a child in his native Denmark. The experience stayed with him for the rest of his long and busy life. At times he seemed to have forgotten this early event. Jens Jacobsen became a wealthy businessman. For many years, he completely immersed himself in work and with accumulating wealth.

But this early encounter never completely left him. At nearly eighty years of age, Jacobsen finally retired from the business world and granted himself the time he needed to make sense out of these early events. In 1992, I met Jacobsen in his home on Lake Geneva. Here is his story, a philosophy of life prompted by to mystical events, as told by him personally:

> In the beginning there was a force, no materia, no space, no time, but this force was a creative force, a life force. Out of it came movement. From movement came development and everything: space, time, and matter.
>
> I was only about eleven when a child in our neighborhood suddenly died. The child was only seven or eight years old. Already then it came to my mind: How could God be so cruel to let something like this happen? The child had suffered incredibly. Already then I got very suspicious about religion. I got very suspicious about the type of God they said was so wonderful. In my eyes this must have been the cruelest thing that could exist to let things like that happen.
>
> Then, when I was about sixteen, I came to the conclusion that God as an entity did not exist. What really existed was a force, a definable force. But what was that force? I didn't know. But my eyes were opened at that time. I was about sixteen. I lived with an uncle of mine who traded with farmers. One day I was asked to go out and visit a farmer who was not able to pay his account. I was supposed to get him to agree to some arrangement to make his payments.
>
> The farmer lived about five or six kilometers away. This was in Denmark where I grew up as a child. I rode my bicycle that morning. On the way I passed a meadow. The sun was just trying to break through the mist. So there was this meadow with a stream running through it, and on the other side there was a forest. The calmness and the view of the sun trying to break

through gave me an extraordinary feeling of the environment in which I was living. I was aware of nature as it presented itself to its product.

And suddenly I was not there any more. I tried to say a prayer, but I couldn't pray to anything. It was out there and it came to its product. I was a product that processed the beauty of it, but it also gave me the idea that I was not there. I was only a product. There were forces out there that were so enormous that it was almost incomprehensible, so overwhelming that it struck me: my goodness, what is the reality of myself? I was not there. I am in reality nature's product and there was a reflection between these two. First there were those enormous physical forces. Then, to imagine the forces it took to evolve an organism that comprehends that. It was so overwhelming that it stayed with me for the rest of my life.

Another event took place at the time I lived in Copenhagen, and I worked at the Central Bank. I worked in the export department. I decided one day with a friend to go to Tivoli Garden, and we decided to go and see a concert in Concert Hall. As we were sitting there, a little frightened chap came on stage. And I said to my friend, "What a terrible thing for the Swedish opera to send out a little frightened chap like that."

But then he started singing. And his humility and his anxiety all of a sudden started to blossom through in the most beautiful singing I had ever heard. That humility that was shown told me that he is not there. He is interpreting nature. He is interpreting something outside of himself. And as the singing went on, the tension grew almost to an explosion point. I noticed the people sitting next to me had tears running down their faces. He sang about forty minutes overtime because of the excitement and the explosive atmosphere. It was so fantastic. When we left the Concert Hall, nobody talked – it was like leaving a church service.

About fifteen years ago I was traveling from Johannesburg to Zimbabwe and next to me was sitting a stout, heavy lady. We started talking about music. She was a professional singer herself. I told her about this experience with Yussi Bjorling, who was the singer at that concert.

She said to me to my horror: "I know all about it." And I said: "You weren't even born." She said: "All singers know about that, you see. All singers know about that because the international press had noticed that there was something extraordinary going on during that performance."

It had been the first time this singer had been allowed to play outside of Sweden. To me this was the first time that I realized how the universal force is interpreted by its product. It gave me a peace of mind for the rest of my life.

I have seen nature. I have seen truth. I have seen what the human organism is in relation to these enormous life forces in the universe, those enormous physical forces that are that organism's environment. From what I had seen I drew conclusions about Nature's purpose, Nature's character, Nature's aim.

Nature's need is to express its character via its product. A product might be an ant, an amoeba, a tiger, a monkey, or a human being. Nature expresses its character via that, its evolutionary process through that – and it does it through life forces.

Life is a universal force, which operates where the environment is suitable for its manifestation. And how does it operate? It operates via definable, understandable behavior patterns, which is preservation – not self-preservation. It is nature that preserves itself via its product. It preserves itself eternally (via its products) in order to achieve its evolutionary process from one generation to the other.

How does self-preservation develop?

When the forces become an internal operation of the product, self-preservation develops. Self-preservation by human beings is negative and destructive because it's not living in truth, it's living in fantasy. This is why there is so much trouble in the world because people live in fantasy. And that is based on self-preservation that does not exist.

Today everything is built on self-preservation, in relation to society, in relation to each other, in relation to politics, in relation to religion, and in relation to the universe. That is the tragedy of us human beings. We are Nature's product which can also be translated into we are Nature's children, not for the children's sake but for Nature's sake. [8]

From his experience and from his discussions with his patients Grof drew the conclusion that once we have such an experience, we cannot help but to incorporate it into our lives. Through years of reflection, I came to the same conclusion. Grof says:

> Transpersonal experiences are so convincing and compelling that the individuals who have had them have no other choice than incorporating them into their worldview. It is thus systematic experiential exposure to transpersonal experiences, on the one side, and the absence thereof, on the other, that sets the technological societies and native cultures so far apart. I have not yet seen a single individual who has had a deep experience of the transpersonal realms and continues to subscribe to the worldview of Western materialistic science. This development is quite independent of the level of intelligence, type and degree of education, and professional credentials of the individuals involved. [9]

Under the guidance of Transcendental Perspectivism, I hope others will no longer judge such transpersonal experiences as mere illness and shun those who have them. We need to find proper scientific ways to explore such experiences and the vast realms of the inner self, just as we have gone to the moon and explored the frontiers of outer space. Under caring and compassionate supervision, we must courageously and successfully undertake further experimentations to give scientific foundation to this last frontier – the vast potential of the human mind that one day can show the way to achieve cosmic consciousness.

Seventeen

TRANSCENDENTAL MEDITATION AND NOWTIME: THE EXPERIENCE OF EMPTINESS

> To see a world in a grain of sand
> And a heaven in a wild flower,
> Hold infinity in the palm of your hand
> And eternity in an hour.
>
> William Blake

Mystical or numinous experiences can fundamentally shape and change a person's life. Even though science cannot easily scrutinize such experiences, we can hardly doubt that they have occurred in the past and still occur today. Just because we cannot scientifically verify them, it should not mean that they do not occur. By the veracity standards of pragmatic philosophy, these events should have at least some truth-value since they produce, in a testable way, effects in the real world.

Yogic meditation (an ancient practice in the East) has become tremendously popular in the Western world. According to Ninian Smart, such meditative journeys into the inner parts of the Self are "another kind of religious experience." Smart says these mystical experiences have been essential for the history of humanity, but they do not have the same qualities of the numinous experience. According to Smart, yogic meditation is aimed at "purifying the consciousness of the individual to such a degree that all images and thoughts are left behind. It is as if the meditator is ascending a kind of inner ladder where at the highest rungs he or she gains a kind of a pure bliss and insight, free from the distractions of ordinary experience."[1]

This higher state, according to Smart, is often understood as a "nondual," state of mind. It is not like our usual experiences where we separate the observer from the observed. The distinction between the subject and the object disappears. According to Smart, "such an ascent of stages of consciousness is usually said to involve the stilling of all feelings and the attainment of a perfect quietness. This is very different from the dynamic and shattering experience of the numinous."[2]

Contrary to what Smart says, I believe that such mystical journeys into the Self can also turn out to be as shattering and devastating as the experience of the numinous in the world of the other. In an earlier book, I described the trip that was undertaken by the Living Theater during their famous adaptation of *The Brig*. Because of its essential theme of a journey into the inner

Self, I will recount here the report by Judith Malina, the wife of the famous director of the legendary Living Theater:

Many critics considered Julian Beck's Living Theater, a radical theater group, the most influential American counterculture group. They practiced an exercise with the intention to send the actor on a trip.

During rehearsals for *The Brig*, the company conducted meditative exercises while also strictly following the training manual established for United States Marines. The play represents a routine day in a Marine prison camp. In recreating the violent and painful routines practiced by the Marines, the Living Theater intended more than mere authenticity in their performance. Beck, a practicing mystic himself, intended to induce mystical experiences in his actors as the result of this exercise.

Malina described the intention of the rehearsal and the effect it had on its participants. A blow to the stomach, exercised routinely by the Marines, was reenacted as a fully expected and contemplated piece of rehearsal and theater. Under the guidance of the director, a blow to the stomach could turn into a contemplative, even a mystic experience. A performer would supposedly transform into a new kind of communication device. Malina called this an "imitative reflex action," known in athletics and circuses. The goal of this exercise was to produce a measurable effect, a contraction in the body of the spectator as well. The secular theater would become a sacred space of spiritual dimension.

Malina discussed the stages of the blow at length. The moment of climax, according to Malina, was brief and vulnerable. It centers in the will "as the mind flicks back from its instant of unconsciousness."[3] This moment had a therapeutic function. Instead of the hatred that we usually connect with violence, the Living Theater intended to use this experience as a cathartic element. "The spectator returns to the world in which this blow, this visceral pain, exists. In prize fights both men fight, and sympathy gets lost in swiftly dealt vengeance. But this blow belongs to the martyrs, the soldiers, and the poor."[4]

Malina described the moment of unconsciousness in which the theater of cruelty occurs. The Living Theater called this Moment of Impact the "trip."

> Each actor brought back travelogues of the trip that he took out into the long silent stretches. Sometimes with his uniform soaking wet, or during and after a bout with the guards, or staring at the wire that hypnotized him with its glittering lines, he stood still inside that stillness within which the physical stillness lies hidden, and in that narrow space, being so strictly confined, took wing into what Artaud calls that "enormous spiral that reveals one perspective after another." The actor felt (some familiarly, some for the first time in their lives) the

other Self, the one that Artaud calls the Double, take flight and soar into that other space where time is not, nor relation, nor anything, but sheer existence, undefined and undefinable, seemingly absolute.

The body of the prisoner is totally captive. The soul of the prisoner is potentially totally free. The trip between these two points is the crucial experience of the play.[5]

Malina reported that in the violent blow to the stomach, the actor experiences the original oneness of mind and body. Mind and body, felt by the ego as independent from each other, suffer from their separation. Suffering, the Living Theater believed, melds a human being and the soul. The physical action of *The Brig* is real, physical, here-and-now. The spirit, according to Malina, needs force to fuse again with the athletic body. Malina asked the actors about the trip. They said: "The space traversed is infinite." and "You can't think further than the next white line."[6]

The Trip assures a reality beyond the limits of the body by revealing physicality as potentially spiritual, a carrier of existential content beyond words and thoughts. Perhaps different from experiments in physical science, the human being becomes the medium of experimentation.

An unfavorable context comes to mind when we recall experimentation with human beings. The Nazis and other eugenics experimenters around the world used human beings for scientific research, much to the shock of the rest of the world. Against their will, the Nazis forced their subjects into the experiments. New science, based on a Perspectivist philosophy, will have to conduct experiments with human beings if we want the occurrences that happen at the borderline of mind and body to become scientifically verified. But Perspectivist experimentation must insist on the voluntary character of all such experimentation. Experimenters must keep participants informed and aware of all possible consequences, even while they may not yet know the full extent of the consequences at times. Perspectivist science will have to assure this, in order to differ from traditional science, which turns into stone, as Toffler once said, everyone who comes in contact with her – much like the ancient Medusa.

The method of the Living Theater has the character of a scientific experiment – though it has lengthy set-up time and training and the results are not always guaranteed. Large sections of the reports are, by necessity, subjective first-person accounts. When reviewing the results of the tests conducted by the Living Theater, we must keep in mind that the participants underwent only a short training. In contrast, Eastern practitioners of meditation are expected to undergo many years of rigorous training in order to reach the full fruit of meditative and yogic submersion. Prospective yogis are often initiated at a young age and then spend the rest of their lives in seclusion while practicing to achieve inner emptiness and oneness with the universe. The goal is the disappearance of duality, which is considered Nirvana. In Tibetan Buddhism, young boys are selected to become monks and then train to become aware of their dreams. Eventually, they can manipulate their dreams with their minds. They believe that after death we enter a stage that is similar to dreaming. Once we can remain aware of our dreams, then we can also master the threshold of death.

One of the most widespread meditation practices that came from the East into the Western world is called Transcendental Meditation, or TM. A meditation master, or guru, instructs the disciple in the techniques of active meditation. The guru gives the acolyte a *mantra*. It consists of a chant, word, or symbol, which only the guru and disciple share. The disciple uses this mantra over and over again in his meditation. The mantra functions as a kind of strange attractor in the brain. In the human mind, the cluster of neurons that constitute self-awareness act like strong magnetic attractors, operating most of the time while we are awake and aware. Here, our conscious Self is at home; however, we lose consciousness or faint when that central command post is vacated.

As we meditate on a mantra, we progressively strengthen the location in the brain where the mantra has been stored. Finally, this cluster of neurons reaches a point where it has become strong enough as an attractor to pull the conscious Self away from the central command post – if only for a split moment. We experience this moment in a similar way as the moment of impact in the Living Theater's practice. The meditator experiences, in the words of Malina, "the original oneness of mind and body." We could also say that we have found the other within our Self.

What we find in the depth of our Self depends on our expectations. We shape these with religious upbringing and cultural context. Recall Faust's remark: "In your Nothing I intend to find my All" or the Living Theater's: "The space traversed is infinite" and "You can't think further than the next white line." For most Buddhists, however, the mystical journey into the inner Self is a journey into emptiness, which we experience as inner peace:

> . . . the mystical (experience) is quiet, but the numinous experience is powerful and turbulent; the mystical seems to be empty of images, while the numinous experience is typically clothed in ideas of encounter with a personal God; the mystical does not give rise to worship or reverence, in so far as there is nothing "other" to worship or revere.[7]

Here Smart describes the non-dual experience of liberation. Buddhists encounter this on their journey into the Self as a freedom. It "consists of an experience of emptiness, or purity of consciousness, together with the perception that this emptiness is the underlying nature of things,"[8] that things are without permanent substance. Already in the *Upanishads* (the sacred text of the Hindus) Brahman (the divine Being, the force that pervades the Hindus) Brahman (the divine Being, the force that pervades everything) and Atman (which is found at the depth of the Self) are one. The sacred text states: "That divine Being which lies behind the whole cosmos, which creates it and sustains it and constitutes its inner nature is the same as what you will discover in the depths of your Self, if you will voyage inward through self-control and the methods of meditation and purification of your consciousness."[9]

"In a flash of insight," Smart says, the Upanishads bring the two together: "the divine Being is found not only out there but also within the heart."[10] Smart correctly sees a similarity of mystical experiences in many different traditions. Many of the Christian mystics have had similar experiences of God, either in a numinous encounter of the divine in the outer world or as a result of contemplative submersion into the Self. The trip into the Self for one can end "at the white line" for another it can "reveal the power of the whole Universe" depending on our metaphysical and religious context, for even others it can be a frightening experience of isolation and death.

In both Western and Eastern mysticism, reports of mystical and numinous experiences that result in the experience of a horrifying emptiness abound. Existentialist artists, for instance, have described their essential experience of oneness with the physical world as a kind of nausea or shock that results in existential despair. As a materialist who believes that the human being is part of the material world, the atheist existentialist undergoes a kind of existential transformation in the experience of oneness with the physical world. For Jean-Paul Sartre, this experience resulted in the supreme command to set our difference and be our God. Or else we are doomed to oneness and sameness with the meaningless earth.

From the same negative experience of emptiness or nothingness at the ground of the material world, the Christian existentialist drew the opposite conclusion. The experience of ultimate meaninglessness of the fallen world shocked them so much that there was only one meaningful thing to do, to flee into the arms of a living God, however logically absurd this may be. Christian existentialism built its case on the existential experience of meaninglessness. Faith provided the way out of this devastating recognition of absurdity.

The question for objectivity or the truth-value of such personal experiences must ultimately remain unanswered. Smart, like Goethe, and numerous others, came to a Perspectivist conclusion to allow individuals to validate their experience as real. In contrast, the relativistic conclusion (most prevalent in our society and in Western medical practice) denies the truth-value and credibility of all such experiences. The Perspectivist conclusion extends the invitation to try out different paths, to each find our perspective, and to have our own experiences. Perspectivism develops and propagates techniques and lifestyles that may lead to the expected results in order to give people techniques and encourage them to explore their own inner space, as

Stanislav Grof recommends. This, too, concurs with Smart's conclusion when he says:

> So the question of whether religious experience tells us the truth at all is a question that depends in part on the worldview with which we start. It looks like a circle. But it is not a circle to be trapped in, for what it shows is that questions of religious truth are a matter of the perspective with which they are viewed. And which perspective – the humanist or the religious – is more convincing depends on a whole array of details.[11]

The universe, it appears, is built in a dreamlike, multiple option fashion, in which for the searching soul all the dreams, from the emptiness of total nothingness to the richness of glorious redemption are possible and available. Christ once said: "In my Father's house are many mansions."[12] I have always taken this to mean in a spiritual way that the universe makes all our dreams come true. We will not have to prove anybody right or wrong. We all are right when it comes to our mind's capability of imagining the reality of the sacred hub.

The experience at the Polish Theater festival gave me these insights and, more than anything, put me on a steady search for the divine in the material world and in relationships. Not by coincidence, I believe, some modern physicists such as Heinz Pagels, Paul Davies, and David Peat have been working on a theoretical understanding of such mystical events. In *The Dice-Playing God,* I asked, whether physical science will "fully grasp the path of the Self into the void?"[13]

Both in the macro world, as well as in the micro world, scientists have found the universe to be enveloped in mystery. A black hole is a physical conundrum, first only postulated by theory, then verified by observation. In *A Brief History of Time*, Stephen Hawking spoke with almost mystical language about the reality of black holes. At one point he speculates about a space traveler approaching a black hole:

> The event horizon, the boundary of the region of space-time from which it is not possible to escape, acts rather like a one-way membrane around the black hole: objects, such as unwary astronauts, can fall through the event horizon into the black hole, but nothing can ever get out of the black hole through the event horizon. (Remember that the event horizon is the path in space-time of light that is trying to escape from the black hole, and nothing can travel faster than light.) One should well say of the event horizon what the poet Dante said of the entrance to Hell: "All hope abandon, ye who enter here." Anything or anyone who falls through the event horizon

will soon reach the region of infinite density and the end of time.[14]

Is this the mythical realm of the dead, the river of silence? On the small scale, each electron, as the French physicist Jean Charon speculated, may be a miniature black hole with an opening to another space-time. In this other space-time, existence, the coordinates of time and space are reversed. The dying mind collapses within the singularity of an electron in fast descent and confronts nothingness. The accounts of many near death experiences seem to confirm this image.[15] Charon speculated about the possibility of the slowly descending mind opening up ever-new spaces of experience and existence. Hawking gave a description of a black hole similar to my experience above. Speaking about the "cosmic censorship hypotheses"[16] Hawking said:

> God abhors naked singularities. . . . Singularities produced by gravitational collapse occur only in places, like black holes, where they are decently hidden from outside view by an event horizon. Strictly, this is known as the weak cosmic censorship hypotheses: it protects observers who remain outside the black hole from the consequences of the breakdown of predictability that occurs at the singularity, but it does nothing at all for the poor astronaut who falls into the hole.[17]

Grof notes that ordinarily when people encounter nothingness they often associate this with something completely unpleasant: a lack of feeling, initiative, or meaning. The Void encountered by the mystic is of a different kind. Grof says:

> When we encounter the Void, we feel that it is primordial emptiness of cosmic proportions and relevance. We become pure consciousness aware of this absolute nothingness; however, at the same time, we have a strange paradoxical sense of its essential fullness. This cosmic vacuum is also a plenum, since nothing seems to be missing in it. While it does not contain anything in a concrete, manifest form, it seems to comprise all of existence in a potential form. In this paradoxical way, we can transcend the usual dichotomy between emptiness and form, or existence and non-existence. However, the possibility of such a resolution cannot be adequately conveyed in words; it has to be experienced to be understood.[18]

Since Western rationalism has consistently denied the validity of such experiences, Western culture has failed to teach methods and techniques to achieve them. For that, our cultural context has become poorer. We need to develop and teach methods of experiencing the Void in a meaningful, cosmic way. Along with techniques, we should also develop new scientific tools to measure the effects, and a new scientific language to adequately describe this experience.

PART SIX

BREAKING NEW GROUND:
PRINCIPLES AND TRENDS OF TRANSCEN-
DENTAL PERSPECTIVISM

Eighteen

PLEASURE AND PAIN:
ARE WE A GENERATION OF VAMPIRES?

> If you need a friend, get a dog.
> Gordon Gekko

This last part of my book deals with the attitudes and qualities that we need to foster in order to nourish Perspectivist sensitivity. In many ways, people today lack compassion as a way to internalize and experience the inner soul of the other person, animals, and the universe. We need to reintroduce compassion so humanity may survive. In order to do just this, we must first ask one thing. Why do we lack compassion? The vampires in Ann Rice's story, *Interview with a Vampire*,[1] are immortal beings who have lost the ability to feel. Tied to their dark destiny of living from the blood of their human victims, their sense of survival commands them to live without compassion or regret. A senior vampire instructs his apprentice, who just killed the woman he loved, as follows: "We must be powerful, beautiful and without regret." The junior vampire hesitates: "What if all I have is my suffering, my regret?" To become fully vampire, he must give up regret. He must become merciless with a heart of stone. Above all, he must lose compassion.

The vampires in Rice's story closely resemble some members of the human species in contemporary society. People involved in every day business affairs often seem to have overcome compassion and feeling. In the world of business, men and women allow mere technical considerations to guide them. They make decisions that affect the lives of people, but they hardly ever take that into account or even have an awareness of it. Like the senior vampire, they go about their business without feeling and without regret. The modern marketplace has no conscience. Corporate boardrooms have no use for sentimentality. For the lead character Gordon Gekko in the movie *Wallstreet,* the world is a battlefield. In the cold world of business only he who has no compassion or regret will survive. "If you need a friend, get a dog," is Gekko's famous advice to his young apprentice. Money is the chip with which the male establishment plays the power game. Pretty women and sexual pleasures are their prize. Emotions and long-term attachments are the bread of the weak and the poor.

According to the Greek master thinkers, lesser gods who didn't know what they were doing created emotions. The chief god, however, wanted us all to be rational, beautiful, and perfect. In such perfection there would also be no place for regret. In the post-capitalist consumer society, the *demiourg*'s rationality is triumphant. But this rationality has no knowledge of the Whole;

it is a functional rationality only, as some have called it – the rationality of the machine.

René Descartes, best known for his *cogito ergo sum,* meant to establish the ultimate logic of life. Following the Greek tradition, he eliminated the emotional part of the human Self. Western human beings became soulless beings – Vampires. In this form, we could take advantage of others, including the animal world, without feeling or regret. Social Darwinism finished establishing Vampire existence as the norm and capitalism became the system of choice for institutionalized selfishness.

This is contrary to the way the rest of the animal world operates. In school we were taught that animals are brute, dumb, and compassionless. But this is not so. Human beings perhaps lacked the compassion to observe animals with enough care. Selfishness exists in nature, but we cannot assume that all of nature is selfish. Nature delicately balances selfish and unselfish, competitive and cooperative behavior. In the long run, as we will see, cooperative behavior must (and will) outweigh selfish behavior. Against the impulse to selfishness, individuals have an urge within them that inspires to become part of a larger whole. But when individuals don't find what they expected from the community, they drop out and try a different combination. In this delicate interplay the gauge of individual satisfaction is pleasure and pain. If this gauge is disturbed or non-existent, then all community creation is in danger.

In twentieth-century America, Ayn Rand,[2] the Russian/American immigrant, fine-tuned capitalist ideology as a philosophy of enlightened and rational self interest. Much of Rand's personal experience, as a Russian, a Jew, and as a woman in a male dominated society, entered into her philosophy and made it one of the most eloquent statements for radical individualism, a statement against compassionate selflessness and ultimately a statement against community.

The "Me-thinking" of the 1980s brought the logic of egoism to full fruition. In her novel *Fountainhead,* which was once required reading for American youngsters, Rand preached the virtues of egoism and opposed the altruistic tendencies of traditional religions and of the welfare state. The main actors in her novels demonstrate the oppressive and often irrational character of emotions. Her leading characters appear totally incapable of showing any real emotions. They show how to manipulate and calculate emotions only to reach their end. This is an accurate observation in regards to the practices of the market place in general. But is this also a statement of ontological truth? Do human beings have to be this way by nature? As a declared "objectivist" Rand makes just this claim.

As a Perspectivist, I know differently. We do not need to be vampires. The rest of the natural world is compassionate and selfish, competitive and cooperative. Human beings alone are in the process of becoming completely compassionless. We are conditioning ourselves to exist like vampires, without regret. The utter neglect of millions of children around the world may stand witness to this.

To the inquisitive reporter in Rice's story the junior vampire reveals, "I am the spirit of preternatural flesh, detached, unchangeable, empty." The characters in Rand's stories are the preternatural creations of our making. They are vampires as the result of human constructions termed metaphysical – a super rationality gone amok.

At the end of the nineteenth century, communities became increasingly replaced by mass society as a result of the industrial revolution. In the large cities, bedroom communities replaced small neighborhoods. Here people lived in anonymity and isolation. Some sociologists questioned whether we might have some vital residue within us that would ultimately resist total alienation. A humanistic hope perhaps inspired these philosophers to believe in a core of goodness within humanity (similar to Anne Frank, the Jewish girl who died prematurely at the hands of fascist murderers). In his theoretical and literary works, Walter Benjamin, the young German/Jewish poet and philosopher, was perhaps the most prominent believer in the basic goodness of human beings. Realizing the alienating power of mass consumerism, he steadfastly believed in the revitalizing power of pure life that would ulti-mately triumph over alienation. When, at the height of fascism, Benjamin realized the extent of twentieth-century barbarism he tried to escape into the safe land across the Pyrenees to Spain. He managed to escape, though hunted by the Nazis. In safety in Spain, Benjamin could not reconcile his loss of faith in the basic goodness of creation and abruptly ended his young life.

Across the ocean, in the safe haven of the United States, my teachers from the Frankfurt School (Max Horkheimer and Theodor W. Adorno, to-gether with Herbert Marcuse and others) started the Institute for Social Re-search. Here they pursued vigorously the question whether an unalienable ground existed in humanity that would ultimately resist complete reification. When they became fully aware of the horrors of fascism (and later of fascist Stalinism) they shifted their research into a comprehensive study of the au-thoritarian personality. The focus of research had turned away from a fruit-less attempt to prove a residue of goodness within humanity to a research into the empirical sources of evil, the nature of the authoritarian personality.

As a father and a teacher I know from experience that greed and self-ishness are naturally not the predominant characteristics in human beings. I have experienced over and over again that the majority of young people want to share, communicate, and live happy lives that they can share with others. As they grow older, a powerful feedback loop that begins with cultural pes-simism breeds cynicism and desperation. School, education, and culture do not teach the necessary skills for survival. The powerful message young peo-ple get over and over again, is one of despair. Life is not worth living. No meaning at all exists. The task of Sisyphus has become the general lot of hu-manity.

The Scottish movie *Trainspotting,* made after a novel by Irvine Welsh,[3] captures the essence of this mentality. "Trainspotting," explained Welsh in an interview with *Time,* "is the compulsive collecting of locomotive engine numbers from the British railway system. But you can't do anything with the numbers once you've collected them."

The message of the rock group Pink Floyd in the legendary movie *The Wall,* in which they proclaim: "Teacher, leave those Kids alone!" and "We don't want no education, we don't want no thought control!" has been taken one step further. At the end of *The Wall,* the main character stares in disgust down a dirty toilet bowl. This is a powerful metaphor for our sick society. When staring into the toilet bowl is all for humanity to do, the next generation of toilet bowl starers is bound to find something beautiful in it. Perhaps this is life's tragic positivity; that, even in insanity, from the perspective of the insane, it is worth living – at least sometimes.

John Hodge adapted *Trainspotting* for the screen. *Time* called the film brilliant, and it became a hit at the Cannes film festival in 1996. The film, according to *Time,* speaks to the "postliterate generation." Hodge succeeds in describing the metaphor of useless collecting as "doing something that gives your life a bit of structure but is ultimately pointless." This Sisyphean absurdity of life, when mixed with a celebratory injection of heavy drugs becomes a deadly mixture of desperation. As a cultural statement this obsession with negativity also indicates the ill and dysfunctional status of our humanity. The cultural feedback loop that propels such diagnostics of cultural decay into the mainstream guarantees the efficiency of cultural decline.

At the same time we can perhaps still find some intrinsic value in this piece of art. As my teacher Adorno said, every artwork, even the most negative one, contains an element of affirmation. The film expresses life from a Perspectivist viewpoint, albeit a suicidal and decaying life. "Death hangs like a crape over Renton and his mates," Brunton and Ressner write in their review in *Time.* They believe that "the film is about joy – in conniving and surviving, in connecting with audiences, in its own fizzy, jizzy style." Therefore, they conclude: "the movie could not be more vital. So say it without irony: *Trainspotting* chooses life."

Art cannot help but to affirm life, even in its most negative form. Gangster rap, too, falls into that category (therefore it can and should not be suppressed). But when cynicism and negativity become the sole, constant, and noisiest beats we drum, when destructiveness and suicidal mania become the apparent essence of the cultural voice, such a culture creates, fosters, and reaffirms the vampire existence in all of us. Those who act out of greed and selfishness need a culture that continuously reaffirms their morbidity and decay as normal. Staring into the toilet bowl of life's garbage becomes an average activity. Since life cannot exist without pleasure, we accept the non-pleasurable as pleasure. Death becomes the ultimate source of such perverted pleasure, and every impetuous drug trip brings us one step closer to our collective suicide.

Nineteen

TRAVEL IN SAFETY:
THE PERSPECTIVE OF EVIL

> For truly to pursue monsters one must under-
> stand them. We must venture into their minds,
> though do we venture letting them into ours?
>
> *The X-Files*

When planning a journey into the dark lands of evil, the *Tourist's Guide to Transylvania*, strongly recommends taking along a guardian or guide. The book itself provides the reader with a semi-serious account of the dark phenomena of life.

In Europe, during the later part of the nineteenth century, the cultural, philosophical bend toward the dark side of existence became fashionable and was underscored by Friedrich Nietzsche's nihilist existentialism. Charles Baudelaire's *Fleurs du Mal*, for instance, and later Herman Hesse's mystical journeys were poetic expressions of this trend. But trips into the Void did not come to full bloom until Eastern and Western philosophies were more closely combined and experimentation with drug trips had reached an unprecedented level – during the post hippie period. As Jay Stevens wrote in *Storming Heaven: LSD and the American Dream,*[1] Aldous Huxley's perennial philosophy was a must-read among Haight-Ashbury hippies. Ultimately, it produced a less then expected effect, even for the author of altered states of consciousness himself. Stevens says, Huxley himself might have been "a trifle disturbed about the amount of occult chaff that was getting mixed in with the grains of perennial philosophy." Stevens continues:

> Although Huxley had predicted that LSD would awaken the Baby Boom's slumbering appetite for spiritual meaning, he hadn't anticipated what would happen once this hunger began searching for something to feed upon. . . in the Height, the perennial philosophy became heavily spiced with astrology, numerology, alchemy, black magic, voodoo; a crazy quilt of arcane practice and contemporary jargon that affronted the trained Western intellect's need to formalize, to abstract out a workable map from anarchic reality.[2]

In poetry, mythology, and religion, traveling to the underworld has been a fairly common practice. Numerous examples of it exist from Christ's three-day descent into hell, to Dante's journey and Faust's wild adventures during the Walpurgis Night. Some seekers went with the aid of a guide and others undertook the trip alone. Johann Wolfgang von Goethe, in *Faust*, let his hero undertake the journey twice. Faust's first trip brings him to the traditional place of evil spirits, the Blocksberg in the Harz Mountains. He undertakes this trip under the experienced guidance of Mephistopheles, the devil. During the second trip, in which Faust descends into the absolute Void, Mephistopheles stays behind. Each individual has to undertake this trip alone. Therefore considerable *angst* is connected with such a "deep self-exploration," because it can reveal ultimate isolation. In this isolation we may encounter what Stanislav Grof calls "the evil demiourg principle" in all its cultural forms. Evil, says Grof, "is a separating force in the universe. . . . ecstatic experiences of unification and consciousness expansion are often preceded by shattering encounters with the forces of darkness, in the form of evil archetypal figures, or passing through demonic screens. This is regularly associated with extreme emotional and physical suffering."[3]

The psychiatrist Grof, like few other scientists, has probed into the reality of altered states of consciousness. "Why is it," Grof asks that "in the process of deep self-exploration we reach a phase when we transcend our individual boundaries and connect with the collective unconscious and the history of our species?"[4] As an empirical scientist, Grof collects narrative accounts of subjects with pertinent experiences. Grof's results agree remarkably with Perspectivist epistemology. Experiential accounts span the gamut of those who believe that they have encountered devils, monsters, or deities, to those who found their journey ending in an absolute Void. The "evil demiourg principle," according to Grof, is a necessary part of all creation. The "negative mirror image" of the divine, says Grof:

> can be experienced in a purely abstract form or as a more or less concrete manifestation. Some people describe it as Cosmic Shadow, an immense field of ominous energy, endowed with consciousness, intelligence, destructive potential, and monstrous determination to cause chaos, suffering, and disaster. Others experience it as an anthropomorphic figure of immense proportions representing the all-pervading universal evil, or the Dark God.[5]

This "shattering confrontation with the dark side of existence," according to Grof, can "culminate in an encounter with a horrifying personification of universal evil." It is ultimately the result of "cosmic partitioning," of separating oneself from the source of all being. Grof's solution follows the experiential insight of Buddhist thought that the trip into the material world reveals the ultimate Void. In the experiential unification with the void, in the so-called Nirvana, the partitioning disappears and universal consciousness reveals its divine creativity.

The human predicament, says Grof, parallels that of a moviegoer. On a different level of existence, we made the decision to incarnate into this material body. As the moviegoer voluntarily enters the cinema and accepts the illusion as real, the conscious mind accepts this world as real, while the advanced mind realizes its illusionary status. Grof sees this ancient model verified by modern science and by philosophers such as Alfred North Whitehead. According to Grof,

> Whitehead calls the belief in enduring existence of separate material objects 'fallacy of misplaced concreteness.' According to him, the universe is composed of countless discontinuous bursts of experiential activity. The basic element of which the universe is made is not enduring substance, but moments of experience, called in his terminology actual occasions. This term applies to phenomena on all levels of reality, from subatomic particles to human souls. [6]

Therefore, just like in the movie theater, "none of the events from our everyday life, and for that matter, none of the situations that involve suffering and evil, are ultimately real in the sense we usually think about them and experience them."[7]

Dealing with ultimate separation, emptiness, and evil in such a way, declaring the whole world a virtual, make-believe reality, may provide a useful therapy for the anxiety-ridden individual to "find the way out of the fly bottle," to use a Wittgensteinian phrase. In the real world, however, the Buddhist solution leaves a multitude of ethical questions and deserves further investigation. Grof concedes that "this way of looking at creation can be very disturbing, in spite of the fact that it is based on very convincing personal experiences in holotropic states and generally compatible with scientific findings about the nature of reality."[8]

When thinking about the practical consequences of such visions, problems arise. Grof contends that "seeing the material world as 'virtual reality' and comparing human existence with a movie seems to trivialize life and make light of the depth of human suffering. It might appear that such a perspective denies the seriousness of human suffering and fosters an attitude of cynical indifference, where nothing really matters.[9]

Grof sees it as equally problematic to accept that "evil is an integral part of creation." This could be construed as "a justification for suspending any ethical constraints and for unlimited pursuit of egotistical goals."[10] We only have to recall the life story of one of Christianity's most revered saints, Augustine in his youth followed just that kind of a philosophy. Believing that human beings were a battleground of the cosmic forces of good and evil, he denied all responsibility for his actions. We can easily see how all kinds of cruelties against humanity can be excused as part of such a "cosmic game." When in the grand scheme of things, human suffering has lost its individual face, we can begin even to justify the holocaust or Stalin's terror. Executioners such as Robespierre, Mengele, or Stalin, when looking into the mirror, see not a bloody murderer but the great arm of history fulfilling its task.

Grof assures that the awareness of emptiness is not genuinely incompatible with love for creation, but no necessary connection exists between these two. What we take away from the experience of the Void largely depends on our psychological state and on the cultural/religious context. In recognizing the duality of the creative source, the Western enlightenment, encoded in the great monotheistic religions and in science, discouraged and even barred the individual seeker from experiencing or searching into the Void. The Eastern enlightenment, in contrast, has at its epicenter the experience of the Void. But in its more popularized forms, Buddhism, too, has largely given up the quest for ultimate emptiness by placing countless visual aids (called bhodisattvas) along the way to guide the seeking acolyte in a more tangible manner.

Central to the experience of the Void is the question of compassion. Does the experience with the Void encourage and increase compassion or does it leave the individual in an ultimate state of separation from the other?

So far we have only dealt with an individual's own personal search into the Void. A person may also encounter another individual who has ventured into the Void, experienced its destructive potential and became affected by it. This can result in a more objective encounter with evil, because the degree of destructiveness in the other is not of our making. Such encounters can be especially dangerous and difficult if they involve emotional attachment and entanglement, or even love.

Experiencing the depth of separation in the other, a shamanic journey into the soul or the mind of others, can be such a trip into darkness and evil. Malevolent thoughts might often fill the other, out to destroy the wandering mind. This is the story of Count Dracula. In a way, the Dracula story reverses the Christ story. Count Dracula dies with a curse of God on his lips. This condemns him to a life in limbo. Unable to find eternal rest, he spends his shadowy existence wandering the streets at night as a ghost. Only a loving soul can redeem him and give him eternal peace. The dark irony: the same loving soul that has the power to save him is also the ideal victim for his insatiable evil desires.

Unfortunately, the story of Dracula is not mere fantasy or as outlandish as it appears on the surface. Few people ever have a relationship with the evil one. Though, many people find themselves in close relationships with abusive spouses, and we are often inclined to call such abuse evil. Just as often, partners who are in love, feel that they can help their lover overcome the abusive behavior by remaining by his or her side.

In such a situation, Perspectivism might have found its limit. While in other relationships, a compassionate, loving exchange of minds and soul can only make the relationship prosper and grow, in an abusive relationship, under the influence of love, things can get worse. In such a case, abused love may devour the lover. Thousands of art works document this. Life, too, is filled with tragic stories of abuse.

In abusive relationships, the abused partner does best to distance herself from the abuser in order to find protection. Let a professional counselor assume the role of the healing shaman. A counselor can make the attempt to cure the ills of the abuser, without loosing his or her soul. Ideally, one individual should not even take on this healing effort alone but it should be a communal effort. Led by a trained professional, group therapy can achieve the desired result. Healing, especially deep psychological healing, works best in community. Just as it takes a village to raise a child, so it often takes a village to heal a broken character. Primal people knew this well; the shaman hardly ever performed his sessions in isolation, but involved the community and the tribe.

Today's hospital treatments of seriously ill patients often shut out friends and relatives, because the medical staff still looks upon healing as a mechanical process. This is even truer for character healing of inmates in prison. One of the main punishments in our maximum-security prisons is to isolate prisoners completely from human contact. No healing can take place in such isolation. In order to heal prisoners have little choice but to accept the prison population as their community. But the "communal healing" they receive among their fellow inmates often only drives them deeper into isolation and crime.

In the process of long-range healing, modern psychology has learned the value of support groups and supportive communities. In the physical and psychological healing of the terminally ill, research has also shown the importance of community.

The world is comprised of a balancing play of creation and destruction: order and chaos, harmony and disharmony. In this natural order, as Grof points out, the shadow side of existence has a legitimate place and will always exist. During his interviews, Grof found verification for this from many different sources. Even though we cannot completely eliminate the shadow side of existence and the archetypal forces, in future experimentation we must purposely nourish less destructive and less dangerous forms of expression for these archetypal principles. According to Grof, "it will be necessary to create appropriate contexts that would make it possible to honor these archetypal forces and to offer them alternative outlets that would enhance instead of destroy life."[11]

The Greeks instituted the Olympic Games as a legitimate outlet for the Dionysian spirit. The wild and chaotic celebrations of that god of ecstasy that often produced altered mind states and uncontrolled sexuality were no longer desirable in an organized and structured society. Similarly, a new partnership-oriented society must create new powerful rituals that could channel and re-focus the destructive and chaotic forces at the basis of existence and employ them again in the sustenance and enjoyment of life instead of denying their existence.

Grof suggests "safe internal channels of expressions" can be found "in powerful rituals involving non-ordinary states of consciousness, dynamic new art forms, or entertainment modalities using the technology of virtual reality."[12] On the way to developing new rituals we will have to take another look at our valuation of pleasure and pain, this elemental way with which nature directs and rewards its products.

Twenty

SACRED PLEASURE: RE-EVALUATING CULTURAL PRIORITIES

> Nature has placed mankind under the govern-
> ment of two sovereign masters, pain and pleas-
> ure. . . . They govern us in all we do, in all we
> say, in all we think: every effort we can make to
> throw off our subjection, will serve but to dem-
> onstrate and confirm it.
>
> Jeremy Bentham

In her recent book *Sacred Pleasure,* Riane Eisler calls for a radical reevaluation of pleasure and pain in modern society.[1] Pain and pleasure, she
says, play a fundamental role in the makeup of culture and society. In her
introduction, Eisler states "neither human society nor human history can be
understood without taking into account the very different ways a society can
use pain or pleasure to motivate human behavior."[2] Eisler says she "began to
see the central, though amazingly ignored, role pain and pleasure have had in
the evolution of culture, and even of life."[3]

Pain and pleasure have played a supreme part in the evolution of life.
To some degree, I believe, pleasure and pain is present at all levels of life.
For Transcendental Perspectivism that means both pleasure and pain are in
everything. The inside/out view that Nick Herbert postulates as a quintessential quality of all things, is therefore characterized, at all levels, by some
sense of pleasure and pain. At the level of atoms, molecules and quarks, or
even at the level of space/time quanta, this inside/out view may mean nothing
more than a "preferred state." Just like a dog has a preferred resting spot, so
do chemical elements. They have preferred states of connecting with other
elements. I am claiming that when these elementary particles move into a
preferred state, they experience excitement. In some rudimentary sense we
can call this pleasure. When groups of micro particles vibrate in unison, as
Roger Penrose and Stuart Hameroff claim in their description of orchestrated
reductions (ORCH R), new, different, and often qualitative stages of existence occur. This kind of self-orchestrated excitement, according to Penrose
and Hameroff, is at the core of what we perceive as the hierarchical development in evolution and life.[4]

A "scaled" image may again help us to visualize this model. From two
thousand feet above, a stampeding mass of people chasing a bull through the
streets of an ancient Spanish city appears like a flowing sea. To the far away
observer, they are like a moving stream within a sea of buildings. Viewed

from a distance, behavior appears uniform and without emotion. Without details such behavior appears predictable as well. But from within that group, we could hardly underestimate the sense of excitement and the extreme emotional high. We can find excitement and pleasure in the minds of each individual. Even though group movement can take over our personal movement and decisions, we never completely loose our sense of individually taking part in a collective action. The pleasure or the excitement is our own.

Moreover, we create a powerful feedback loop between our excitement and the excitement of the group. In such collective actions, something qualitatively new may occur. This may result in actions, for which the individual no longer has full responsibility. The group, we are inclined to say, "has acted as one." On rare occasions, this "acting as one" of a group may produce astounding evolutionary results. When the individual members of such a collective "decide" not to abandon the group again, but to remain one organism, a new individual state of evolution can manifest. I have called this evolutionary process "collective orchestration."

The power of Perspectivist imagination can help us recreate in our minds the extreme excitement of each person running through the streets chasing or being chased by a bull. Artistic renderings of the event usually attempt to recreate this feeling. Herein lies the power of art; it can bring distant moments into the present and make them available again for emotional identification. This is why Perspectivism goes hand-in-hand with creativity and art.

Considering the immense brutality that human beings have brought upon each other during the course of the twentieth century, we could quickly conclude that human beings have gone too far in acting out their emotions. Or, perhaps, such brutal acting-out demonstrates a lack of emotions, a frightening absence of compassion? Many considered World-War-I the war to end all wars, mostly because of the immense cruelty that it inflicted on millions of civilians. Many hoped that this would help end wars. We all know the result of that wishful thought.

Perhaps in recognition of the human inability to act without emotions, we have made killing in wars more automatic, more removed from direct human intervention, and more distant. We have turned killing into a game on a computer screen. Who can score the highest points? In the thousands of high-tech video arcades in the country our young people train to kill as a virtual activity. The military uses such video games as a training tool for soldiers. Once soldiers perceive the enemy as a dot on the screen, they do not need compassion and, often, it is no longer even possible. Losing our once-compassionate humanity is a highly sophisticated game that is not only part of the training in military camps, but is also a necessity in training good consumers.

Post-Kantian philosophers, in search for truth, chose creativity as the most promising arena where the individual could still meet the divine in a compassionate encounter. Friedrich Nietzsche saw this possibility. For him it was the only way out of mechanical formalism; it was a way out of hell, as one of his followers once said. In the conflict between mediocre society and the self, Nietzsche who in many ways was one of the prime promoters of the dominator philosophy chose the creative ego to transcend the boundaries of the beleaguered self and of society. The human Self became its own god. In this cataclysm, Nietzsche was bound to lose his mind, not because the self is not capable of becoming its own god, but because society and his contemporary culture did not allow it.

German sociologists such as Max Weber and Georg Simmel were influenced by Nietzsche's search for the creative divine within the Self. They observed the struggle between the individual and society as a never-ending epic in which we ultimately deal the shorter hand to the individual. Each individual, according to those early sociologists, creates new forms. Aesthetic forms are the legitimate offspring of human selfhood. But inevitably, once released into society, these forms take on an independent life. And again, inevitably, they come back to haunt and oppress the individual. They become so powerful, so distant from the individual person, and so alienated, as Karl Marx said, that the single person feels completely manipulated and powerless. Social forms, born from subjective creation, become objective social norms. In turn, they stifle and even murder the creative life of the individual and become tools for the dominator mentality to justify and maintain its existence.

Simmel, at the end of his life after World War I, saw no further chance for the individual to exist freely. He perceived rational explanations of social interaction as fiction. The powerless self, constituting itself only through its own creativity, is confronted with the totalitarian power of society. As the dominator model spirals to ever-higher levels, the power game becomes destructive, irrational, and ultimately suicidal.

The result of such social and institutional oppression, which in post-industrial society is ever-present, is an overabundance of pain: physical pain, neuroses of all kinds, mental, and psychic pain. Modern society has become a pain-focused society. As a culture we spend so much energy to alleviate and eliminate pain, mostly unsuccessfully, because our chemical remedies seldom cure the source of the pain. True to the objective philosophy from where modern medicine grew, we try to replace pain with some kind of a neutral state that we could somehow characterize as perfect functioning. Instead, we should look for a steady state of excitement, of heightened sensuality, a state of "wow," as the inventors of the modern empowerment movement have called it.

In *Pleasure and Pain,* the famous German neuroscientist Ernst Pöppel quotes Albert Einstein, who said: "Everything done and thought by human beings is directed toward the satisfaction of emotional needs and the elimination of pain."[5] This, according to Pöppel, is a fundamental principle of human life. According to Pöppel, his book "demonstrate[s] how indeed pleasure and pain are hidden in all our experiences, and sometimes they push only too evidently into the foreground." Pöppel begins with the assumption that every event (*Erlebnis*) is flavored by pleasure or pain. He says:

> A state of total disinterestedness (*Gleichgültigkeit*) is in my opinion something unnatural and foreign to the true essence of us humans as spiritual beings. Whether we observe, hear, feel, smell, or taste, whether we contemplate something, plan something, discuss and even research something, the subjective event is always more than the objective information about the real world or about an event in our own self. Every experience (*Erlebnis*) is from the onset always also pleasant or unpleasant, beautiful or ugly, pleasurable or painful, and in the extreme case, intoxicating or disgusting. [6]

Pöppel rejects here a traditional objectivist position in the human sciences. The German *Gleichgültigkeit* means "objectivity." The philosopher Immanuel Kant called such objectivity "disinterestedness." We can directly connect the Aristotelian ideal of balance and the Kantian concept of disinterestedness. Kant, this pivotal German schoolmaster and philosopher had declared disinterestedness as the voucher of authenticity for morality, art, and science.

In dealing with judgments of morality, art and especially science, a need for objectivity exists. In order to reach a fair assessment, we need to compare, find standards, and judge. But all this must not loose sight of compassion and care. Disinterestedness, lacking compassion and care turns into a lifeless, cruel and dead objectivity. Such disinterestedness has proven to be not the solution but the culprit. Robbed of the creative fire, the "objective" eye of the scientist has turned nature into a lifeless machine as Donald Schoen pointed out in his book *The Reflective Practitioner*.[7] Artists, too, were required by Kantian aesthetics to become disinterested. They became manipulators of style and form, which made them easy prey for commercial exploitation. Moralists and their modern version of sociologists and social scientists, remain number crunchers and interpreters of norms. Other scientists became amoral inventors and operators of deathly machines. All of them became willing defenders of the status quo – as long as the pay is right.

Our survival demands that we, as human beings, understand how our life connects intrinsically to the natural world, and we need to reevaluate this connection. Any ethical consideration must grow out of this cosmic connectedness of all life. Earlier, I elaborated on the reasons for the neglect of pain and pleasure as motivators for cultural development in Western societies. The Greeks relegated feelings to the lower, the animal part of the human existence. As human beings became more rational they overcame these momentary feelings and focused on more permanent achievements. Such achievements, the Greeks believed, are generally based on logical considerations.

For the Greeks, reason was the charioteer who guides the unruly horses of emotion and spirit in the right direction. In this, they saw the guarantee for an action not to end up in foolhardiness, gluttony, or similar excesses. Achieving the right balance remained the noble goal for the Greek classical thinkers. Their art and architecture superbly exemplifies this goal.

Greek moral thought (mostly shaped by Aristotle) however, provided for a less fortunate marriage between emotion and reason. Once they established a hierarchy between emotion and reason (with reason at the apex), it was only a matter of degree to eliminate emotions completely. An individual could only assess happiness at the end of our life. Reason should guide every action in between, because emotions inevitably lead human beings astray. While we could interpret Aristotle's works in different ways, this was the reading that Aristotle's ethics received from Christian interpreters. It also became the standard among American Aristotelians such as Mortimer Adler, who exerted a major influence on American conservative thought. Throughout the Christian occident and in agreement with biblical orthodoxy, Christians began to see emotional devotion as the work of Satan in an evil world. American neo-conservatives, inspired by Greek thought, developed a specific brand of Protestant work ethic that views emotions as distracting from the right path of good and decent work. In spite of a whole profession dealing with emotions, many reach for emotional fulfillment fleetingly. Practitioners of higher intellect, universities and colleges, places of learning, and theories of educational strategies, are frighteningly bare of emotional training (at least in regards to pleasure, not so much in regards to pain).

Our public educational institutions almost eagerly provide pain in a myriad of disguises. For example, even though corporeal punishment has been outlawed in most American institutions, we frequently hear the cry to re-instate it. Only ten years ago, the practice of paddling a child was still a recognized form of punishment in many American schools. In Michigan, where we brought up our five sons, schools only had to send a regulatory note to the parents. This memo detailed the length of the stick and the way the enforcer would administer the punishment. It even included a guarantee that at least one other person besides the punisher would oversee the punishment, usually the principal.

The administration of pain in our public school systems today is often more subtle, but not less cruel. To give an example: in an elementary school in a suburb of Chicago, where we moved after leaving our farm in Michigan, students were prepared for months for outdoor education days. It was billed as the highlight of the school year – the highlight of the children's stay in the school. The outdoor education program lasts three days. Students go to a forest preserve campground and spend hours and presumably days full of fun activities. The teachers carefully prepare the activities to provide education as well.

The best part for boys and girls during outdoor education days is the evening around the bonfire. The time my son took part in this activity, a small group of students (boys) had "misbehaved." Some of them had entered a cabin, locked and bolted the door from the inside, and then had exited through a window, so the rightful occupants of the cabin could not gain easy access. Compared with school shootings and other random violence, it was a harmless prank. The way the teachers dealt with the situation reveals the underlying educational spirit that can create further frustration for school children. I believe it also has the potential to foster violent reactions in later years. Since none of the boys came forward to "confess" to the deed, the educators excluded all boys from the evening bonfire – even though only a handful had committed the "crime." While the girls sat around the fire and had fun, the boys had to stay inside. The principal spent the whole time lecturing them on proper behavior. Afterwards, I asked my nine-year-old to describe the most exciting thing during outdoor education. He dryly said, "A dead rat floating on top of the swimming pool."

We could extend the list of such incidences, anecdotal as they may be, into a book. Underlying them is the general perception, that education cannot be fun, as life is not fun. Instead life is a continuous fight for superiority, survival, and discipline. We receive fun as the reward for work well done. We must always connect work with sweat. For this is the sanction of the Holy Bible: when work appears fun, something is wrong with it.

This may also tell us why employees that have jobs that provide some emotional satisfaction, as teaching often does, are dismally underpaid. You need less pay for work that is also fun. The more boring and alienated your job is, the higher the monetary rewards. After firing thirty thousand people in the name of downsizing, the corporate manager of a large telecommunication company recently received a pay raise of eighty thousand dollars.

We can find obvious exceptions to this rule. A minute minority in our society receives tremendously high salaries while doing the work they love to do. I am talking of those highly paid individuals we call stars: athletes, movie stars, and some media workers. Most often, they pay for the price of stardom with the total loss of their private lives. A hungry public registers and marks any emotional move they make. But for each star who "makes it," a thousand others in the industry don't. And they often work for minimum wages while pursuing the occupation they love.

The lack of pleasure in education is complemented by an overabundance of "pleasure for sale" in the market place. Not that the marketplace itself is a pleasant home, because of its extreme hostility and cutthroat competition. To immerse oneself in its activities is like taking part in an all-out war, as Gekko in the movie *Wallstreet* said so poignantly.

The more appropriate image to characterize the marketplace is that of a brothel. If consumer capitalism is to work, then pleasure must remain a commodity. In consumerism, we teach our children that pleasure is for sale. The real and true educational lesson should be that pleasure is inside each of us and in our relationships with each other. But we seldom teach that lesson. Children should learn that they do not need to buy pleasure. Their birthright is to have fun with whatever they do. It is a vital ingredient for survival. But this attitude would be counterproductive in a growth-oriented consumer world. So we hide the real source of pleasure and fun, and instead we spend all our energy (and bitterly earned money) to buy pleasure and avoid pain. To what avail? Is it only to reach a state of equanimity, a state of disinterested objectivity, and a state of passionless boredom? In as much as we have involved our educational system in this process, education is bound to fail in its real purpose: survival and happiness.

The relative short space dedicated to the subject of pleasure in most modern encyclopedias indicates that the classical philosophical approach to pleasure still abounds today. The famous *Encyclopedia Britannica* deals with pain in over twenty articles, mostly as a physiological phenomenon. Pain is in need of elimination, often through chemical intervention. The encyclopedia only deals with the concept of pleasure in a few short paragraphs. As Riane Eisler observed, our culture has made pain more sacred than pleasure. She says, "the capacity to inflict pain, rather than to give pleasure, has been idealized in so many of our epics and classics."[8]

Even a philosopher such as Epicurus (who believed that pleasure is the supreme good and main goal of life) ultimately chose intellectual pleasures over sensual ones. Sensual pleasures, Epicurus said, tend to disturb the peace of mind. True happiness is the serenity resulting from the conquest of fear of the gods, death, and the life thereafter. We can only find happiness when we rid ourselves of such fears. Sensual pleasures seldom bring such happiness. By discrediting sensual pleasures and immediate satisfaction as insecure, unreliable, and disturbing, Epicurus concurred with Aristotle. He postponed the achievement of happiness to some distant future, just as Aristotle did. To overcome the fear of death, many Epicureans chose to die by their own hand. What a strange solution to a perceived problem!

In Christianity, we could not even find real pleasure in this world at all, but in a distant heaven. Aristotle's concept of happiness, as Mortimer Adler understands it, is a heaven in disguise, an eternal bliss, achievable only after life ends. Promising happiness as an unalienable right but making it impossible to achieve in a lifetime offers the perfect ideology to fit a consumption-oriented, dominator world.

Ever since our philosophical, religious, and economic models have led us to lose sight of pleasure as a healthy, whole, and happiness-promoting activity, we have increased our focus on pain. Whenever past cultures became fixated by pain and lost sight of real pleasures that life gives, they could not withstand the evolutionary game and soon disappeared. When the Roman Empire had run its course Aristotle's so-called masses "who live the life of mere beasts" as Aristotle put it, replaced the degenerated civilization. Throughout history, common people again and again rose from the bottom and regenerated a decadent culture, often by sweeping it off the face of the globe in a violent revolution. The danger we face today: our global culture transfixed by pain could likely take down all of humanity in a final cataclysm.

Our bodies yearn for health and no pain. When our bodies are healthy, we experience a happy daily existence. As psychologists have found, physical and mental pain often results from a continuous lack of pleasurable moments. When constant pains plague us, we have a miserable existence. Then we perceive the world in which we live as the construction of an evil demon.

The Christian Middle Ages taught the evils of the human body, which they chastised and bound into a tight corset legitimized by the Church and the bible. Even though the history of the Christian West is marked by waves of revolt against these unnatural restrictions, we still feel the result of these doctrines today in our cultural and especially educational inadequacies. In the culture at large, gigantic industries use pain and pleasure as tools to sell products. In terms of our enlightened and spiritual life, those feelings that have the potential of connecting us with the Sacred have lost nearly all relevance.

With the attempt to control excesses of immediate pleasure and pain, Western culture has nearly completely eliminated pleasure as a tool of learning. Through pain and pleasure the human animal, like any other creature in this world, adjusts to life's demands. In the name of rationalism and of science, pleasure (and with it the elements of fun and joy) has been all but eliminated from our educational process. Pleasure and pain have become the cynical tools of an "enlightened" elite to control, manipulate, and exploit the masses. Even education, which could bring this enlightenment to the people, teaches them that they must overcome pleasure and pain if they want to succeed in a rational world.

The new picture that emerges from Perspectivist philosophy puts emphasis on the necessity to experience pleasure and happiness as a daily, even hourly practice. The picture of a newly-developing holistic medicine stresses the need for pleasurable experiences, happiness, and laughter as a vehicle to good mental and physical health. Besides musical and creative dramatics training early childhood education should teach children how to gain happiness and pleasure from fully completing a task as the Waldorf and Steiner schools suggested and practiced. Instead in our public schools children are interrupted in their work by hourly bells and moved on to a new subject regardless of their individual stage of completion. This is an outdated model shaped after the conveyer belt of the industrial age.

Perspectivism stresses the good and happy feelings that come from reaching a goal, physically or intellectually. Finishing a task, completing something, bringing a problem to its solution, somehow makes us feel good. Such completeness also produces happiness. Our educational systems must take advantage of this.

We can assume that the Minoans had the experience of happiness and pleasure available on a daily basis. For the Greeks, this way of life had faded into a dim memory; therefore, they called the Minoan age the Golden one. As pleasure became disconnected from the experience of the Sacred, direct contact with the gods was interrupted. In Aristotle's *Poetics*, one of art's roles was to re-establish fractured communication with the gods. This happened for the spectator during the cathartic moment, when the experience of the divine influence on human affairs cleanses the emotions. The simple and naive happiness of the Golden Age gave way to a reflective, melancholic sense of unity with the divine. The Dionysian yielded to the Apollonian, to use Nietzsche's terms.

The church's influence further diminished the sacred experience of the divine in the aesthetic catharsis. It eventually turned into a disciplined exercise of "making the right choices." The arts, too, had to turn away from a celebration of the fullness of life and were turned into moralizing agents. Under the influence of science, art evolved into a showcase for social conditions. Finally, capitalist consumerism turned the arts into a vehicle to sell goods. Ever-increasing secularization severed the arts further and further from their origin in the practical experience of the divine. We lost the spiritual dimension of art, the experience of human connectedness with the whole universe, forever.

While first the separation of art from the divine might have been experienced as a liberation from ancient shackles of dogmatism, secular art as a totally "free" art was only too willing to go into the service of another master, the promotion of consumption. Avant-garde art, as an art form perhaps truly free of all masters, subsisted for a while only at the bare fringes of society. But whenever it became successful, the mainstream quickly co-opted it. With a few exceptions, it joined the establishment and was put in service again, the service of profit and wealth.

Today, the commercial art industry, mostly unrestrained by religious and ethical considerations, uses the results of newest psychological, physiological, and biological research to influence people in their choices of consumption of goods and products. Behaviorist psychologists long knew how to manipulate people's perceptions of needs and wants through purposefully administered pleasure and pain. They easily swept aside moral deliberations when it came to maximizing profits. That way we could all live a "pleasure-filled" if not perfectly happy life. While promising personal happiness, the happiness of the dominator is dished out at whim and for pay. We no longer have happiness as our natural right, but it comes as a reward for work, in exchange for money. Pleasure becomes pleasure for sale.

In *Sacred Pleasure,* Eisler proposes to re-ground the experience of happiness in our bodies. She says that we need a major revolution in consciousness, to accomplish the shift from a dominator culture to a culture of partnership. According to Eisler,

> The dominator and partnership models have for the whole span of social and cultural evolution been two basic "attractors" for social and ideological organization. Drawing from chaos theory and other contemporary scientific theories that show how living systems can undergo transformative change in a relatively short time during states of extreme disequilibrium, *cultural transformation theory* shows how these same principles apply to social systems. . . . proposes that in our chaotic time of escalating disequilibrium we have the possibility of another fundamental cultural shift: this time in a partnership rather than dominator direction.[9]

The dominator system has institutionalized and sacralized pain. Much of what we allow to happen in our time, says Eisler, "can be seen as an attempt to shift to a system where pleasure – not in the sense of short-term escape or distraction, but in the sense of healthy long-term fulfillment – can instead be institutionalized, and even sacralized."[10]

In the following chapters I will show how pleasurable experiences can become a vital ingredient for good learning.

Twenty-One

LIFE CONTROL AND SELF-EMPOWERMENT: CAN PERSPECTIVIST TECHNIQUES REVERSE THE COURSE OF SELF-DESTRUCTION?

> Deep within man dwell those slumbering powers; powers that would astonish him, that he never dreamed of possessing; forces that would revolutionize his life if aroused and put into action.
>
> Orison Swett Marden

During a three-day seminar, conducted by the Robbins Research Institute, I learned how heightened sensitivity and a steady state of excitement could be used to create a "state of wow." In the course *Unleash the Power Within,* the charismatic Anthony Robbins demonstrates how to use empowerment techniques to educate ourselves. Robbins leads people out of the dark past and makes their future appear bright and hopeful.

When I signed up for the course I was extremely skeptical. My son had urged and persuaded me to come along. He himself had studied empowerment techniques for many years. I was skeptical for several reasons.

Most of these enterprises are surrounded by commercialism. This becomes evident by the way they advertise through so-called "infomercials" on cable television. I am usually appalled by everything connected with unsolicited sales whether by phone or any other medium. For the average consumer empowerment seminars generally are far too expensive.

Secondly, a strong sense of "guruism" permeates this and similar movements, since they generally focus on the personality of one charismatic leader. As a devout individualist trained in Western enlightenment, I have an aversion for following a guru.

The idea of teaching techniques to manipulate the subconscious mind also evokes all kinds of red flags in me. As a German of the post-World-War-II generation, I have been endowed with a healthy dose of anti-fascist education. The mere possibility of making such manipulative techniques available sends shivers down my spine.

My earlier experiences with the empowerment movement had done little to dispel my suspicion. During the seventies, when the whole empowerment movement got underway, I learned from one of my students about EST, a self empowerment group. What I heard aroused my suspicions. It seemed like a manipulative scheme that, at best, was out to get people's money, with not much in return; at worst, it seemed a dark scheme of manipulative domination, a sign of impending fascism. The personality of EST's leader, Werner Erhard, seemed dictatorial and intimidating. Another student of mine familiarized me with a book by Sheldon D. Glass, *Life-Control: How to Master the Phases of Success.* At the time a popular empowerment guru, Glass, offered his followers total control over their lives. He began his best-selling book saying: "Imagine what it would be like if you were able to predict, with complete accuracy, everything that would happen to you. Suppose you had every part of your life completely under control – that your every success was the result of your own careful and systematic planning, and that no mishap would ever catch you unaware."[1]

Glass provides a typical example of a rationalist, cognitive approach to empowerment that grew out of the Western enlightenment model. The approach is super-structured and organized. People following this venue put every detail in a little box and leave nothing to chance. If this method succeeds it tends to achieve super efficiency, but ultimately lacks creativity. Followers become legions of Salieries, who might end up arguing with God about endowing slops like Amadeus with all that genius. (In Mozart's time, Salieri was a diligent and even successful composer, who was in competition with the young Mozart and envied his genius.) Many psychologists in the academic world today still favor this cognitive approach.

Glass begins with the questionable assumption that most human beings want complete and absolute control over their lives. Only then can they obtain true happiness. I perceive such a premise as the surest recipe for failure. Many people, I believe, exist quite comfortably with only a limited control over their lives. As an artist, I learned to trust in the faculties of my subconscious mind. Academically, I was trained in the tradition of continental rationalism. But I also learned to use Georg Wilhelm Friedrich Hegel's dialectic and Adorno's negative aesthetics as theoretical justifications for a creative trust in the power of the subconscious mind and the wisdom of nature. While writing my first book, *The Dice-Playing God,* I had an extended discussion with my editor who would not accept the phrase: "wisdom of nature." From a traditional, rationalist perspective, nature works automatically, while wisdom requires a conscious mind and logical thinking. Today we have changed the paradigm; we accept much more readily the idea that nature has wisdom.

The highest command of the European enlightenment was to take charge of your life. But a difference exists between taking charge of those things that we can influence or control and in assuming that we take total control over everything. This makes the presumption that we can control everything. We assume God's perspective while the rest remains a machine universe, ready for us to manipulate and control.

Last year, I trained as an instructor for a leadership course compiled by the National Honors Society *Phi Theta Kappa.* Again, I felt an overwhelming sense of applying rational solutions to all personal problems. The trainers assumed that once we have a rational awareness of the reasons for acting in a specific way, that we should also act that way. This assumption, I believe, is unrealistic and often times plainly wrong. Many times, even when faced with survival decisions, people know what they should do, but lack the energy, will, or motivation to do it. Even though many would like to quit smoking and know all the reasons why they should, they lack inner motivation and strength. Academic psychology, grown out of and influenced by the Western rationalistic paradigm, has little to offer in regards to deep motivation.

This is true for individuals and also for the whole of humanity. The World Watch Institute found that, based on empirical science and from a rational point of view, we well-understand all the reasons that point to the destruction of planet earth. Humanity knows that once we render this green planet uninhabitable (as a result of human mismanagement and waste) we have no convenient planet to escape to. In other words, we know all the reasons, why we should stop the destruction, but we lack the collective will to do so. We do not know how to motivate ourselves.

A giant industry exists that is completely occupied and absorbed with techniques of persuasion and motivation. This industry has become so powerful that it virtually controls every aspect of our lives – on a local as well as a global level. It not only designs what we wear, the kind of transportation we use, how we furnish our homes, which music we listen to, and how we spend our vacations. This industry also directs the course of our social lives. It designs and manipulates public opinion and even politics. It ultimately tells us what to think. This powerful industry is by no means homogeneous, but as diverse as the clientele it serves. It is an industry driven by the idea of service, serving any master who will pay the price.

This selling out is especially ominous in the field of politics. Not infrequently political strategists switch between parties or, less often perhaps, serve candidates of adversary parties simultaneously. For instance, the Russian president Boris Yeltsin paid a team of American political strategists to assist him with the first democratically organized elections in that country after the iron curtain came down. Yeltsin won the election. One of president Bill Clinton's most influential advisors, Richard Morris, had previously been an advisor to Jesse Helms, an ultra-conservative politician.

Efficiency and depth of research make the techniques of the political and advertising industries so effective. With empirical precision, psychologists determine what the public wants. They then design a product to fulfill that need. In the democratic political process such a "dialogical" approach may on the surface be appropriate. Ironically, it results in a subtle, but obvious, manipulation of minority views. Moreover, it renders politicians into populist puppets. Far from trying to win the electorate with a defined political agenda, these strategists first conduct in-depth studies of what the populace wants to hear. Then they adjust their client's message to match the profile of popular opinion as closely as possible. Everything becomes packaging and the underlying truth does not matter. The people who exercise this total relativism have not hidden it from the public. This has contributed to the complete cynicism with which many view the American political process.

The experts of this industry base their strategies and techniques on extensive research into the ways we can manipulate the human mind to receive messages. Often these messages operate on a subliminal level and achieve their effects without the manipulated subject becoming fully aware. Far from ignoring the emotional part of the human psyche, these experts know that the brain receives and retains informative messages if they are tagged to a pleasant – or in some cases even unpleasant – impression. The emotionally expressive context or marker becomes the key to learning. Emotions, in other words, provide the key to retaining and remembering information. They make us want things, and therefore they become the solution to the question how to sell goods. Nobody knows this better than the commercial industry. This controlling industry must continuously create new needs and wants and then persuade the customer to fulfill these needs by buying their client's product. To this end, the commercial industry has studied the human psyche more thoroughly than any academic department. Unimpeded by past history, the leaders of this powerful industry are only motivated by what works. It is thoroughly pragmatic. But this pragmatism only focuses on short-term efficiency. Hardly ever does it have a long-range goal – other than maximizing profit.

Cross-cultural sensitivity, for instance, has become fashionable, and we have increasingly interjected it in teaching schedules. Often we even teach it as a separate subject. We do this, not just because someone thinks that it is the right and human thing to do, to foster mutual understanding. But we do it because we must know the customs of these countries and their culture in order to sell our products in foreign countries.

From prior readings, I knew that Robbins (who has been advisor to many business giants, presidents, and royalty) bases his empowerment techniques on deep conscious and subconscious manipulation and conditioning. This, then, was my strongest concern. If these techniques are made available to political opportunists and bandits, a new fascism could await us just around the corner.

During the seminar I learned among many other things the following:

Methods and techniques to influence and manipulate the subconscious mind are well known and documented. The advertising industry and government agencies already widely use these methods, both domestically and abroad. These agencies often employ public relations firms to reach the minds and lives of their constituencies.

The larger social and political powers have used these effective and simple methods for their purposes. The only way to prevent these agents from using these methods for exploitation is by increasing the public's awareness of them. By learning how to use these techniques on a personal level we can empower ourselves to prevent abuse of these techniques by authorities on a large scale.

Therefore these methods of subliminal manipulation are a vital and necessary link to promote true democracy. On a large scale this knowledge will set into motion what I call the third enlightenment, the enlightenment of the Body. Robbins calls the connection between pleasure, learning, and empowerment the E^3 Revolution: Entertainment, Education, Empowerment.

Twenty-Two

THE E³ REVOLUTION: ENTERTAINMENT, EDUCATION, EMPOWERMENT

> Maybe you should be asking yourselves, "How am I going to live the next ten years of my life? How am I going to live today in order to create the tomorrow I am committed to? What am I going to stand for from now on?"
>
> Anthony Robbins

Reservations aside, Anthony Robbins has redefined the link between emotions and education, which Greek rationalism and the Protestant work ethic originally had severed. We must reintroduce this vital connection into education if we want it to compete effectively in a child's mind with the constant bombardment of commercial advertisement.

Our current educational system presents work as serious, hard, and uncompromising. Children receive fun as a reward for work done. If work is not completed, fun is taken away. In the real world we get paid for hard work and then use this money for buying fun. The essential message a child learns in our current educational system is this: work is hard and is rewarded by fun and pleasure. During instructional sessions teachers often minimize children's emotional involvement. The student must sit perfectly still in neatly arranged rows of chairs and desks while a serious teacher instructs somber material, often in boring lectures. The students may only talk with the teacher's permission. Teachers do not permit socializing at all. Only during recess can the students have time for relaxation and fun, and the administrators often cut this to a minimum. When a student misbehaves (often no more than expressing a spontaneous feeling) the teacher takes away recess time. Teachers often use this punishment for work done in an untimely manner. A child's natural reaction is to revolt against such a boredom and rigor. But this is exactly the lesson they must learn: life is treachery and jobs are boring. If you accept this reality, you get rewarded with a good paycheck, which, in turn, enables you to buy fun.

Primal societies used a measure of fun and entertainment in all work (even during the most repetitive task). When slaves were acculturated to American society they continued this combination of enjoyment and work, which they had brought over from Africa. The songs that accompanied their fieldwork integrated this part of their tribal heritage into their slave existence. White slave-owners realized that the slaves would work more efficiently

when they were allowed the pleasure of singing, and therefore did not interfere much with the singing. From these beginning spirituals evolved.

Today, in the larger American society, employers are not inclined to
sanction singing during work time; if workers try to ease the burden of repetitive work employers are ready to enforce the status quo with a catalogue
of ethical taboos and punishments.

Neurolinguistic programming informs us that learning happens more effectively when tagged onto an emotional marker. This makes sense from a
historical, evolutionary perspective. Our emotions are aroused in dangerous,
life- threatening situations. Our chance to survive depends on our quick responses. When I encounter the same situation again, I react better if I can
quickly recall the responses that saved my life. These responses occur almost
automatically. The Eastern arts of self-defense make use of this connection.
In Karate training, teachers choreograph defensive responses until they become automatic. Then the students do not need a planning strategy by the
self-conscious mind to recall them. When needed, martial artists can perform
them with the spontaneity of a dance.

On the surface, the three-day fire walk seminar I participated in was
like a giant party. More than a thousand people participated. When my son
and I arrived at the convention center in suburban Chicago, people crowded
the hallways, waiting to gain access. Next to me in line was a father from
New York who had participated in the same seminar for the sixth time. He
had brought his twelve-year-old son along to give him an experience of this
empowerment party as well.

Loud pop music played in set intervals. Youthful dancers animated the
audience to participate in rhythmic movement. "Motion is emotion" is one of
Robbins's golden rules. We did little, if anything, without accompanying
rhythmical movement. Colorful lighting heightened the sense of a festive
occasion. During and in-between stretch exercises, instruction and learning
took place. The whole process challenged traditional assumptions of education and set new standards for learning. Robbins is not only a master enter-
tainer; he sets excels as a successful public speaker as well. His conversa-
tional lecture is extremely entertaining and accessible. He avoids big words
and difficult lingo, which academic speakers often use in abundance. Robbins entertains as well as provides his knowledge. Most of all, he appears to
genuinely care and listen. His excitement sweeps over his audience, until he
engages most people in a celebrative mood. Contrasting with many academic
lectures, Robbins's presentation complies with simple statistical findings
about retention by the average student. Statistics say that the average adult
retains: "10% of what he or she reads, 20% of what he or she hears, 30% of
what he or she sees, 50% of what he or she hears and sees, 70% of what he or
she says and hears and sees, 90% of what he or she says and does and hears
and sees."[1]

Participants in Robbins's seminars hear, speak, repeat, see, visualize and often also act out. These are the optimal ways of presenting material for retention.

A few days after this seminar, I took part in a public middle school awards ceremony for one of my sons. The two principals and the dean of discipline patrolled up and down the isles spotting every slightest disturbance, intervening and stopping it immediately. Teachers herded silent rows of children in, and they filed into their uncomfortable seats. The students had absolutely no place for spontaneity and there was little excitement. The whole scene reminded me of a prison. This is education in one of the wealthiest suburban schools of America.

Many schools have installed metal detectors to prevent students from bringing weapons to school. Some consider even a fingernail file a weapon. Though we generally consider indiscriminate searches unconstitutional, they are common in public schools. Two out of every five students will get into a fight. What is wrong with this picture?

Teachers expect and force children to sit nearly motionless in their seats. During learning they focus on only training the mind. The emotional landscape of our young people is often a wasteland, marked by broken families and callused through the intake of perpetual TV violence.

Robbins's strategy reconnects body and mind. His methodology presupposes that the mind cannot learn without an accompanying pleasurable physical experience. We call this "experiential learning." The effectiveness of this type of learning has widely been documented. Periodically we attempted to use it in public education. One of America's great educators, John Dewey, ardently defended experiential education. But by and large, teachers and administrators have not effectively adopted experiential learning for use in the classroom. In an environment driven by output numbers, the difficulty of grading and accounting makes experiential learning so unattractive.

Perspectivist epistemology suggests that learning does not take place in an isolated organ called brain while the rest of the body exists superfluously or even as a hindrance. The process of learning involves the whole body. Each organ learns when the brain learns. When in a learning process, we only exercise part of the brain and when in the classroom, we teach only abstract concepts, the rest of our physical being remains unattached, disinterested, and bored. According to the new science of neurolinguistic programming, which underlies Robbins's techniques, we associate a powerful signal that combines the physical experience with the mental one within a student's memory. In a traditional classroom students store the experience of the informational material in the brain with the associated boredom of the rest of the body. The brain concludes that the material itself is boring. Robbins teaches that we need to activate each cell and neuron in our body for good learning to take place.

The human animal is most alert in life threatening situations. In such situations, every fiber of our body tenses. We pay attention. Such situations exert a powerful influence on our memory. Second only to life threatening situations are fun filled, exciting situations. These, too, leave powerful marks in our memory that we can recall and relive later. Robbins's empowerment techniques make use of this fact. Our whole body must vibrate to allow effective learning. That is what happened during the fire walk seminar, and it should become a key ingredient in any future education.

Twenty-Three

EMOTIONAL INTELLIGENCE: THE THIRD ENLIGHTENMENT

> The only questions worth asking today are
> whether humans are going to have any emotions
> tomorrow, and what the quality of life will be if
> the answer is no.
>
> Lester Bangs

If a quantum animistic operational ontology is the foundation of the third enlightenment, emotional intelligence is its catalyst. In this book, I tried to advance the basic knowledge of the world as body, mind, and consciousness. This will lead humanity to a new level of awareness that includes full scientific knowledge of us as emotional beings. I have come to call this new awareness the third enlightenment. Theoretical and ontological considerations, however, were only one part of my research. The other component is comprised of strategies, especially when it comes to getting in touch with our emotions. I mark these strategies by their radical focus on emotional involvement and happiness.

Western medicine, to give one example, has been traditionally concerned with developing scientific and rational techniques to prolong life. In this it has been extremely successful. Under the new paradigm medical science puts a new emphasis on the quality of life. Human life, prolonged by technical means, and without a strong focus on qualitative measures, can become miserable. In its 1997 general meeting, the American Medical Association adopted a resolution that would help to acquaint and train doctors in more effective pain management. It also teaches them a more accepting attitude in the management of death and dying.

This new sensitivity, a deep and sincere care for the quality of life, must extend beyond medical science and become an intrinsic part of all fields of the scientific enterprise. While a critical analysis of Western civilization uncovered an emphasis on rational survival, with all its shortcomings, the third enlightenment will stress the importance of emotional survival. Emotional survival must become a constitutive part of all sectors of our lives, a pivotal element of family and community life. We must practice it in education, art, and in the entertainment industry.

In his groundbreaking book *Emotional Intelligence: Why It Can Matter More Than IQ*,[1] Daniel Goleman observed an "uptick in emotional ineptitude, desperation, and recklessness in our families, our communities, and our collective lives." This, Goleman said, couples with a visible "disintegration of civility and safety, an onslaught of mean-spirited impulse running amok."[2] While tracking the progress of our scientific understanding of the realm of the irrational, Goleman, a science writer for the *New York Times* and senior editor of *Psychology Today*, found that despite its bad news, the last decade has seen "an unparalleled burst of scientific studies of emotion."[3] New brain-imaging technologies allowed us to see the brain at work. "For the first time," says Goleman, can we see "what has always been a source of deep mystery: exactly how this intricate mass of cells operates while we think and feel, imagine and dream."[4] Goleman asserts: "This flood of neuro-biological data lets us understand more clearly than ever how the brain's centers for emotion move us to rage or to tears, and how more ancient parts of the brain, which stir us to make war as well as love, are channeled for better or worse. This unprecedented clarity on the workings of emotions and their failings brings into focus some fresh remedies for our collective emotional crisis."[5]

Goleman's book collects such remedies. He offers strategies and techniques to enhance our emotional development and well-being. Much of this has to start at an early age; but we should continue to pursue our emotional training for the rest of our lives. In the chapter on "Schooling the Emotions," Goleman cites educational projects and schools around the nation where teachers have successfully practiced emotional training for years. In these schools, says Goleman, "teachers and students focus on the emotional fabric of a child's life – a focus that is determinedly ignored in almost every other classroom in America."[6]

Schools that have an interest in emotional learning should, according to Goleman, begin by instituting "an ongoing series of school-based prevention programs, each targeting a specific problem: teen smoking, drug abuse, pregnancy, dropping out, and most recently violence." Such programs, however, become increasingly more effective if they "teach a core of emotional and social competencies, such as impulse control, managing anger, and finding creative solutions to social predicaments."[7] Different from information and retention of facts, teachers must repeat emotional learning over and over again until it becomes ingrained in a child's daily behavior. According to Goleman, "as experiences are repeated over and over, the brain reflects them as strengthened pathways, neural habits to apply in times of duress, frustration, hurt. And while the everyday substance of emotional literacy classes may look mundane, the outcome – decent human beings – is more critical to our future than ever."[8]

For instance, under the general title of Self-Science and included in their basic science curriculum, these schools teach classes in cooperation. Teachers devote other sessions in Self-Science to conflict-resolution. Here Goleman finds that "the point is not to avoid conflict completely, but to resolve disagreement and resentment before it spirals into an out-and-out fight." This devotes much time to the development of proper linguistic and communicational ability. Being assertive, listening actively to each other, making eye contact, interpreting silent cues, such psychological tools for these boys become "more than just empty phrases on a quiz – they become ways of reacting that the boys can draw on at those moments when they need them most urgently."[9]

A vital part of social ability, according to Goleman:

> is empathy, understanding others' feelings and taking their perspective, and respecting differences in how people feel about things. Relationships are a major focus, including learning to be a good listener and question-asker; distinguishing between what someone says or does and your own reactions and judgments; being assertive rather than angry and passive; and learning the arts of cooperation, conflict resolution, and negotiating compromise.[10]

Not by coincidence, Perspectivists take these same ideas as the main values and goals of Perspectivism. Consistent training in emotional intelligence is a long-term positive conditioning of each individual's behavior toward altruism, cooperation, and peacefulness. This was without any doubt one of the main goals of most human communities at all times. Whether these communities were nomadic groups, farming villages with their extended family structures, or the nuclear family of the industrial age, as a major part of their upbringing, members of a group have always tried to teach their offspring how to get along with each other. As we have learned from observation of animal groups, this holds true for groups of primates and other animals.

As we have seen without a doubt, the tendency to aggression is part of the human physiological and psychological makeup. This is especially true for the male child. From ancient times, we aggressively respond to enemy attacks; this response is "hardwired" into our brain, as we commonly say. But the term "hardwired" is a relic from the machine paradigm, the time when the human body and the brain's responses were seen as a machine or computer. This gives the false impression that we cannot change; because if a machine is hardwired, it cannot change its behavior. The human "machine" is different: we continuously learn, not only in our lifetime, but over hundreds of thousands of years. We are a self-organizing system capable of change. Today we have developed tools to achieve such changes faster.

Neuroscience has recently found the seat of passionate responses, the part of the brain called the amygdala. The amygdala calls our body to action even before the neocortex (the place where we process logical and consciously aware information and make decisions) registers a situation. "This smaller and shorter pathway – something like a neural back alley," as Goleman calls it, "allows the amygdala to receive some direct inputs from the senses and start a response *before* they are fully registered by the neocortex." According to Goleman:

This discovery overthrows the notion that the amygdala must depend entirely on signals from the neocortex to formulate its emotional reaction. The amygdala can trigger an emotional response via this emergency route even as a parallel reverberating circuit begins between the amygdala and neocortex. The amygdala can have us spring to action while the slightly slower – but more fully informed – neocortex unfolds its more refined plan for reaction.[11]

This discovery amounts to the recognition that we have two minds. According to Goleman, we have two "fundamentally different ways of knowing." They interact to construct our mental life. The rational mind is "the mode of comprehension we are typically conscious of: more prominent in awareness, thoughtful, able to ponder and reflect. But alongside that there is another system of knowing: impulsive and powerful, if sometimes illogical – the emotional mind."[12]

Transcendental Perspectivism suggests that many tiny "minds" direct our actions and care for our well-being. Our body is a complex system of conscious cells making continuous decisions. Without these, our body could never sustain its existence. A hierarchy of such minds begins at the lowest level and ends up at the neocortex as its main organizing unit, the center of self-awareness. Many "lower grade switching stations" operate in between. These conscious stations (the amygdala, the brain stem, and the immune system) are older parts of our natural makeup. They process information and plan reactions according to ancient response patterns. By far, the majority of these decisions never come to our conscious awareness. Decision-making, based on prior experience stored in memory banks, is one of the main characteristics of a living organism. This characteristic, as we have seen, repeats over and over again down to the level of primitive quanta. Today we have techniques available to influence and teach these lower level "minds."

As a neuroscientist at the Center for Neural Science at New York University, Joseph LeDoux first discovered the key role of the amygdala in the emotional brain. He said of the amygdala that it "can house memories and response repertoires that we enact without quite realizing why we do so because the shortcut from thalamus to amygdala completely bypasses the neocortex. This bypass seems to allow the amygdala to be a repository for emotional impressions and memories that we have never known about in full awareness."[13]

In the mapping of the human brain, scientists have found exact locations for many of our most vital functions. But they have never identified a precise place for the location of memory. Perspectivism suggests that all the cells in our system are capable of memory. Using Jean Charon's model, cells cooperatively assemble lower dimensional elementary particles, which themselves hold the memory of their past. Electrons are perhaps nothing more than a string of memory (brought into being in the present moment by the energy each electron draws from its location in space and time).

We should not be surprised that responses that draw their rationale from such memories seem automatic, and somehow appear "hardwired" into our system. Often their pace of change is much too slow for us to recognize. It may often take hundreds, perhaps thousands of years for the emotional response of our cells to change. But cells do change and learn, and somehow this memory gets passed on to the next generation (most likely in the DNA of the single egg and cell that creates the next human being). Today, we have developed techniques to affect change at these levels. They are based on meditative practices and visualization.

Nature offers examples for both selfish and altruistic behavior. Biologists and socio-biologists have long been searching for the root of altruism. But if selfishness and aggression are "hardwired" into our system, how can we explain altruistic behavior? Whereas selfishness is often the norm, outright altruism is also present, but perhaps harder to discern. Rationalistic social scientists often interpreted altruism within a group as a "natural" response to scarcity as well as to plenty. According to this theory, when things are "normal," a "healthy" group sees no specific reason to exhibit altruism. Each individual in such a group is justified therefore to go about his or her business in quite a selfish way, disregarding the need of the others. When scarcity arises, through natural disaster, wars, or mismanagement, the group – according to those scientists – reverts back to its altruistic ways. This gives the comforting impression that in times of plenty we have no special need or purpose in teaching and practicing altruism.

This description of altruism, I believe, misses the mark in several ways. The scarcity/plenty/cooperative curve results from empirically-observed altruistic human behavior. It overlooks that in the past human groups may have maintained a level of altruistic "training" even during times of plenty. As individuals become more and more self-centered and cooperative behavior becomes less frequently the norm, a future scarcity on earth may be met by an apathetic and numb humanity, incapable of altruism. This lack results from human families neglecting to nourish their offspring in a way that would teach them warmth, and give them a feeling of togetherness and belonging (from which altruistic and heroic acts of selflessness can grow).

Goleman believes that the ability to show empathy (the root of altruism and the passionate involvement with the other) is deeply connected with our emotional being. Emotional intelligence hinges:

> on the link between sentiment, character, and moral instincts.
> There is growing evidence that fundamental ethical stances in
> life stem from underlying emotional capacities. . . the root of
> altruism lies in empathy, the ability to read emotions in others;

lacking a sense of another's need or despair, there is no caring.[14]

The crisis of humanity then, is in large part, a crisis of emotional intelligence. Western civilization has produced an atomized individual, without emotional connection to others beyond the physical and economic bonds. As of now, science has done little to underscore the importance of emotional development, as Goleman so rightly pointed out. "The place of feeling in mental life has been surprisingly slighted by research over the years, leaving the emotions a largely unexplored continent for scientific psychology."[15]

Empathy, the ability to see through the eyes of the other, being emotionally with the other in compassionate union, is essential for the survival of humanity on earth. This should become the main purpose of family life, education, and the media.

At the core of Western civilization there was a misjudgment of human nature that, if not corrected in time, will ultimately lead to our demise. This misjudgment stems from the patriarchal and domineering culture that developed at the dawn of recorded history; and because of its successes in science and technology, this culture still carries us today.

Twenty-Four

MULTIPLE INTELLIGENCES: THE PERSPECTIVIST BRAIN

The Brain is wider than the Sky.
Emily Dickinson

Imagine the human brain as a well-organized city. Groups and subgroups of individuals inhabit this city. There are shopping areas, ethnic neighborhoods, entertainment centers, and administrative bodies. On one level they all have their agenda and goals. On another, they collaborate in a highly cooperative manner. The neurons in the brain are the individual occupants of the city. Each citizen has its needs, wishes, and desires. Each neuron has its own history. In this highly organized city, the needs of all individuals are generally met. They collaborate like a giant symphony orchestra to fulfill common tasks, almost appearing as one. This is the miracle of the human brain and the self that manifests itself in it. How do we measure the potential of the human brain?

In Western societies we use the same yardstick to measure all brains. We consider intelligence the same in all brains, regardless of cultural context and location on the map. This "uniform" view of the human mind has its roots in Greek philosophy and the Judeo-Christian belief that God created man in his image. As we conceived God as one, so we believed was the mind. Aristotle's teleological view projected a uniform image of the educated mind. Teleological science continued this view after René Descartes re-emphasized the mind's special relationship to the Divine.

In the twentieth century, under the influence of science, education became more and more fixated on measuring. The uniform view of the mind merged with the uniform results of IQ tests. IQ testing, according to Howard Gardener, reinforced the uniformity principle in public education. In the uniform school, according to Gardener:

> there is a core curriculum, a set of facts that everybody should know, and very few electives. The better students, perhaps those with higher IQs, are allowed to take courses that call upon critical reading, calculation, and thinking skills. In the "uniform school," there are regular assessments, using paper and pencil instruments, of the IQ or SAT variety. They yield reliable rankings of people; the best and the brightest get into the better colleges, and perhaps – but only perhaps – they will also get better rankings in life.[1]

Bringing up five children and nursing them through the public school system provides me with many examples that demonstrate the ill effect of uniform education. This education focuses only on training one sector of the human mind. I have personally experienced the uselessness of standardized tests. As a college teacher I have witnessed how the needs of administrators, politicians, and public institutions have gradually turned educational institutions into pseudo-efficient production mills. As if students were products, like toasters or television sets, we measure the efficiency of a system by its output. But what might work for UPS may be a slow-death sentence for education.

In elementary school, teachers of my children generally complained that they "did not get their work done." Often their teachers kept them in from recess, one of the few enjoyable experiences left in our schools. The more problems a child has, the more often teachers keep them in from recess. As problems accelerate, the school resorts to suspension instead of dealing with the problems. As a result the child is home alone, or spends the day out on the streets. There he learns the real lessons of life.

One day I decided to observe the nature of the work that my son did not complete. I went to school with him to observe the class. The work consisted of fourteen different individual tasks. These tasks, to the credit of the teacher, stressed several types of intelligences, to use Gardener's term. But when it came to evaluating the completion of the work, the teacher only measured and rewarded efficiency and speed. The teacher did not take into account the different time frames of task completion that students need when different intelligences are at play. Let me make this a little clearer.

For one of the tasks each child had a bag with cutout letter types. The letters of the alphabet were all mixed up. Students had to spell the names of the numbers from zero to ten. When my son had reached number four, he realized that the typefaces of the letters were all different. Some were larger and some were smaller. In other words, the letter types did not match. He put all the letters back in his bag and started over again, this time carefully choosing the matching letter-types. But, in the final evaluation, the teacher did not pay any attention to how the work was completed, much less whether it was aesthetically pleasing. The student just had to complete the assignment.

Another task combined recognition skills with drawing skills. Children had to recognize words with long vowels. For this they were given pictures of different animals, some with long vowels some with short ones. A duck was next to a goose. I asked my son which of the words had a long vowel and which had a short one. He had no problem identifying this. It took him less than ten seconds. Then he started coloring the pictures with crayons. He carefully chose the right color for the right animal and tried to stay within the lines. In other words, he did his best to make his work appealing. This took him fifteen minutes. I observed some of the so-called super-achievers who always "got their work done." One of them identified three animals with long vowels right next to each other. He took a crayon and scratched over all three pictures at once without any sense for color or harmony. This kid received the reward in a system that values efficiency and speed. What message does this send to the other kid?

Reading is another case in point. All five of our kids were avid and proficient readers. From early on we read to them, and books were all around them, long before they entered kindergarten. In school we noticed that the scores they received in standardized tests were generally below average. On several occasions during conferences we asked the teacher about this. Much to our surprise, teachers assured us not to worry about anything, our son was reading well. But then, what was the problem with his test? In standardized reading tests, the teacher explained, the standardized answers must closely reflect the content of the story. This makes the job easy to score for the tester, but a creative mind will freely associate and make connections that are not contained in the legitimate answer book. New ideas develop in this way and new imaginative perspectives open. Just like multiple choice tests train young minds to narrowly focus on the one "correct" answer, so do standardized tests train the mind to assume the average answer. No discovery happens and everything becomes a repetition of old information.

Much to our dismay, our oldest son found the same sentiment in his English class at the quite prestigious Illinois Institute of Technology. Here teachers are supposed to train young minds to become engineers and computer scientists, city planners, and architects. While reviewing an essay on Charles Dickens's *The Tale of Two Cities*, my son's English professor crossed out every sophisticated word, even though the word use seemed quite correct in the context. (My son took pride in expanding his vocabulary continuously. He did this on his own.) The teacher replaced every "unusual" word with a simpler, more popular word. When questioned, the professor responded that most Americans read at a twelfth-grade reading level. Therefore, in order to be widely understood, students were taught to write at that level. If the class had been labeled a journalistic or technical writing class that teaches writing skills for the mass-market, this might have made some sense. But this was supposed to be a college literature class. What is the real message presented in this case?

As Gardener found, different children come equipped with different kinds of intelligences by nature. Gardener distinguished between seven different intelligences, which have equal claims. These are: Linguistic intelligence: poets use this best. Logical-mathematical intelligence: the ability best suited for traditional science. Spatial intelligence: the ability to form a mental model of a spatial world and to operate and use that model. Musical intelligence. Bodily-kinesthetic intelligence: the ability to solve problems or to fashion products using the whole body. Interpersonal intelligence: the ability to understand other people, what motivates them, how they work, and how to work cooperatively with them. Intrapersonal intelligence: the ability to form an accurate, veridical model of oneself, and the ability to use that model to operate effectively in life.[2]

Gardener sees these intelligences more or less as "raw, biological potentials." They seldom exist in pure form. In individuals they almost always combine to favor their development into vocations and avocations. I remember a time when we called these inborn potentials talents.

In the small rural community in Germany where I grew up, different children had different talents for different things. I will never forget an elementary school teacher of mine who early on discovered my love for creative writing. Instead of any other home assignment, this teacher had the courage to let me write a composition of my choosing whenever I wanted. For a whole year, I wrote a story a day and was seldom burdened with math or other problems. In time I learned the concepts of math, too. I never lost my passion for the written word because early in life a courageous teacher completely validated my love for writing. Today's students, who we drill in a technical way of writing from early on, take creative writing and journaling classes much later in life. Often they struggle to find creative expressions – an ability many of them most likely lost in early childhood.

In our society, a false sense of equality demands the same "work" from everyone and judges everyone with the same measure. Except, perhaps, our athletes. Star athletes often pass through the educational system without regard to giving them a real education. Often we leave them with nothing to fall back on when their bodies give out (because of injury or old age).

From a critique of the universalistic view of mind, Gardener deduces the notion "of an individual-centered school, one geared to optimal understanding and development of each student's cognitive profile."[3] Maybe these ideas are utopian, as Gardener contends, but can we afford not to use them?

In different elementary school grade levels I have conducted a simple test with small groups of children. I have them close their eyes for a few minutes. Then I call them back and let them report on what they saw or experienced. These children read the pictures they saw in their mind. First and second graders bubble over in excitement. By the time children reach fourth grade, their mind is often blank. The empty slate that some prominent philosophers projected at the beginning of a child's life may be the result of zealous education. The right brain is silenced so the left brain can triumph. How different our world would look if we truly allowed our children to think creatively and instructed them in *How to Think Like Leonardo da Vinci*,[4] doubtlessly one of the most creative and imaginative persons to walk this earth.

Our public schools today are creations of the industrial age. Their model is the factory and their mode of operation is the conveyer belt. When time is up a shrill bell rings and the belt moves them on to a different subject. While our way of industrial production has by and large changed and moved on, our educational system is slow to do so. As we move rapidly into a new age dominated by information, a standardized education that suited the workers of the industrial age will no longer do. The problems facing humanity in the twenty-first century are massive, and we will need all our creativity if we want to survive.

Against the backdrop of uniformity, the recognition of multiple intelligences is one of the foremost achievements. Recognizing multiple intelligences in our children and developing techniques to nourish them and help them grow must be the goal of a compassionate philosophy. It is the essence of Transcendental Perspectivism.

Twenty-Five

TEACHING PERSPECTIVES: THE PARTNERSHIP WAY

> ... still lacking, and urgently needed, is an integrated partnership curriculum that will not only help today's and tomorrow's children build healthy bodies, psyches, families, businesses, governments, and communities but also give them a clearer understanding of our human potential, our place in history, our relationship to nature, and our responsibility to future generations.
>
> Riane Eisler

The International Partnership Way Center in Tucson trains students of all ages to become teachers and educators in partnership education. In this election year, as for many years in the past, presidential candidates promise to reform a failing educational system. Many proposals have been on the table, from increasing monetary spending to school vouchers and even to do away with schools all together, "de-" or "un-schooling" society.

In *Tomorrow's Children*, Riane Eisler develops a different vision. Eisler begins with this premise:

> At the core of every child is an intact human being. Children have an enormous capacity for love, joy, creativity, and caring. Children have a voracious curiosity, a hunger for understanding and meaning. Children also have an acute inborn sense of fairness and unfairness. Above all, children yearn for love and validation and, given half a chance, are able to give them bountifully in return.[1]

According to Eisler's analysis, the dismal state of humanity at the beginning of the new millennium results from an epidemic spread of dominator thinking. This virus affects our families, communities and, most of all, our educational system. Dominator thinking, at its core, pits one half of humanity against the other. As outlined earlier, dominator thinking began in the distant past and has never ended, affecting human beings in the most negative ways. In *The Chalice and the Blade*, Eisler gave a foundational analysis into the sources and the spread of the dominator paradigm. When first published in 1988, the book became an instant bestseller and eventually was translated into seventeen major languages, including Chinese, Spanish, Russian, and Japanese. Eisler's message struck a chord in many people's minds and hearts.

The anthropologist Ashley Montagu called Eisler's *The Chalice and the Blade*, "the most important book since Darwin's *Origin of Species*," and novelist Isabel Allende said that it was "one of those magnificent key books that can transform us."[2] In the wake of the book's publication, partnership groups formed around the country, and partnership had an impact around the world. The first wave of enthusiasm culminated in the First Minoan Celebration of Partnership on the Island of Crete in 1993. This international meeting brought together nearly five hundred committed partnership people from around the world for a week of reflection, discussion, dance, and celebration.

Considering the almost instant popularity of Eisler's message, we could ask why, so many years after the publication of her book, her ideas have not yet found a way to mainstream education. Why is her work not yet fully accepted in the academic world, or even widely discussed?

The answer is both simple and complex. Violence, the necessary expression of the dominator paradigm, is systemic in our society. We have woven violence into the social fabric, as the necessary means to perpetuate a dominator culture. Many institutions in our society reveal their inherent hierarchies, when seen through the lens of the dominator/partnership model (as democratic as they may appear on the surface). These dominator hierarchies, (for instance the ones of teacher over students, parent over child, father over mother, policeman over citizen, soldier over civilian) are far from being natural and unavoidable, for they are maintained by force and, if necessary, by violence. We have made violence such a part of our culture that we don't give it a second thought when we propagate defending our democratic values with military might instead of negotiations. Often, we maintain that we need violence on television because it expediently gets consumer's attention and sells goods. When we encounter violence in our schools (as in the many school shootings during the past few years), we commission research to establish a profile of the youngsters most prone to violent actions. Instead, we should establish a profile of the culture that makes such violence possible and nearly inevitable. We can credit Eisler with establishing such a profile. But changing age-old habit amounts to nothing less than a paradigm shift of enormous dimensions.

The conservative answer to this epidemic of violence calls for a return to traditional family values. This remedy does not take into account the dismal state of families and children in America. In these times of immense budget surplus and unprecedented economic boom, over twelve million American children still live below the poverty level. Since 1979, guns have killed more than 80,000 American children. Almost twelve million children have no health insurance. One in five children are poor.[3] Ethicist James Sterba from the University of Notre Dame, reflects about the state of families and children in America saying that we share with Italy the highest infant mortality rate in the industrialized world. Except for Bolivia and Haiti, America has:

> the lowest vaccination rate for children under the age of two in the Western Hemisphere, that each day 135,000 children take a gun to school, that one in seven claim to have been sexually abused as a child, that the home is actually a more dangerous place for women than the city streets, that typically more women are abused by their husbands than get married in a given year, that one-third of all women who require emergency hospital treatment are there as a result of domestic violence, that 50 percent of first marriages and 60 percent of second marriages are likely to end in divorce, that 42 percent of the children whose father had left the marriage had not seen him in the past year. . . .[4]

Would a return to traditional family values help? Are the so-called traditional family values not just a fiction of conservative imagination? In Eisler's analysis, the rapid decline in traditional values is not primarily the result of the evil influence of modernism and progress (as conservative critics often claim), but it is the culmination of two thousand years of dominator mentality. Undoing this will not be easy.

Attempts to return to a more partnership-oriented social structure are by no means new. We have tried them in many variations throughout history. Only recently, however, were we able to isolate the dominator model itself as the main culprit that underlies the many faces of human misery. We must credit Eisler with this achievement. In education, too, the partnership model has a firmly rooted history, even though it has failed to reach mainstream education.

One of the early reformers of education in the direction of a more cooperative, partnership-oriented model was the famous Swiss educator Johann Pestalozzi (1746–1827). Influenced by Jean-Jaques Rousseau, Pestalozzi insisted that education had to be concrete and practical. Instead of dealing with words alone, Pestalozzi believed that children should learn through activities and through contact with objects and things. Children should also have the freedom to pursue their interests and draw their conclusions. Education reformers such as Rudolf Steiner, Maria Montessori, and John Dewey adopted many of Pestallozzi's ideas. During the twentieth century, educators practiced their ideas in numerous alternative schools around the world. In America, the movement became known as holistic education – an education that speaks not only to the mind, but to the whole human being.

In *Tomorrow's Children*, Eisler has provides us with an extensive "Blueprint for Education in the 21st Century." She filled this new book with curricular details for all ages. In a society where families often no longer do the work of teaching children how to develop empathy, love, and coopera-

tion, Eisler charges our educational institutions to prepare for this monumental shift in human thinking. Without this shift, humanity may be doomed. The
shift in thinking will have to come on three levels: partnership process, partnership content, and partnership structure. Partnership process is "about how
we learn and teach. It applies the guiding template of the partnership model
to educational methods and techniques."[5] The partnership education model's
main concern lies in bringing joy back into learning. We must fill children
with excitement and passion for knowing. This excitement, Eisler concedes,
is a natural gift of each child; but our current educational system, steered by
the dominator model, tends to extinguish the flame. The teacher who tries to
implement the partnership model must ask these questions:

> Are each child's intelligences and capabilities treated as
> unique gifts to be nurtured and developed? Do students have a
> real stake in their education so that their innate enthusiasm for
> learning is not dampened? Do teachers act primarily as lesson-
> dispensers and controllers, or as mentors and facilitators? Is
> caring an integral part of teaching and learning? Are young
> people learning the teamwork needed for the postindustrial
> economy? Or must they continuously compete with each
> other? Are students offered the opportunity for both self-
> directed learning and peer teaching? In short, is educating
> children merely a matter of filling an "empty vessel," or are
> students and teachers partners in the adventure of learning?[6]

Though how we teach and learn is vital for the partnership model to
succeed, Eisler dedicates by far the largest part of her book to developing
partnership content. Here, Eisler offers an unprecedented plan for a partnership curriculum, ready for anyone interested in partnership education at an
elementary and secondary level to use. In order to develop competent and
caring citizens, workers, parents, and community members, Eisler believes
that besides the three Rs, a school also needs to model the life skills students
so desperately need. Eisler gives a detailed analysis of the view of "human
nature" our children take away from their education. She asks whether what
young people learn about human nature limits or expands their human potential? Does a school teach young people the difference between the partnership and dominator models "as two basic human possibilities and the feasi-
bility of creating a partnership way of life?"[7] Transforming the curriculum,
Eisler believes, "is basic to transforming education."[8]

Eisler shows how teachers can use partnership values in many traditional subjects such as science, mathematics, psychology, history, and literature. Her book provides a valuable guide for those who like to use the partnership model in their classroom.

At the partnership training workshop participants spent much time and
energy discussing structural questions. Developing a partnership structure is

Eisler's third concern. With their overwhelmingly top-down approach, current organizational structures have grown from the dominator model. This is especially obvious when we consider the style of discipline enforcement practiced in most public schools. Deans of discipline enforcement often run these large overcrowded school systems with little input by the student body. Military style structure and a prison-like atmosphere prevail in institutions that supposedly teach our children the principles of democracy and freedom.

The Nova School in Seattle provides one example of a school organized according to partnership principles. Here "students play a key role in formulating and enforcing school rules."[9] According to Eisler, "this practice not only encourages responsibility; it offers hands-on experience in democratic process and leadership."[10] A high percentage of Nova High school graduates go on to prestigious universities, and Nova High school ranked first among area high schools in Seattle in educational climate surveys. In other words, this experimental use of the partnership model has shown excellent educational and scholastic results.[11]

Inspired by Partnership principles, a novel element has been developed for the Nova curriculum that we can use as a model for other institutions. Eisler believes that from preschool to graduate school we must integrate some aspects of what she calls a "Caring for Life" curriculum into the educational fabric. At lower levels this might mean caring for animals and plants. Older children can care for younger children by teaching them necessary skills in writing and math in conjunction with their adult teachers. At higher grades "Caring for Life" may expand into Service Learning, Peace Corps activities, and community involvement.

Contrary to traditional education with its emphasis on information, the partnership model emphasizes caring, care giving, and compassion. According to Eisler:

> Practicing caring and care giving helps meet our human needs for meaning, for spiritual awareness, for larger purpose. The deeply imbedded human yearning for connection that is the evolutionary mainspring for love is also the evolutionary mainspring for spirituality–for the sense of awe and wonder that comes from the intuitive understanding that we are not isolated blips on the evolutionary screen, that we are in a mysterious, and truly miraculous, way actively interconnected with all that is, was, and can be.[12]

In her partnership approach, Eisler does not advocate the elimination of hierarchies, but she distinguishes between two types of hierarchies: hierarchies of domination and hierarchies of actualization. Hierarchies of domination are, according to Eisler, "imposed and maintained by fear" and held in place by the power "to inflict pain, to hurt and kill."[13] Hierarchies of actualization, in contrast, are:

primarily based not on power *over*, but on power *to* (creative power, the power to help and to nurture others) as well as power *with* (the collective power to accomplish things together, as in what is today called teamwork). In hierarchies of actualization, accountability flows not only from the bottom up but also from the top down. That is accountability flows in both directions.[14]

While following this model of interaction, in the classroom as well as in partnership training sessions, we must give much emphasis to collaboration and group work. In a collaborative effort students develop ideas in small groups and then share them with the larger assembly. The teacher's position is often that of a neutral coordinator who facilitates the group process.

As the partnership workshop in Tucson showed, effective hierarchies of actualization require a new type of leadership. First, these new leaders and managers must "inspire rather than coerce. They empower rather than disempower, making it possible for the organization to access and utilize the knowledge and skills of all its members."[15]

To this end, partnership leaders must allow for flexibility and spontaneity in the agenda. They must resist the bureaucratic model of super-efficiency to plan every moment of the day, while weary participants are left "to fill in the blanks."

While partnership content may be an essential component of partnership learning, partnership structure is the most difficult to develop and the hardest to achieve. Perhaps largely because of its efficiency the dominator model has been quite successful in human history. Following orders, at least on the surface, gets things done expediently. In dominator systems of the past, individual rulers, even despots or tyrants, were able to react to changes in an adequate, often even creative way. If these individuals lost their creative edge, they were swept away by intrigues and revolutions. But as democracies replaced the old dominator hierarchies, large bureaucracies evolved to manage the status quo. These bureaucracies maintain the so-called democratic systems. In reality, however, the bureaucracies have a tendency to become dictatorial monsters and often obstruct real change.

Top-heavy educational bureaucracies have replaced the one-room schools of yesterday where the principal often doubled as a teacher. Educational managers with little knowledge of teaching make policies and sometimes almost outnumber classroom teachers. Bureaucracies draw their meaning and their justification from the structure they perpetuate. Education's problems today stem from bureaucracies exerting their dominator structure on the educational process (which we should solely define through caring and care giving). But the caring element inherent in teaching often cannot exist amidst the rules, regulations, and testing tools that administrators impose on teachers from above.

As our society shifts from a consumer-oriented mass society to an information society we hear more demands for a more flexible and creative approach to education. Our current mass-schools view students as output like goods produced by traditional factories. But these reified products, who have lost the ability to enjoy life and learning, are poor inhabitants of a creative, ever-changing world.

We must dismantle the bureaucratic structures along with the huge school systems and replace them with smaller systems in which the caring compassionate individual will become the center of the educational agenda. Partnership education based on Perspectivist philosophy can show the way.

Inspired by the partnership model, teachers and educational institutions will find new ways to let children and students express their individual creativity. They will put caring for growth and joyful fulfillment over a mere striving for brilliance and excellence. Confronted with moments of chaos and disorder, they will not immediately resort to strict discipline and harsh punishment, but let chaos take its course. They must be well aware that chaos is the birthing place of new order. In the end, they will even employ the self-organizing power of chaos to let this most miraculous of all symphonies happen, the growth of a child's mind to full fruition in happy union with the universe.

Twenty-Six

IN MEMORIAM EASTER ISLAND: WHITHER HUMANITY

> We are close to dead. There are faces and bodies
> like gorged maggots on the dance floor, on the
> highway, in the city, in the stadium; they are a
> host of chemical machines who swallow the
> product of chemical factories, aspirin, preserva-
> tives, stimulant, relaxant, and breathe out their
> chemical wastes into a polluted air. The sense of
> a long last night over civilization is back again.
>
> Norman Mailer

The story of Easter Island is as short as it is mysterious, painful, and shock-ing. It could provide a frightening parable for the fate of our mother earth. Easter Island is one of the world's most isolated and inaccessible lands. Only 64 square miles large, it lies in the Pacific Ocean more than 1,400 miles away from any other inhabited place. When the Dutch explorer Jacob Roggeven, the first Western explorer, set foot on Easter Island in 1722, he found a de-serted island with little vegetation. The only inhabitants were primitive head-hunters.

The island Roggeven saw was grassland without a single tree or bush over ten feet high. There were only two types of small trees less than ten feet tall and woody shrubs on the island, no firewood to keep the islanders warm during the cold and wet island winters. For domestic animals, the islanders only had chickens.

Investigating the island more closely, explorers found gigantic stone statues, that the islanders evidently had transported from an ancient quarry from the center of the island to the coast. Some of the statues were over 33 feet tall. Further inland, explorers found abandoned statues that were over 65 feet tall and weighed as much as 270 tons. These statues could not have been built and transported by the primitive people that inhabited the island when Europeans came there. But who constructed them and for what purpose?

Speculations ran rampant as to the origins of these gigantic sculptures. For over two-and-a-half centuries, anthropologists wrote volumes speculating about the origin of these figures. Europeans generally believed the Polyne-sian islanders incapable of anything remotely as sophisticated as these statues represented. In one of the most far-reaching theories, the Swiss writer Erich van Däniken even speculated that space visitors with advanced technology had erected the statues there. Did extra-terrestrial astronauts build them for some alien cult?

The last two decades revealed a different story, however. Careful research of soil samples, using most advanced analytical tools, concluded that the first human beings were most likely Polynesian colonists from neighboring islands. When they first came to Easter some 1,600 years ago, they found a paradise filled with rich vegetation, birds, animals, and a great variety of exotic creatures. Jared Diamond reports:

> For at least 30,000 years before human arrival and during the early years of Polynesian settlement, Easter was not a wasteland at all. Instead, a subtropical forest of trees and woody bushes towered over a ground layer of shrubs, herbs, ferns, and grasses. In the forest grew tree daisies, the rope-yielding hauhau tree, and the toromiro tree, which furnishes dense mesquite-like firewood. The most common tree in the forest was a species of palm now absent on Easter, but formerly so abundant that the bottom strata of the sediment column were packed with its pollen.[1]

When the first human beings settled in this pristine paradise, a rich abundance of birds, fish, dolphins and other animals to hunt for meat existed. The island provided an ideal nesting-site for many species of seabirds. The pollen analysis and soil samples tell a grim story of what happened after human beings arrived and began using the natural resources freely and carelessly.

Since everything they needed was there in abundance they saw no reason to ever leave the island again. Over generations they even forgot their origins from a distant land. This and their long sea-journey may have provided the mythical background for the statues they built in veneration of some unknown gods. We still cannot reconstruct their true purpose.

The story, however, reveals a slow but steady decline that accompanied the constant use of the island's resources without a thought of replenishing them. Eventually they harvested the last tree; they ate the last larger animal. Diamond says:

> The fifteenth century marked the end not only for Easter's palm but for the forest itself. Its doom had been approaching as people cleared land to plant gardens; as they felled trees to build canoes, to transport and erect statues, and to burn; as rats devoured seeds; and probably as the native birds died out that had pollinated the trees' flowers and dispersed their fruit. The overall picture is among the most extreme examples of forest destruction anywhere in the world: the whole forest gone, and most of its tree species extinct.[2]

With no plan for escape, the civilization on Easter had condemned itself to slow extinction. As the food supply on the island dwindled, they eventually even resorted to cannibalism.

Today, the story of Easter Island serves as a grim reminder of the state of the earth. Our tenure on earth began a mere 150,000 years ago. By the best scientific accounts, human beings were the culmination of millions of years of developing life on this planet. Traditional science believes this was an accidental result, a humbling notion at best. Only our pride, fed by religious fervor could make us believe that the whole planet with all its teeming life was there for our taking, for us to waste and exploit. As human beings, we have, like the Easter islanders, forgotten our origin. We have created mythologies and religions that justified our exploitation while they secured for us a separate place in creation, a mythical escape in the sky.

Today we can no longer ignore the destruction we brought to the planet. Human beings destroy an ever-greater amount of life forms on this earth at a staggering rate, many of which we haven't even named and catalogued. Others who have been living along side us for the whole length of our tenure as faithful companions such as the elephant, tiger, and whooping crane are nearing extinction.

"How are we doing it?" asks Richard Swift in an article in the *New Internationalist*, and answers, "Simply by demanding more and more space for ourselves." This has lead to what Swift calls "planetary overload."[3]

What can we learn from Easter's example? Given the current situation and course of humanity on earth, unfortunately the general level of intelligence, judged by the state of the earth and its ecological health, is hardly much more advanced than that of the so-called savages on Easter Island. Though alerted by many scientists to the dangerous destruction of our natural resources that human beings already inflicted on Earth, the general course of humanity is still designed by selfishness, greed and ruthless exploitation.

In my youth, people still commonly believed that if we exhausted Earth we could escape to another nearby planet, such as Mars and colonize it. Back then we had no understanding of the technologies of how to do this. There was a general optimism that if humanity could somehow survive the threat of nuclear extinction, we could find the technological means to colonize space. Today we may have the technological know-how that could transport at least some of us to a hospitable nearby planet, but the same technological sophistication has shown unmistakably that we cannot easily colonize any of our neighbors. No other earth around exists, at least not in our neighborhood.

A new urgency must focus human development to preserve this planet for the use of future generations. Even though some efforts have been made, we are far from having reached a global consensus. The doomsday clock is still ticking and every new nuclear explosion, every missed treaty to prevent global warming, any selfish use of the scarce rain forests, brings us one second closer to experience Easter Island's fate.

Twenty-Seven

TALKING TO HEAVEN: THE COMMUNICATING UNIVERSE

> And I heard a voice from heaven, as the voice of
> many waters, and as the voice of a great thun-
> der: and I heard the voice of harpers harping
> with their harps.
>
> Revelation, 14:2

This book is about communication and finding ways to reach the other. We have seen that in the search for the other we can no longer narrowly focus on other people who speak our language. We must see the other in all human beings inhabiting this globe. Transforming the enemy into a friend was one of the noble goals found in the message of Jesus Christ, of Mahatma Gandhi, and Martin Luther King, Jr., alike. Modern peace studies and theories of conflict resolution have shown us techniques of transformation that leave both sides with a feeling of gain, while a simple "turn of the other cheek" often left the recipient with a feeling of hurt and shame. Recovery from such a position of serfdom and underdog may need metaphysical strength and divine support. The win-win outcome of modern conflict resolution, can provide both sides with an optimal base for empowerment and strength.

Beyond fostering positive communication between human beings, Perspectivism also embraces new ways to communicate with animals and plants who live on this planet with us and whose birthright is much older than ours. As previous sections of this book have shown, Transcendental Perspectivism wants to go even further. It wants to encourage communication with the so-called inorganic world and even with the universe.

The attempt of communication with the universe is by no means new to humanity, even though, coming from the perspective of modern science, it might at first sight be an impossible task. When people of ancient civilizations gazed into the starry heavens, perhaps sitting on top of a mountain peak on a clear and cold night, they frequently imagined that the heavens talked back to them. Have our chattering minds, so filled with images, information, and sounds of our noisy world, lost this ability? Has our placement of orbiting telescopes and satellites (our technological ears and eyes in outer space) replaced our ability to hear the voices of the dead, the music of the spheres, and the melody of creation?

While Western civilization went all out to change the surface of this earth and make it more hospitable for people, the Eastern tradition shows us another way, in experiencing the great silence of the universe, not as our enemy, but as a friend. While Christ undertook the task of reconciling the universe with humanity, and left Christians to the task of helping their brothers and sisters, Buddha asked each person to take on the cross of discovery, to personally undergo the task of communicating with the Void. Which mission satisfies more? Which mission is the more worthwhile and deserving? In the end, who can tell? Both are part of the Way.

Oddly enough, in following Christ, Western civilization enabled a feminine kind of caring among its followers as perhaps best exemplified by the image of Mother Teresa. Christianity, to some extent, eliminated the need for individual search into the spiritual Void. This task was, according to Christian faith, fully accomplished by Christ the Savior. Christians could more fully embrace the second task of loving thy neighbor as well as thy enemy as yourself. Christ had put this command on equal footing with the first law of loving thy God. Combined with the Greek faith in education and progress that spurred scientific development and technology, Western civilization went about the giant task of making this world more habitable for human beings. By following a male instinct of subjugation and dominance, Western civilization all but forgot its connection and its utter dependence on the rest of the natural world, the animals, plants, ecosystems, and ultimately humanity's real dependence on the awe-inspiring powers of the universe.

Science tells a story of an unresponsive, accidental universe. The unlikely story: out of the billions and billions of random events that resulted from that first blind accident (the Big Bang – from which supposedly everything began) eventually life developed, again by sheer accident. If life occurred as a quirky fluke, no wonder many find it hard to buy into the myth of science. Science tells us that by far the largest part of this universe is lifeless, unpredictable chaos, more bare than even the Easter Island after the invasion of human beings. With such a universe, it makes no sense to even attempt communication.

After we first isolated ourselves from communication with the universe, we developed sophisticated machines and directed them toward the far reaches of the sky – gathering faint signals that would indicate that we do not exist alone. These signals, we expect, would have to have the imprint of intelligence, human intelligence, if they were to assure us of other life in the universe. Scientists have developed the most sophisticated tools to take the pulse of a dead universe. At the same time, the nation's bestseller lists are filled with books about angels, near death experiences, and communication with spirits and the dead. Talk show circuits have given modern shamans, media who supposedly communicate with the dead, worldwide exposure. Psychic media such as James van Praagh[1] and John J. Edwards[2] even take calls over the air. They claim that they communicate with the dead loved ones by giving surprising details (often only known by the deceased). While to us children of a secular age this kind of dialogue with dead people appears weird, it was not so strange to many people as recent as one or two generations back. My grandmother and my mother both reported frequent visits with their passed-on loved ones, mostly in dreams. They gave great significance to those dreams. The current Dalai Lama says he has met with several dead Dalai Lamas in his dreams. Most world religions encourage dialogue with dead ancestors, saints, spirits or angels.

Religions generally have a concept of the continuation of life after the death of the physical body, which they often see as the shell or vehicle for a higher consciousness, often called soul. The idea that the soul somehow becomes reborn or reincarnated goes back into ancient prehistory. Perhaps by observing nature and its recurring cycles of life and death, this belief first developed. Native Americans often believe in a dual soul – a human one (bound to the body) and a free one that can reach the land of the dead and survive.

African religions encourage a lively dialogue with the deceased ancestors who live in the world of the lower spirits and maintain, at least for some time, an active interest in the affairs of the living. In African religions, ancestors are a powerful force. Often their descendants hold them responsible for droughts, famines, and earthquakes. They are a force in need of appeasement and respect. They make certain that their descendants observe the customs faithfully and punish wrongdoing. We can find the same reverence for ancestors in Chinese, Japanese, and Indian traditions. Hindu families traditionally have a shrine in their houses with a picture of the patriarch of the family (with whom the living members communicate in prayer).

Modern children of science lack such communication. The extreme success of psychic media and books about this subject demonstrates the human need for psychic reassurance. Perhaps Karl Marx's lasting shortcoming was that his philosophy failed to recognize the extreme need of human beings to find their place in the universe and to find ultimate meaning. While his critique of religions as co-conspirators of oppression was justified, his blind trust in rational atheism was not, and ultimately this may have caused the demise of communism. Many people under atheist communism felt a need for spiritual fulfillment and flocked to the churches. They then used the churches as a base for their protest against oppression.

In this postmodern age, we have placed a renewed emphasis on securing a scientific base for the possibilities of communication with the universe beyond mere measuring of data and facts. We have tested and scrutinized the healing power of faith and belief. We have developed and applied scientific methods to investigate phenomena such as faith healing, clairvoyance, telepathy, and teleportation. On the cosmological front, a handful of scientists push at the confines and probe new frontiers. In *In the Beginning*,[3] the astrophysicist John Gribbins promotes the idea of a living universe. While holding on to a strictly evolutionary model, Gribbins claims that the universe on the large scale is not at all just random chaos, but exhibits the characteristics of a living system. According to Gribbins:

It may be outrageous to claim that our Galaxy, a collection of stars, gas and dust (plus the still mysterious dark matter), should be alive. Even those astronomers who use words like "evolution" to describe the structure of an individual galaxy and the nature of galaxies in general change as the universe ages do not claim that this is anything other than an analogy, or a metaphor. But I believe that it is more than an analogy, and that we have been misled into thinking of objects like galaxies as merely inanimate collections of matter by the accidents of scale – the distance scale and the time scale.[4]

Similar to the quantum animist's contention that we lack the ability to observe life at the quantum scale, the cosmologist Gribbins claims that we lack the same ability on the large scale of galaxies. On the large scale of whole galaxies, observed over millions of years, the same non-equilibrium conditions that indicate life here on earth are apparent. According to Gribbins, they work against mere physical laws of entropy that would soon drive such systems toward unstructured equilibrium. "If you had a lifespan of a few billion years, so that you could sit and watch galaxies rotate, and if you had the vantage point in the far depth of space, high above the Milky Way, looking down on its spiral pattern, you would see individual stars moving through the spiral pattern, following their orbits in obedience to the simple laws of physics."[5]

According to the laws of physics as we know them, the movement of the stars should disrupt the larger movement of the galaxy. But somehow the pattern resists disruption. From this Gribbins concludes that something akin to a living system is at work here:

It would be as obvious to you that something odd was going on as it would be to an alien spectroscopist that there is something odd about the atmosphere of the Earth. And as you watched the spiral arms grow, and move around the Galaxy seemingly independently of the differential rotation of the stars, it would be obvious that you were watching a living system.[6]

In the evolutionary process of assembling higher, more complex forms of life, why should the universe have succeeded only in us, a carbon based variety of life? Following Perspectivist philosophy, all energies in the universe continuously try to assemble new combinations and cooperate with each other to reach higher levels of complexities. In these attempts to organize themselves, many projects end in failure. Only some succeed and move on to higher organization. The failures eventually result in the death and destruction of the unsuccessful system, only to make place for new experimentations. Carbon based life may only be one of these attempts that has produced successful results. Human beings hope that our lives are somehow under the special guardianship of a living, caring universe. Perhaps such a personal, conscious power exists in the universe somewhere. If our faith assures this, I believe that the universe will respond. Others yet believe that the complex spirits of their ancestors care for them and guide them along the difficult route of experimentation toward complexity and higher levels of consciousness.

As Van Praagh and other psychics report, these spirits try to help us, but they, too, don't have full knowledge. Perhaps the center of the universe, while consistently trying to assemble possibilities for new life and higher forms of consciousness, is oblivious to the individual life that makes you and me. Perhaps some day a cosmic community will span and connect the whole universe. This may include our ancestors, too, who will join us in that cosmic dance. Talking to heaven, for a variety of reasons, could be a worthy task.

Twenty-Eight

TOWARD A COSMIC CONSCIOUSNESS

> We live between two worlds; we soar in the at-
> mosphere; we creep upon the soil; we have the
> aspirations of creators and the propensities of
> quadrupeds. There can be but one explanation of
> this fact. We are passing from the animal into a
> higher form, and the drama of this planet is in its
> second act.
>
> W. Winwood Reade

The film, *The Mission*, provides an excellent tool with which to analyze an ideal community. I ask my students to compare the community, which the Jesuits tried to create among the Indians of the Amazon, with their own experience of community.

The community of the Indians is characterized by a family-like mutual support, shared rituals, leisure activities, education, and above all, equally shared economic advance. Compared to this ideal of a community, the reports I receive from students about their experiences of community are somber, but could hardly come as a surprise. Often, their experience of community is not much more than a place to live, go to school and pay taxes. The idea of community has suffered like little else in these post-modern times. What is the cause for this demise?

Good reasons exist why modern urbanites generally act suspicious of community and would live in atomistic isolation instead. Almost everyone yearns for the "good old days" when people talked to each other while sitting on the stoops of their houses or when shopping in the mom and pop grocery store. Gone are the times when people would come together and help each other on a regular basis, join forces when a neighbor was in need, celebrate when a child was born, or mourn together when one of them died. True, in times of real disasters (when a tornado strikes or a flood wipes out whole villages, or in times of national emergencies such as the recent terrorist attacks on New York) people will mostly still root together. But when the immediate emergency is solved, people will once more go their ways down their individual paths to isolation and loneliness. When they meet again in the mall, or a church service, they hardly know each other anymore. We generally go our separate ways while relegating most of our neighborly cares and duties to institutions.

We teach our children at an ever-earlier age not to talk to strangers. As justification, we often hear that violence and high crime rates cause our suspicion. But we fail to see that crime, especially violent crime, is an effect of our loneliness and atomization, not its cause.

We must answer two questions: why do we need community and why have we lost it? Many would blame the loss of community on the rapid development of Western individualism. Individualist theory goes back to the philosophers Immanuel Kant, Georg Wilhelm Friedrich Hegel, and in more recent times, John Rawls. While most communitarians believe that laws and morality grow out of and must be grounded in community, these philosophers contend that the individual is fundamentally self-sufficient. Individualists do not think that we have to see laws and morality in a social, cultural, or historical context, but moral laws are instead derived from the rational underpinning of morality and are therefore universal. This conception of morality absolved the individual of any reference to community when making moral choices, and absolved the state to teach morality. It was sufficient for public schools to teach rationality and discipline.

The complete exclusion of community in the formulation of morality is, however, a new invention of the twentieth century. The positivistic attempt to emulate the objectivity of science in the field of ethics caused this neglect. Hegel still saw the world-spirit as the foundation of morality. But the Hegelian world-spirit, was not a pseudo-rational abstraction but the living will of the people, which became objective in the laws of a nation. This Hegelian view, driven to its extreme, became the intellectual corner-stone of fascist ideology.

The fear of the recurrence of fascism may keep many modern intellectuals from promoting the need for community. That fear helps to justify the defense of extreme individualism, often to the detriment of giving any direction to our youth at all. But neither a rational, objective approach nor an atomized individualistic one can produce the moral fabric our society so desperately needs.

Believing in the failure of the cognitive rational program to produce a sensible morality, both the narrative approach found in postmodernism and the contextual approach of the new communitarians try to counteract the loss of moral fiber in society. Conservatives propose to hold on to a universal set of values grounded in the Bible and encoded, as they would like to see it, in the constitution of the land. Often, however, these ideas clash with each other and create great confusion.

Perspectivist research shows that we need community in order to survive. Moreover community is a vital part in reaching a higher level of evolutionary development. As of now, we have only a vague idea of what such a cosmic community will be like, though several visionary proposals have been put on the table.

With the communitarians, Perspectivism assumes that morality is grounded in community. Abstracted from community, no rational ground of goodness exists and happiness remains elusive. Community creation in the form of collective orchestration appears to be the natural tool that drives the evolutionary process to new plateaus. Collective orchestration is the third leg of evolution besides natural selection and the random creation that provides plurality and options. It adds the second-person perspective to the so widely acclaimed third and first-person perspectives of modernism and postmodernism respectively.

As described above, collective orchestration is the process by which groups of individuals of a lower dimensional structure and existence come together and perform cooperative activities in order to perform tasks that we cannot accomplish alone. On rare occasions, these communities remain connected permanently and as a new single individual, they actualize and reach a new level of awareness and existence. Tasks that they could not accomplish individually are now permanent property and an intrinsic part of the biological makeup of the new creature. It can perform them whenever desired and needed. For the amoebas, this meant having a variety of organs with a clear distribution of labor and the ability to move from one place to another. This was a qualitatively new structural arrangement of life. It fits the description of having reached a higher dimension, without doubt a great evolutionary achievement. Life had moved from one-celled organisms to the level of multi-celled organisms. Structurally, parts which once were external and separated became internal parts and structure of one new individual. What such a collective move could mean for human beings is unknown territory. What new degrees of freedom, new avenues of development, and new ways of communication will open up, once humanity collectively moves on to the next higher dimension?

There may be already ten or fifteen such dimensions available as string theory proposes. Have human beings reached the highest level? We cannot be sure. From observation of less complex, perhaps lower-dimensional creatures that live within us (such as bacteria, microbes, electrons, and space/time quanta), we may assume that our existence as a member of a higher collective order would perhaps not need to be fully conscious to each individual. Each single neuron in my brain is on one level a functional individual in its own rights. It may only be dimly aware of being part of my whole self. In a similar way, I could perhaps be a member of a larger community, without the full experience of that community's existence.

The possibility of reaching a new and higher dimensional awareness with one more step of collective orchestration may be at hand. Once we reach a critical mass of like-minded people, collective orchestration will make this goal come true. Throughout history, humanity's continuous attempt to build communities in all shapes and forms indicates a subconscious urgency to fulfill this potential. This perhaps is the ultimate promise of the second-person enlightenment and of Transcendental Perspectivism.

The communal organization of insects, for example, is one of the most efficient systems of organization we know. A subconscious awareness that through collective orchestration they will eventually reach a higher dimension may also drive insect colonies. Evolution has gone that route by creating higher dimensional organisms such as mammals.

What would a higher-level cosmic community of human beings be like? We can only speculate. Would there be the distinct awareness in each community member that on the higher level a perfect, inseparable communion of all those individual minds exists? Would it be a spiritual community that collectively reaches into the next higher dimension and there realizes a common bond? A striking image of such a bond is the idea of the mystical body of Christ projected in the Christian faith. But there may well be other spiritual unions that also are able to fulfill that image.

A problem in the formation of such a cosmic community would be the question of free will. Would individual members loose their identity and merge into the collective whole so completely that nothing of their individuality would remain? Would they have to relinquish the possibility of free choice for the larger good? I don't think that this would need to be the case. I believe that our individual minds could continue to function at the present dimensional level. We would reach the knowledge of the higher dimension as a result of collective activities such as meditation, prayer, contemplation, healing, and dancing. Membership in the higher community would be a joyous and happy one that would in no way let authoritarianism and fascism resurface. The philosopher Ken Wilber has developed the vision of a union guided by what he called "new dharma."

Perspectivism subscribes to such a new dharma because it integrates the best of the wisdom traditions with the best of what science and Western social advances have to offer. Wilber says, "New dharma is set in the political freedom of the West, which doesn't force itself on people but invites them to transcend themselves through a culture of encouragement and example."[1] In his dialectical approach, Adorno of the Frankfurt School developed the intellectual tools for such a communal ideal. In my earlier book I have developed these ideas in the chapters on "Community Creation through Art" and "Toward a Materialist Spirituality."[2] Transcendental Perspectivism will make use of all these aids.

Perhaps humanity is approaching a new turning point, as many have predicted. Taking Perspectivism with its second person perspective seriously will initiate a revolution. If, shortly before the Cambrian explosion, single-celled amoebas could have spoken to each other, they might have developed a dream of coming together and collectively moving up into a higher dimension. One wise amoeba, gifted with a greater vision than all the others, would have said:

"Listen up, my fellow amoebas. For many million years now, longer than we amoebae can remember, we have performed the Great Ritual of Coming Together. We all know the purpose of the Great Ritual. Without it we amoebas would have been extinguished a long time ago. In times of need the Great Ritual has saved our lives over and over again, even though each time many of us have to lay down their lives so our kind can survive. For the sake of our young ones let me recall the Great Ritual, so you may remember when we old amoebas are no longer around.

"We amoebas are a strange bunch indeed. We like to do our thing, go our separate ways for most of our lives. We feed on bacteria and other food sources as long as they are available.

"But when resources become scarce, since ancient times we have rooted together and have acted as one. In the Great Ritual a super-mind takes over and leads us from scarcity to where there is plenty. This is the greatest miracle indeed. Millions of us become one, and together we find a better tomorrow. Some will become the mouth of the new being, others the stomach, and some of us will have to die on the journey. Before we reach the Promised Land we will go through many transformations, but once we arrive, there will be great joy and plenty of food. Those of us, who finish our journey, will never forget the encounter of the Great Spirit working through all of us to give us a land of milk and honey, a land of plenty, and a new purpose for all.

"My fellow amoebas, I can assure you, once you have gone on that journey, once you partake in that Great Ritual, you will never forget the experience of discovery and fulfillment. Traditionally, once we have arrived at the Promised Land, we disband and become our individual selves again, each fighting alone until new scarcity strikes.

"But let me tell you of another vision. Let me speak as one who has been there and has come back. I can foresee a time, when we amoebas will have matured enough to put aside our individual desires, wants and wishes. Then the greatest miracle of all will occur. United we will remain there on the other side, as one individual, with a new vision, a new purpose, and a new beginning. Then we will no longer yearn for the time when each of us did our own thing, went our own way, and had our own goals. We will stand there as one, in a new time, a new era, and new dimensions will open before us. Let us prepare for this great time and let us once more perform the Great Ritual of Collective Orchestration. But this time we will perform it not because scarcity and need compelled us, but because we choose to do so with our own free will. A New World, a new dimension, waits out there for us to grow into. United, we have the vision and united, we are strong. This will begin the Great Cambrian Explosion."

A new Cambrian explosion is at hand, and humanity will be its main actor. Many of the great religions on earth have formulated a vision of a higher dimension of being, a cosmic community. Struggle, infighting, and selfishness have kept us from fulfilling that dream of evolution. Having found Collective Orchestration at the base of natural evolution, we must climb the obvious ladder. Many leaders have spoken from the mountaintop about the new vistas they could see on the other side. When will humanity reach a critical mass of like-minded people? When will we freely chose to merge with the other so that we can advance to the next higher level?

AFTERWORD

As the events of 11 September 2001 unfolded, I was like millions of others paralyzed by the immensity of the terrorist acts. The collapsing towers on the screen in front of my eyes hammered in the fact that this was real, that this meant the death of thousands of individual lives, right this very moment. How could anyone see this as the mere destruction of symbols? How could anyone merely enjoy the aesthetic power of the visuals without feeling the pain? Could such destruction be executed in the name of a God they call "the Compassionate One?"

In the days that followed I tried to make sense of this horrific event. At a local mosque I joined our Muslim brothers and sisters in reflection and prayer. Later, even before the bombing of Afghanistan had started, I attended a meeting of a quickly revived peace group. In the past, pacifist actions had come to me a lot easier. This time it seemed different. And still I was shocked, when I read that my good friend Riane Eisler, whom I have known as the promoter of peace, partnership and cultural transformation, had come out in an interview in support of military action. As the missiles and bombs rain down on Afghanistan I am still asking myself: Is there no other way? Is this not just another way of America showing its patriarchal might?

What a different world this could be if all the nations could commit themselves to the principles of true partnership! Does the mightiest nation in the world not have a sacred obligation to bring true justice to all? Not through guns and bombs, but by letting all people share in the wealth of this planet. This alone could bring the end of terrorism and promote a lasting peace.

In the wake of 11 September, Americans have asked themselves over and over again, why do they hate us so much? A lot of Perspectivism will be needed to answer that question. We will truly have to see ourselves through the eyes of the other if we ever want to understand the depth of their hate.

These events have forced me, too, to rethink my life in America. My father was a simple foot soldier in Hitler's army. Fighting a senseless war, he was gunned down by an American tank advancing over a hill in the Bavarian Alps. His body was thrown in a mass grave. He died only three days before the end of the Second World War. And here I am, living and thinking as an American.

Growing up in postwar Germany, I would perhaps not have survived without American food aid. Never mind the possible ulterior motives of the victor to secure a partner in the global market place, the Marshal Plan saved this child's life. For the sake of the children in this world, wars must never again be seen as the solution to a problem. Compassion must extend beyond national borders to embrace the whole of humanity.

What makes this conflict different from others, perhaps comparable only with Hitler's fascism, is that the enemy is driven by an ideology that chooses death over life. Religions have sometimes tried to instill in their followers a deep belief that eternal life is awaiting the martyr. This has often been interpreted that this life is of lesser worth, that the earth is not our real home, that pleasure and rewards are reaped in heaven only. Such anti-life, anti-earth ideology, I believe, is the most dangerous outgrowth of human thinking, whether it is grown and nourished on Christian, Muslim, or Shinto soil. As human beings we must preserve this earth of ours and keep it inhabitable for future generations. If life is not sacred, what else is?

Shortly after 11 September, I attended a peace conference at which five outstanding South African activists, among them Ela Gandhi, activist granddaughter of Mahatma Gandhi, talked about the struggle they endured to transform their country from one of the world's most repressive apartheid systems to an open democratic society. Enshrined in South Africa's new constitution is the peaceful coexistence and celebration of diversity. As an overt expression of the acceptance of diversity eleven languages are equally sanctioned and used by parliamentarians and in the society at large. The new South African constitution makes the conscious attempt to include inter-religious understanding and cooperation in the fabric of daily life. Religions and spirituality are not relegated to the private sphere, but are publicly encouraged and celebrated. They remain mindful, however, that religions have the tendency to be exclusive and oppressive to others. The new political leaders under the wise guidance of Nelson Mandela have encoded the equal rights for people of all religions into the very fabric of their constitution. Truth in the new South Africa is not the property of one religion or one church; all have the right to share it equally. When asked about truth Gandhi answered with unequaled wisdom: "Each eye sees only one part of the truth, the more eyes we have, the more we will know of the truth." This is Perspectivism in action.

At the center of the assault on America is the attempt to return the world to a total and complete subjugation of women. The attack on the World Trade Center is only in part an attack on Western trade and commerce, it is also an attack on a civilization for making the attempt to overcome patriarchy and to eliminate the inequality of the sexes. The attack has been called evil, and the mastermind of such violence was named the Evil one. This conjures up an apocalyptic scenario of universal powers engaging in a superhuman battle. Such wallowing in mythical absolutes can serve no practical purpose, as Stanley Fish, dean of liberal arts at the University of Illinois at Chicago, and tireless promoter of postmodernism, in an article in the *New York Times* pointed out.[1] Condemnation is called for, but it does not need to revert back to old absolutes. Fish instead suggests the Perspectivist practice "of putting yourself in your adversary's shoes, not in order to wear them, but in order to have some understanding (far short of approval) of why someone else might want to wear them."

While we can "prefer our own position," as Fish puts it, we do not need to condemn the enemy to death. Instead, Perspectivist ethics suggest analysis and creative problem solving. Fundamentalism generally entails the return to patriarchal dominator forms of government and society. True freedom, creativity, and happiness flourish when partnership with its acceptance of otherness is encouraged and celebrated. Under the guidance of Perspectivist philosophy and using the principles of the partnership ideal we must further the struggle for peace and justice now more than ever.

NOTES

INTRODUCTION

1. Kathy A. Svitil, "Virtual Gorillas," *Discover*, 18:4 (April 1997), p. 26.
2. *Ibid.*

PART I: TRANSCENDENTAL PERSPECTIVISM

Chapter One
The Voodoo Connection

1. Karen McCarthy Brown, *Mama Lola, A Voodoo Priestess in Brooklyn* (Berkeley: University of California Press, 1991), p. 8.
2. Miriam Therese Winter, "Feminist Commentary is 3 lb., Must–Read Text," *The National Catholic Reporter* (6 October 1995), p. 18.
3. *Ibid.*
4. *Ibid.*
5. CNN: Worldnews.
6. Ruth Behar, "Dare We Say 'I'? Bringing the Personal into Scholarship," *The Chronicle of Higher Education*, 40:43 (29 June 1994), p. B2.
7. *Ibid.*
8. *Ibid.*
9. *Ibid.*
10. *Ibid.*
11. *Ibid.*
12. David Peat, *Superstrings and the Search for the Theory of Everything* (Chicago: Contemporary Books, 1989), p. 276.
13. Kim A. McDonald, "Scientists Rethink Anthropomorphism," *Chronicle of Higher Education*, 41:24 (24 February 1995), p. A8.
14. *Ibid.*
15. *Ibid.*

Chapter Two
The Sacred Wheel

1. *A Global Ethics: The Declaration of the Parliament of the World's Religions* (New York: Continuum, 1993).
2. *Ibid.*
3. Joel Beverslius, ed. *A Sourcebook for the Community of Religions* (Grand Rapids, Mich.: The Sourcebook Project, 1993).
4. *Ibid.*
5. Gotthold Ephraim Lessing, *Nathan the Wise,* trans. Bayard Q. Morgan (New York: Ungar, 1955), pp. 75–80.
6. John, *Gospel*, 14:2.
7. *Quuran,* 5:48.

Chapter Three
Perspectives from the Edge of Chaos

1. *The Egyptian Book of the Dead; the Papyrus of Ani in the British Museum.* Introd. by E. A. Wallis Budge (New York: Dover Publications, 1967).

2. *New Larousse Encyclopedia of Mythology* (New York: The Hamlin Group, 1968), p. 89.

3. Nick Herbert, *Elemental Mind: Human Consciousness and the New Physics* (New York: Penguin Books, 1993), p. 167.

4. Ilya Prigogine, *Order out of Chaos* (New York: Bantam Books, 1984), p. xii.

5. *Ibid.*

6. *Ibid.*

7. Allen Bloom, *The Closing of the American Mind: How Higher Education has Failed Democracy and Impoverished the Soul's of Today's Students* (New York: Simon and Schuster, 1987), p. 183.

8. Joanne Wieland-Burston, *Chaotische Gefühle* (Zurich: Kreuz Verlag, 1989), p. 19.

9. *Ibid.,* p. 110.

10. D. S. Wilson "Dora, Nora and Their Professor: The 'Talking Cure' 'Nightwood,' and Feminist Pedagogy," *Literature and Psychology* 42:3 (Summer 1996), p. 48.

11. Prigogine, *Order Out of Chaos,* p. 6.

12. Paul Davies, *Prinzip Chaos: Die neue Ordnung des Kosmos* (München: 1988), p. 106.

PART II: THE HUMAN PERSPECTIVE

Chapter Four
The Quest for Happiness: Perspectivist Ethics, A Way Out of the Confusion

1. Bernie Zilbergeld, *The New Male Sexuality* (New York: Bantam Books, 1992), p. 139.

2. *Ibid.*

3. Gay Norton Edelman, "Show Me the Presents," *McCall's* (February 1998), p. 48.

4. Derald Wing Sue and David Sue, *Counseling the Culturally Different: Theory and Practice* (New York: John Wiley and Sons, 1990).

5. *Ibid.,* p. 4.

6. Sam Keen, *To a Dancing God* (New York: Harper and Row, 1970).

7. *Ibid.,* p. 24.

8. *Ibid.*

9. *Ibid.*

10. *Ibid.*

11. Mahatma Gandhi, "All Men are Brothers," *Beyond the Western Tradition* (Mountain View, Cal.: Mayfield, 1992), p. 250.

12. *Ibid.,* p. 250.

13. Sharon Begley and Claudia Kalb, "Learning Right from Wrong," *Newsweek* (13 March 2000), p. 30.

14. *Ibid.*

15. *Ibid.*

16. *Ibid.*

17. *Ibid.,* p. 31.

18. Arthur Waskow, "Proclaim Jubilee!" *The Other Side*, 34:5 (September, October 1998), p. 10.

19. *Ibid.*

20. *Ibid.*

21. *Ibid.*

22. *Ibid.,* p. 34.

23. Scott R. Sanders, *The Force of Spirit* (Boston: Beacon Press, 2000).

24. *Ibid.,* pp. 85–90.

25. *Ibid.*

Chapter Five
The Partnership Way

1. Matthew Fox, *Original Blessing* (Santa Fe: Bear, 1983).

2. Riane Eisler, *The Chalice and the Blade* (San Francisco: Harper Collins, 1988).

3. *Ibid.,* p. 6.

4. David Loye, *Darwin's Lost Theory of Love* (Web Publishing, 2000).

5. Roger Lewin, *Complexity, Life at the Edge of Chaos* (New York: MacMillan, 1992).

Chapter Six
The Year the Horses Came: The Roots of Domination

1. Marija Gimbutas, *The Civilization of the Goddess: The World of Old Europe* (San Francisco: Harper, 1991).

2. Riane Eisler, *Sacred Pleasure: Sex, Myth and the Politics of the Body* (San Francisco: Harper, 1995).

3. *Ibid.,* pp. 58–59.

4. http://www.isa.it/tuscia

5. Lewis Hopfe, *Religions of the World* (Upper Saddle River, N. J.: Prentice Hall, 1998).

6. Karen Anderson, *Chain Her by One Foot: The Subjugation of Native Women in Seventeenth-Century New France* (New York: Routledge, 1993).

7. Mary Mackey, *The Year the Horses Came* (San Francisco: Harper Collins, 1993).

Chapter Seven
Chasing Amy: Our Sexual Selves

1. Kevin Smith, dir., *Chasing Amy,* (View Askew Productions, 1997).

2. *Ibid.*

Chapter Eight
Men Are from Mars, Women Are from Venus

1. John Colapinto, *As Nature Made Him: The Boy Who Was Raised as a Girl* (New York: Harper-Collins, 2000).
2. Deborah Blum, "The Gender Blur: Where Does Biology End and Society Take Over?" Utne Reader (September, October 1998), pp. 45–48.
3. *Ibid.*, p. 46.
4. *Ibid.*
5. John Gray, *Men Are from Mars, Women Are from Venus* (New York: Harper-Collins, 1992).
6. *Ibid.*
7. *Ibid.*

Chapter Nine
Healing the Body and the Mind

1. *Jet*, 93:1 (24 November 1997) p. 14.
2. Charles Marwick, "Should Physicians Prescribe Prayer for Health? Spiritual Aspects of Well-Being Considered." *JAMA, The Journal of the American Medical Association*, 273:20 (24 May 1995), p. 1561.
3. *Christian Science Monitor*, 88:52 (2 September 1996), p. 17.
4. Daniel Goleman and Joel Gurin, ed. *Mind Body Medicine* (Yonkers, N.Y.: Consumer Reports Books, 1993).
5. Bill Moyers, *Healing and the Mind* (New York: Doubleday, 1993).
6. Candice Pert, "The Mind Body Connection," *Healing and the Mind,* pp. 177–194.
7. *Ibid.,* p. 178.
8. *Ibid.,* p. 180.
9. *Ibid.,* p. 181.
10. *Ibid.,* p. 186.
11. Deepak Chopra, *Ageless Body, Timeless Mind: The Quantum Alternative to Growing Old* (New York: Harmony Books, 1993).

Chapter Ten
Mission or Mission Impossible: Community

1. Jeremy Rifkin, "Choosing Our Future," *Utne Reader*, 69 (May, June 1995), p. 57.
2. *Ibid.*
3. *Ibid.*
4. *Ibid.*
5. *Ibid.*
6. *Ibid.*
7. *Congressional Quarterly: Weekly Report*, 50:29 (18 July 1992), p. 2128.
8. Encyclopedia Britannica, *Macropedia*, 4, p. 660.
9. Roger Lewin, *Complexity: Life at the Edge of Chaos* (New York: MacMillan, 1992), p. 20.

10. *Ibid.,* p. 21.
11. *Ibid.,* p. 22.
12. Carl Zimmer, "The Slime Alternative," *Discover* (September 1998), p. 88.
13. Stuart Hameroff and Roger Penrose: "Conscious Events as Orchestrated Space-Time Selection," *Journal of Consciousness Studies,* 13:1 (1996).

PART III: The Animal Perspective

Chapter Eleven
Animals, Our Teachers and Healers, Our Brothers and Sisters

1. Peter Singer, *Animal Liberation: A New Ethics for Our Treatment of Animals* (New York: Random House, 1975).
2. Ken Simonsen, "Shooting Elephants in Zimbabwe: An Intellectual Journey," Manuscript, p. 5.
3. *Ibid.*
4. Rebecca Tavernini, "Return of the Wolf," *American Times* (May 1993).
5. *Ibid.*
6. *Ibid.*
7. Kim A. McDonald, "Peacemaking Among Primates" *Chronicle of Higher Education,* 41:43 (7 July 1995), p. A6.
8. *Ibid.*
9. *Ibid.*
10. *Ibid.*
11. *Ibid.*
12. *Ibid.*
13. *Ibid.*

Chapter Twelve
Horse Whispering

1. Paul Shephard, "The Others: How Animals Made Us Human," *Utne Reader,* 73 (January, February 1996).
2. *Ibid.*
3. *Ibid.*
4. Vicky Hearne, *Adams Task: Calling Animals by Name* (New York: Harper Perennial 1994).
5. *Ibid.* p. ix.
6. *Ibid.,* p. xi.
7. *Ibid.*
8. *Ibid.,* p. 3.
9. *Ibid.,* p. 9.
10. *Ibid.,* p. 4.
11. *Ibid.,* p. 9.
12. Robert Redford, dir., *The Horse Whisperer,* (Touchstone Pictures, 1998).
13. *Ibid.*
14. Robert Redford, http://www.movieweb.com/movie/horsewhisp /horsewis.txt.

15. *Ibid.*

16. Stan Allen, http://www.horsemastership.com.

PART IV: INANIMATE NATURE

Chapter Thirteen
Where Does Mind Originate? Plotting Out a New Science of Awareness

1. Jean Charon, *Der Geist der Materie* (Wien: Zsolsnay, 1979).

2. *Ibid.,* p. 85.

3. *Ibid.,* p. 88.

4. *Ibid.,* p. 90.

5. *Ibid.,* p. 104.

6. *Ibid.,* p. 182.

7. Lee Smolin, *The Life of the Cosmos* (New York: Oxford University Press, 1997).

8. *Ibid.,* p. 292.

9. Nick Herbert, *Elemental Mind: Human Consciousness and the New Physics* (New York: Penguin Books, 1993).

10. *Ibid.,* p. 121.

11. *Ibid.,* p. 123.

12. *Ibid.,* pp. 119–120.

13. *Ibid.*

14. Roger Penrose, *The Emperor's New Mind: Concerning Computers, Minds, and the Laws of Physics* (New York: Oxford University Press, 1989).

15. *Ibid.,* p. 8.

16. *Ibid.,* p. 9.

17. Herbert, *Elemental Mind*, p. 17.

18. *Ibid.,* p. 18.

19. Stuart Hameroff and Roger Penrose, "Conscious Events as Orchestrated Space-Time Reduction," *Journal of Consciousness Studies*, 3:1 (1996), pp. 36–53.

20. Stuart Hameroff, "Did Consciousness Cause the Cambrian Evolutionary Explosion?" *Toward a Science of Consciousness II: The Second Tucson Discussions and Debates (Cambridge:* MIT Press, 1998), pp. 421–437.

21. *Ibid.,* p. 423.

22. Herbert, *Elemental Mind,* p. 36.

23. *Ibid.,* p. 37.

24. *Ibid.*

25. Paul Davies, *About Time* (New York: Touchstone, 1995), p. 209.

26. *Ibid.,* p. 216.

Chapter Fourteen
Panexperientialism, Panpsychism, and Quantum Animism

1. Nick Herbert, *Elemental Mind: Human Consciousness and the New Physics* (New York: Penguin Books, 1993), p. 187.
2. *Ibid.,* p. 187.
3. *Journal of Consciousness Studies* (Richmond, Va,: Virginia Commonwealth University, USA).
4. Alfred North Whitehead, *Science and the Modern World* (New York: Free Press, 1967).
6. David Ray Griffin, "Panexperientialist Physicalism and the Mind-Body Problem," *Journal of Consciousness Studies*, 4:3 (1997), pp. 248–268.
7. *Ibid.,* p. 254.
8. *Ibid.*
9. *Ibid.*
10. *Ibid.,* p. 255.

PART V: INFINITY, THE SUPER PERSPECTIVE OF THE ABSOLUTE

Chapter Fifteen
Numinous and Mystical Experiences

1. *Maitri-Upanishad*, Book 6, ch. 17.
2. Goethe, *Faust*, trans. by Stuart Atkins (Cambridge, Ma.: Suhrkamp, 1984) p. 161.
3. *Ibid.* p. 162.
4. Ninian Smart *World Views, Cross-Cultural Explorations of Human Beliefs* (Upper Saddle River, N. .J.: Prentice Hall, 1995).
5. *Ibid.,* p. 58.
6. *Ibid.*
7. *Ibid.,* p. 59.

Chapter Sixteen
Holotropic States of Consciousness and Mystical Encounters:
Two Case Histories

1. Stanislav Grof, *The Cosmic Game, Explorations of the Frontiers of Human Consciousness* (Manuscript, 1996).
2. *Ibid.,* p. 10.
3. *Ibid.,* p. 5.
4. *Ibid.*
5. *Ibid.,* p. 14.
6. *Ibid.,* p. 15.
7. Werner Krieglstein, *The Dice-Playing God: Reflections on Life in a Postmodern Age* (Lanham, Md.: University Press of America, 1991), p. 174.
8. Jens Jacobsen, Personal Interview (Evian les Bains, France, 1995).
9. Grof, *The Cosmic Game*, p. 14.

Chapter Seventeen
Transcendental Mediation and Nowtime:
The Experience of Emptiness

1. Ninian Smart *World Views, Cross-Cultural Explorations of Human Beliefs* (Upper Saddle River, N. .J.: Prentice Hall, 1995), p. 61.

2. *Ibid.*

3. Kenneth H. Brown, *The Brig* (New York: Hill and Wang, 1968), p. 89.

4. *Ibid.,* p. 90.

5. *Ibid.,* p. 101.

6. *Ibid.*

7. Smart, *World Views*, p. 61.

8. *Ibid.,* p. 62.

9. *Ibid.*

10. *Ibid.*

11. *Ibid.,* p. 72.

12. John, 14:2.

13. Werner Krieglstein, *The Dice-Playing God: Reflections on Life in a Postmodern Age* (Lanham, Md.: University Press of America, 1991).

14. Stephen W. Hawking, *A Brief History of Time* (New York: Bantam Books, 1988), p. 89.

15. For examples, see "NDE, Near Death Experiences," *Omni* (February 1982).

16. Hawking, *A Brief History*, p. 88.

17. *Ibid.,* pp. 88–89.

18. Stanislav Grof, *The Cosmic Game, Explorations of the Frontiers of Human Consciousness* (Manuscript, 1996), p. 40.

PART VI: BREAKING NEW GROUND, PRINCIPLES AND TRENDS OF
TRANSCENDENTAL PERSPECTIVISM

Chapter Eighteen
Pleasure and Pain: Are We a Generation of Vampires?

1. Anne Rice, *Interview with a Vampire* (1995) http://www.angelfire.com /la/krysan/script.html

2. Ayn Rand, *The Fountainhead* (New York: Penguin Books, 1993).

3. Irvine Welsh, "Trainspotting Review," *Time Magazine* (15 July 1996), p. 64.

Chapter Nineteen
The Perspective of Evil

1. Jay Stevens, *Storming Heaven: LSD and the American Dream* (New York: Grove Press, 1998).

2. *Ibid., p.* 303.

3. Stanislav Grof, *The Cosmic Game, Explorations of the Frontiers of Human Consciousness* (Manuscript, 1996), p. 130.

4. *Ibid.,* p. 130.

5. *Ibid.*, p. 106.
6. *Ibid.*, p. 112.
7. *Ibid.*
8. *Ibid.*, p. 114.
9. *Ibid.*
10. *Ibid.*
11. *Ibid.*, p. 117.
12. *Ibid.*

Chapter Twenty
Sacred Pleasure

1. Riane Eisler, *Sacred Pleasure: Sex, Myth and the Politics of the Body* (San Francisco: Harper, 1995).
2. *Ibid.*, p. 3.
3. *Ibid.*
4. Stuart Hameroff and Roger Penrose, "Conscious Events as Orchestrated Space-Time Selection," *Journal of Consciousness Studies*, 13:1 (1996), pp. 36–53.
5. Ernst Pöppel, *Lust und Schmerz: Über den Ursprung der Welt im Gehirn* (München: Siedler, 1993), p. 9.
6. *Ibid.*
7. Donald Schoen, *The Reflective Practitioner: How Professionals Think in Action* (New York: Basic Books, 1983).
8. Eisler, *Sacred Pleasure*, p. 3.
9. *Ibid.*, p. 11.
10. *Ibid.*

Chapter Twenty-One
Life Control and Self Empowerment

1. Sheldon D. Glass, *Life-Control* (New York: M. Evans and Co., 1977), p. 11.

Chapter Twenty-Two
The E³ Revolution: Entertainment, Education, Empowerment

1. Tony Jeary, *Inspire Any Audience* (Tulsa: Trade Life Books, 1997).

Chapter Twenty-Three
Emotional Intelligence: The Third Enlightenment

1. Daniel Goleman, *Emotional Intelligence: Why It Can Matter More than IQ* (New York: Bantam Books, 1995).
2. *Ibid.*, p. x.
3. *Ibid.*, p. xi.
4. *Ibid.*
5. *Ibid.*,
6. *Ibid,*, p. 261.
7. *Ibid.*, p. 262.
8. *Ibid.*, p. 263.

9. *Ibid.*, p. 266.
10. *Ibid.*, p. 268.
11. *Ibid.*, p. 18.
12. *Ibid.*, p. 8.
13. *Ibid.*, p. 18.
14. *Ibid.*, p. xii.
15. *Ibid.*, p. xi.

Chapter Twenty-Four
Multiple Intelligences: The Perspectivist Brain

1. Howard Gardener, *Multiple Intelligences* (New York: Basic Books, 1993), p. 6.

2. *Ibid.,* pp. 8–9.
3. *Ibid.,* p. 10.
4. Michael J. Gelb, *How to Think like Leonardo da Vinci* (New York: Delacorte Press, 1998).

Chapter Twenty-Five
Teaching Perspectives: The Partnership Way

1. Riane Eisler, *Tomorrow's Children: A Blueprint for Education in the 21st Century* (Boulder: Westview Press, 2000), p. 6.
2. Riane Eisler (Promotional Material, 2000).
3. "The State of America's Children," *The Children's Defense Fund Publication* (Yearbook, March 2000).
4. James P. Sterba, *Three Challenges to Ethics* (New York: Oxford University Press, 2001), p. 56.
5. Eisler, *Tomorrow's Children* (2000), p. xv.
6. *Ibid.*
7. *Ibid.*
8. *Ibid.,* p. 17.
9. *Ibid.,* p. 20.
10. *Ibid.*
11. *Ibid.*
12. *Ibid.,* p. 234.
13. *Ibid.*
14. *Ibid.*
15. *Ibid.*

Chapter Twenty-Six
In Memoriam Easter Island: Whither Humanity?

1. Jared Diamond, "Easter's End," *Discover* (August 1995), pp. 63–69.
2. *Ibid.*
3. Richard Swift, et al., "Endangered Species," *The New Internationalist* (http://www.internationalistbooks.com).

Chapter Twenty-Seven
The Communicating Universe

1. James van Praagh, *Talking to Heaven: A Medium's Message of Life after Death* (New York: Dutton, 1997).
2. John J. Edward, *One Last Time: After-Death Communication*, (video tape).
3. John Gribbin, *In the Beginnning: After Cobe and Before the Big Bang* (New York: Little, Brown and Company, 1993).
4. *Ibid.,* p. 191.
5. *Ibid.*, p. 193.
6. *Ibid.*

Chapter Twenty-Eight
Toward a Cosmic Consciousness

1. Mark Matousek, "Up Close and Transpersonal with Ken Wilber," *Utne Reader* (July, August 1998). pp. 51–107.
2. Werner Krieglstein, *The Dice-Playing God: Reflections on Life in a Post-modern Age* (Lanham, Md.: University Press of America, 1991), pp. 179–219.

Afterword

1. Stanley Fish, "Condemnation Without Absolutes," *The New York Times* (15 October 2001).

BIBLIOGRAPHY

Anderson, Karen. *Chain Her by One Foot: The Subjugation of Native Women in Seventeenth-Century New France.* New York: Routledge, 1993.

Begley, Sharon, and Claudia Kalb. "Learning Right from Wrong," *Newsweek* (13 March 2000), p. 30.

Behar, Ruth. "Dare We Say 'I'? Bringing the Personal into Scholarship," *The Chronicle of Higher Education* (29 June 1994), B, p. 2.

Beverslius, Joel. Editor, *A Sourcebook for the Community of Religions.* Michigan: The Sourcebook Project, Grand Rapids, 1993.

Bloom, Allen. *The Closing of the American Mind: How Higher Education has Failed Democracy and Impoverished the Souls of Today's Students.* New York: Simon and Schuster, 1987, p. 183.

Blum, Deborah. "The Gender Blur, Where Does Biology End and Society Take Over?" *Utne Reader, 89* (September, October 1998), pp. 45–48.

Brown, Kenneth H. *The Brig.* New York: Hill and Wang, 1968.

Charon, Jean. *Der Geist der Materie.* Wien: Zsolsnay, 1979.

Chopra, Deepak. *Ageless Body, Timeless Mind: The Quantum Alternative to Growing Old.* New York: Harmony Books, 1993.

The Christian Science Monitor. 88:52 (9 February 1996).

Colapinto, John. *As Nature Made Him: The Boy Who Was Raised as a Girl.* New York: Harper-Collins, 2000.

Congressional Quarterly: Weekly Report, 50:29 (18 July 1992), p. 2128.

Davies, Paul. *About Time.* New York: Touchstone, 1995.

––––. *Prinzip Chaos: Die neue Ordnung des Kosmos.* München: Heyne, 1988.

Diamond, Jared. "Easter's End," *Discover* (August 1995), pp. 63–69.

Edelman, Gay Norton. "Show Me the Presents," *McCall's* (February 1998), p. 48.

Edward, John J. *One Last Time: After Death Communication.* Video tape.

The Egyptian Book of the Dead: The Papyrus of Ani in the British Museum. Introduced by E.A.Wallis Budge. New York: Dover Publications, 1967.

Eisler, Riane. *The Chalice and the Blade*. San Francisco: Harper Collins, 1988.

—–. *Sacred Pleasure: Sex, Myth, and the Politics of the Body*. New York: Harper Collins, 1995.

—–. *Tomorrow's Children: A Blueprint for Education in the Twenty-First Century*. Boulder, Col: Westview Press, 2000.

Fox, Matthew. *Original Blessing*. Santa Fe: Bear, 1983.

Gandhi, Mahatma. "All Men are Brothers," *Beyond the Western Tradition*. Mountain View, Calif.: Mayfield, 1992, p. 250.

Gardener, Howard. *Multiple Intelligences*. New York: Basic Books, 1993.

Gelb, Michael J. *How to Think like Leonardo da Vinci*. New York: Delacorte Press, 1998.

Gimbutas, Marija. *The Civilization of the Goddess: The World of Old Europe*. San Francisco. Harper, 1991.

Glass, Sheldon, D. *Life-Control*. New York, M. Evans and Co., 1976.

A Global Ethics: Text of Declaration and Principles. Council for a Parliament of the World's Religions, 1993.

Goethe, J. W. *Faust*. Translated by Stuart Atkins. Cambridge, Ma.: Suhrkamp, 1984.

Goleman, Daniel, and Joel Gurin. Editors. *Mind Body Medicine*. Yonkers, New York: Consumer Reports Books, 1993.

Goleman, Daniel. *Emotional Intelligence: Why It Can Matter more than IQ*. New York, Bantam Books, 1995.

Gray, John. *Men Are from Mars, Women Are from Venus*. New York: HarperCollins, 1992.

Gribbin, John. *In the Beginnning: After Cobe and Before the Big Bang*. New York: Little, Brown and Company, 1993.

Griffin, David R. "Panexperientialist Physicalism and the Mind-Body Problem," *Journal of Consciousness Studies*, 4:3, 1997, pp. 248–268.

Grof, Stanislav. *The Cosmic Game: Explorations of the Frontiers of Human Consciousness*. Manuscript, 1996.

Hameroff, Stuart. "Did Consciousness Cause the Cambrian Evolutionary Explosion?" *Toward a Science of Consciousness II, The Second Tucson Discussions and Debates.* Cambridge: MIT Press, 1998, pp. 421–437.

Hameroff, Stuart, and Roger Penrose. "Conscious Events as Orchestrated Space-Time Selection," *Journal of Consciousness Studies,* 3:1 (1996), pp. 36–53.

Hawking, Stephen W. *A Brief History of Time.* New York: Bantam Books, 1988.

Hearne, Vicky. *Adams Task: Calling Animals by Name.* New York: Harper Perennial, 1994.

Herbert, Nick. *Elemental Mind: Human Consciousness and the New Physics.* New York: Penguin Books, 1993.

Hopfe, Lewis. *Religions of the World.* Upper Saddle River, N. J.: Prentice Hall, 1998.

http://www.horsemastership.com

http://www.isa.it/tuscia

Jacobsen, Jens. Personal Interview at Evian les Bains, France, 1995.

Jeary, Tony. *Inspire Any Audience.* Tulsa, Okla.: Trade Life Books, 1997.

Jet, 93:1 (24 November 1997), p. 14.

John. *Gospel.* 14, 2.

Keen, Sam. *To a Dancing God.* New York: Harper and Row, 1970.

Krieglstein, Werner. *The Dice-Playing God, Reflections on Life in a Post-Modern Age.* Lanham, Md.: University Press of America, 1991.

Lessing, Gotthold Ephraim. *Nathan the Wise.* Translated by Bayard Quincy Morgan. New York: Ungar, 1955.

Lewin, Roger. *Complexity: Life at the Edge of Chaos.* New York: MacMillan, 1992.

Loye, David. *Darwin's Lost Theory of Love: A Healing Vision for the Twenty-First Century.* New York: ToExcel/iUniverse.com, 2000.

Mackey, Mary. *The Year the Horses Came.* New York: Harper Collins, 1993.

Maitri-Upanishad. Book 6, ch. 17.

Marwick, Charles. "Should Phycisians Prescribe Prayer for Health? Spiritual Aspects of Well-Being Considered," *JAMA, The Journal of the American Medical Association,* 273:20 (24 May 1995), p. 1561.

Matousek, Mark. "Up Close and Transpersonal with Ken Wilber," *Utne Reader, 88* (July, August 1998), pp. 51–107.

McCarthy Brown, Karen. *Mama Lola: A Voodoo Priestess in Brooklyn.* Berkeley: University of California Press, 1991.

McDonald, Kim A. "Scientists Rethink Anthropomorphism," *Chronicle of Higher Education,* 41:24 (24 February 1995), p. A8.

–––––. "Peacemaking Among Primates," *Chronicle of Higher Education*, 41:43 (7 July 1995), p.A6.

Moyers, Bill. *Healing and the Mind.* New York: Doubleday, 1993.

New Larousse Encyclopedia of Mythology. New York: The Hamlin Group, 1968.

Peat, David. *Superstrings and the Search for the Theory of Everything.* Chicago: Contemporary Books, 1989.

Penrose, Roger. *The Emperor's New Mind: Concerning Computers, Minds, and the Laws of Physics.* New York: Oxford University Press, 1989.

Pert, Candice. "The Mind Body Connection," *Healing and the Mind*, Bill Moyers, Editor. New York: Doubleday, 1993, pp. 177–194.

Pöppel, Ernst. *Lust und Schmerz: Über den Ursprung der Welt im Gehirn.* München: Siedler, 1993.

Prigogine, Ilya. *Order Out of Chaos.* New York: Bantam Books, 1984.

Quuran. 5:48.

Rand, Ayn. *The Fountainhead.* New York: Penguin Books, 1943.

–––––. *Atlas Shrugged.* New York: Signet Books, 1957.

Rice, Anne. *Interview with a Vampire.* http://www.angelfire. com/la/krysan/script.html, 1995.

Rifkin, Jeremy. "Choosing Our Future," *Utne Reader*, 69 (May, June 1995), p. 57.

Sanders, Scott R. *The Force of Spirit.* Boston: Beacon Press, 2000.

Schoen, Donald. *The Reflective Practitioner: How Professionals Think in Action.* New York: Basic Books, 1983.

Shephard, Paul. "The Others: How Animals Made Us Human," *Utne Reader*, 73 (January, February 1996).

Simonsen, Ken. *Shooting Elephants in Zimbabwe: An Intellectual Journey.* Manuscript.

Singer, Peter. *Animal Liberation: A New Ethics for Our Treatment of Animals.* New York: Random House, 1975.

Smart, Ninian. *World Views: Cross-Cultural Explorations of Human Beliefs.* Upper Saddle River, N. J: Prentice Hall, 1995.

Smolin, Lee. *The Life of the Cosmos.* New York: Oxford University Press, 1997.

Sterba, James P. *Three Challenges to Ethics.* New York: Oxford University Press, 2001.

Stevens, Jay. *Storming Heaven: LSD and the American Dream.* New York: Grove Press, 1987.

Svitil, Kathy, A. "Virtual Gorillas," *Discover*, 18:4 (April 1997), p. 26.

Swift, Richard, (*et al.*). "Endangered Species," *The New Internationalist* (March 1997).

Tavernini, Rebecca. "Return of the Wolf," *American Times* (May 1993).

Van Praagh, James. *Talking to Heaven: A Medium's Message of Life after Death.* New York: Dutton, 1997.

Waskow, Arthur. "Proclaim Jubilee!" *The Other Side* (September, October 1998), p. 10.

Welsh, Irvin. "Trainspotting Review," *Time Magazine* (15 July, 1996), p. 64.

Whitehead, Alfred North. *Science and the Modern World.* New York: Free Press, 1967.

Wieland-Burston, Joanne. *Chaotische Gefühle.* Zurich: Kreuz Verlag, 1989.

Wilson, D. S. "Dora, Nora and Their Professor: The 'Talking Cure,' 'Nightwood,' and Feminist Pedagogy," *Literature and Psychology*, 42:3 (Summer 1996), p. 48.

Wing, Derald and David Sue. *Counseling the Culturally Different: Theory and Practice.* New York: John Wiley and Sons, 1990.

Winter, Miriam Therese. "Feminist Commentary is 3 lb., Must–Read Text, " *The National Catholic Reporter* (6 October 1995).

Zilbergeld, Bernie. *The New Male Sexuality.* New York: Bantam Books, 1992.

Zimmer, Carl. "The Slime Alternative," *Discover* (September 1998), p. 88.

ABOUT THE AUTHOR

Werner Krieglstein came from Germany to the United States as a Fulbright scholar in 1968. Born in Czechoslovakia, Krieglstein studied at the Goethe University in Frankfurt and at the Freie University in Berlin. He received a Ph.D. from the University of Chicago in 1972. Krieglstein taught at the University of Helsinki, Finland, and Western Michigan University, Kalamazoo, USA. He currently teaches philosophy and religious studies at the College of DuPage in Glen Ellyn, Illinois.

At the Goethe University, Krieglstein directed the "neue Bühne," one of Europe's leading avant-garde theaters of the 1960s. Later he founded the Whole Art Theater in Kalamazoo. His theater productions received awards at International Theater festivals. Krieglstein also has a career in professional acting. Most recently, he acted as a guru in the independent film, *Urban Ground Squirrels*. He played Henry Kissinger in the Buffalo Theater Company production of *Nixon's Nixon*. Krieglstein published a book: *The Dice-Playing God: Reflections on Life in a Post-Modern Age* (University Press of America, 1991). He wrote numerous articles in national and international journals and newspapers.

Krieglstein is a charter member of the International Society for Universal Dialogue and currently serves as a member of the governing board.

INDEX

VIBS

The **Value Inquiry Book Series** is co-sponsored by:

Adler School of Professional Psychology
American Indian Philosophy Association
American Maritain Association
American Society for Value Inquiry
Association for Process Philosophy of Education
Canadian Society for Philosophical Practice
Center for Bioethics, University of Turku
Center for Professional and Applied Ethics, University of North Carolina at Charlotte
Center for Research in Cognitive Science, Autonomous University of Barcelona
Centre for Applied Ethics, Hong Kong Baptist University
Centre for Cultural Research, Aarhus University
Centre for Professional Ethics, University of Central Lancashire
Centre for the Study of Philosophy and Religion, University College of Cape Breton
College of Education and Allied Professions, Bowling Green State University
College of Liberal Arts, Rochester Institute of Technology
Concerned Philosophers for Peace
Conference of Philosophical Societies
Department of Moral and Social Philosophy, University of Helsinki
Gannon University
Gilson Society
Ikeda University
Institute of Philosophy of the High Council of Scientific Research, Spain
International Academy of Philosophy of the Principality of Liechtenstein
International Association of Bioethics
International Center for the Arts, Humanities, and Value Inquiry
International Society for Universal Dialogue
Natural Law Society
Personalist Discussion Group
Philosophical Society of Finland
Philosophy Born of Struggle Association
Philosophy Seminar, University of Mainz
Pragmatism Archive
R.S. Hartman Institute for Formal and Applied Axiology
Research Institute, Lakeridge Health Corporation
Russian Philosophical Society
Society for Iberian and Latin-American Thought
Society for the Philosophic Study of Genocide and the Holocaust
Society for the Philosophy of Sex and Love
Yves R. Simon Institute

Titles Published

66.   John R. Shook, *Pragmatism: An Annotated Bibliography, 1898-1940*. With contributions by E. Paul Colella, Lesley Friedman, Frank X. Ryan, and Ignas K. Skrupskelis

67.   Lansana Keita, *The Human Project and the Temptations of Science*

68.   Michael M. Kazanjian, *Phenomenology and Education: Cosmology, Co-Being, and Core Curriculum*. A volume in **Philosophy of Education**

69.   James W. Vice, *The Reopening of the American Mind: On Skepticism and Constitutionalism*

70.   Sarah Bishop Merrill, *Defining Personhood: Toward the Ethics of Quality in Clinical Care*

71.   Dane R. Gordon, *Philosophy and Vision*

72.   Alan Milchman and Alan Rosenberg, Editors, *Postmodernism and the Holocaust*. A volume in **Holocaust and Genocide Studies**

73.   Peter A. Redpath, *Masquerade of the Dream Walkers: Prophetic Theology from the Cartesians to Hegel*. A volume in **Studies in the History of Western Philosophy**

74.   Malcolm D. Evans, *Whitehead and Philosophy of Education: The Seamless Coat of Learning*. A volume in **Philosophy of Education**

75.   Warren E. Steinkraus, *Taking Religious Claims Seriously: A Philosophy of Religion*, edited by Michael H. Mitias. A volume in **Universal Justice**

76.   Thomas Magnell, Editor, *Values and Education*

77.   Kenneth A. Bryson, *Persons and Immortality*. A volume in **Natural Law Studies**

78.   Steven V. Hicks, *International Law and the Possibility of a Just World Order: An Essay on Hegel's Universalism*. A volume in **Universal Justice**

79.   E. F. Kaelin, *Texts on Texts and Textuality: A Phenomenology of Literary Art*, Edited by Ellen J. Burns

80.   Amihud Gilead, Saving Possibilities: A Study in Philosophical Psychology. *A volume in Philosophy and Psychology*

81.   André Mineau, *The Making of the Holocaust: Ideology and Ethics in the Systems Perspective*. A volume in **Holocaust and Genocide Studies**

114.   Thomas M. Dicken and Rem B. Edwards, *Dialogues on Values and Centers of Value: Old Friends, New Thoughts.* A volume in **Hartman Institute Axiology Studies**

115.   Rem B. Edwards, *What Caused the Big Bang?* A volume in **Philosophy and Religion**

116.   Jon Mills, Editor, *A Pedagogy of Becoming.* A volume in **Philosophy of Education**

117.   Robert T. Radford, *Cicero: A Study in the Origins of Republican Philosophy.* A volume in **Studies in the History of Western Philosophy**

118.   Arleen L. F. Salles and María Julia Bertomeu, Editors, *Bioethics: Latin American Perspectives.* A volume in **Philosophy in Latin America**

119.   Nicola Abbagnano, *The Human Project: The Year 2000*, with an Interview by Guiseppe Grieco. Translated from Italian by Bruno Martini and Nino Langiulli. Edited with an introduction by Nino Langiulli. A volume in **Studies in the History of Western Philosophy**

120.   Daniel M. Haybron, Editor, *Earth's Abominations: Philosophical Studies of Evil.* A volume in **Personalist Studies**

121.   Anna T. Challenger, *Philosophy and Art in Gurdjieff's Beelzebub: A Modern Sufi Odyssey*

122.   George David Miller, *Peace, Value, and Wisdom: The Educational Philosophy of Daisaku Ikeda.* A volume in **Daisaku Ikeda Studies**

123.   Haim Gordon and Rivca Gordon, *Sophistry and Twentieth-Century Art*

124.   Thomas O Buford and Harold H. Oliver, Editors *Personalism Revisited: Its Proponents and Critics.* A volume in **Histories and Addresses of Philosophical Societies**

125.   Avi Sagi, *Albert Camus and the Philosophy of the Absurd.* Translated from Hebrew by Batya Stein

126.   Robert S. Hartman, *The Knowledge of Good: Critique of Axiologic l Reason.* Expanded translation from the Spanish by Robert S. Hartman. Edited by Arthur R. Ellis and Rem B. Edwards. A volume in **Hartman Institute Axiology Studies**

127.   Alison Bailey and Paula J. Smithka, Editors. *Community, Diversity, and Difference: Implications for Peace.* A volume in **Philosophy of Peace**